Akmolinsk

ogorsk

Namangan

L:ISSYK-KUL'

Przheval'sk

Aksu

C H I N

Andizhan

Kokand Sko-belev Osh

F E R G A N A

I N D I A

A N

S E M

Vassal States

Governor-generalships of the Steppe and of Turkestan

Province boundaries

Uyezd boundaries

REGMARAD

Mission to
TURKESTAN

Being the Memoirs of
COUNT K. K. PAHLEN
1908–1909

Count Pahlen, *c.* 1920

Mission to
TURKESTAN

Being the memoirs of
COUNT K. K. PAHLEN
1908–1909

Edited and Introduced by
RICHARD A. PIERCE

Translated by
N. J. COURISS

Published in Association with the
CENTRAL ASIAN RESEARCH CENTRE

LONDON
OXFORD UNIVERSITY PRESS
NEW YORK · TORONTO
1964

Oxford University Press, Amen House, London E.C.4

GLASGOW NEW YORK TORONTO MELBOURNE WELLINGTON
BOMBAY CALCUTTA MADRAS KARACHI LAHORE DACCA
CAPE TOWN SALISBURY NAIROBI IBADAN ACCRA
KUALA LUMPUR HONG KONG

Printed in Great Britain at the Pitman Press, Bath

CONTENTS

The endpaper maps show the regions
travelled by Count Pahlen in
his Mission to Turkestan

INTRODUCTION

COLONIALISM is a term much used, but ill-defined. Bearing an implied rebuke, it sums up the ambiguities of propaganda directed against one-time colonial powers. The colonial régimes of former times are condemned in the light of present day concepts, while surviving régimes have attributed to them the motives and procedures, real or alleged, of the past.

In its day, however, the 'colonialism' of the nineteenth and earlier part of the twentieth centuries had many positive achievements to its credit. These as well as negative features must be acknowledged and understood if we are to comprehend the problems facing the many peoples recently or soon to become independent.

Perhaps least known of any colonial régime has been that of pre-Revolutionary Russia, obscured before 1917 by remoteness and western indifference, and since then interpreted mainly by Soviet propaganda distorting the past to better portray the present or to magnify the Russian 'progressive' role.

This book is concerned with one of the principal colonial possessions of Imperial Russia, western Turkestan, the vast area lying between the Caspian Sea and China. This region consisted of five provinces, which with the then semi-independent vassal states of Khiva and Bukhara corresponded roughly with the present Uzbek, Turkmen, Tadzhik, and Kirgiz, and part of the Kazakh, Soviet Socialist Republics.

From the eighteen-sixties, when Russia began the conquest of this region, a régime was established which in many ways was exemplary among nineteenth century colonial administrations. Peace and order, the abolition of slavery, a lightened tax burden, inclusion in a large trading area, and improved transportation facilities brought a rise in economic prosperity and a substantial improvement over early conditions. A *laissez faire* policy was adopted toward the Muslim religion and other aspects of native culture.

By 1908, however, many of the defects inherent in a paternal, centralized régime had made themselves felt. The corruption of the Turkestan administration had become a byword, while mismanagement of the settlement problem, squabbles between local authorities and the ministries in St. Petersburg, and weakness of local officials in coping with the revolutionary disturbances of 1905 and 1906 caused the Imperial Government increasing concern. On 18 June 1908 Emperor Nicholas II ordered the Governing Senate, one of the highest state bodies, to undertake a complete investigation of affairs in Turkestan.

The investigation was entrusted to Count Konstantin Konstantinovich Pahlen, who was provided with a staff of twenty-five assistants and given full powers to examine all aspects of the region's administration and economy, and to prosecute offenders.

Pahlen was well qualified for the task. He came from a family with a long tradition of service to the Empire. Established as landowners in Livland (present-day Latvia) in the late twelfth century, von der Pahlens were long under Swedish rule. After Peter the Great conquered the Baltic provinces in the early eighteenth century they became subjects of Russia. They typified the Protestant Germanic element in the Empire, whose western orientation and concepts of order and duty provided a major contribution to Russian political and military leadership. However, in spite of religious and cultural similarities, their long separation from the main German stream engendered subtle differences in character and a deep affinity for the land in which they were rooted.

Pahlen's father, Count Konstantin Ivanovich Pahlen (1830–1912), served as Governor of the *guberniya* (province) of Pskov, and later, as Minister of Justice, carried out the judicial reforms of Emperor Alexander II. While chairing a committee appointed in February 1883 to draft new legislation to deal with the Jewish problem he boldly, though fruitlessly, urged abolition of discriminatory laws.

K. K. Pahlen was born in St. Petersburg on 26 March 1861. He spent his childhood there, at Pskov, and on the family estate of Gross-Autz in the province of Livland. After the customary early training by tutors, through which he acquired facility with Russian, German, French, English and Latvian, he attended the Jurisprudence School in the capital, which provided an education from the earlier grades through three years of law study. Here he obtained the wide-ranging and thorough liberal arts training which placed the Russian higher schools among the best in Europe.

Born with a slight foot deformity, Pahlen was never called to military service. In school, his physical handicap set him apart from other children and helped to develop the more serious side of his nature. Officially he was an Evangelical Lutheran, but while visiting England in the early eighteen-eighties he became influenced by Lord Radstock,[1] an Irish evangelist well-known for his drawing-room preaching in England and on the Continent. Radstock's preaching had a deep effect on Pahlen. His religious faith became a vital force in his life, influencing his attitudes and conduct of official duties.

Upon completing law school Pahlen, at the request of his father, undertook the management of the family estate, some 8,000 *desiatins* (21,600 acres) of farm land and forest. There he developed a keen interest in agriculture, particularly the breeding of fine cattle.

In 1890, he married Baroness Sophie Nicolay, daughter of a former Russian minister to Denmark and descendant of French *émigré* nobility who fled to Russia after the French Revolution. They settled on a smaller estate, of about 1,000 desiatins, 18 kilometres from Gross-Autz. Drawn gradually into local administration, he served first as *Volost* Elder (a post resembling that of a French *maire*), then as commissar for peasant affairs in the *uyezd* (county) of Goldingen, and finally as permanent member of the peasants' provincial board in Mitau, the chief town of Kurland. During these years he gained administrative experience, and knowledge of agricultural problems.

In 1896, Pahlen's father, Chief Marshal of the Coronation of Nicholas II, asked him to be his secretary during the investigation of the Khodynka tragedy which followed the Coronation. In 1897, Pahlen was named Vice-Governor of the guberniya of Warsaw, serving three years there. He enjoyed this period in his official life very much, making lasting friendships among the Polish aristocracy, who did not like the Russians but accepted the Balts sympathetically. In 1900 he was transferred in the same capacity to Pskov, where his father had served fifty years before, and in 1902, as Governor, to Vilno. This too was an interesting period for him. The population there consisted of many ethnic groups, chiefly Russians, Poles, Lithuanians, Germans, and many Jews. Like his father he was sympathetic toward the Jews, and took their part in his official reports.[2]

---

[1] Granville Augustus William Waldegrave, 3rd Baron Radstock (1833–1913).
[2] One of these reports, although secret, somehow fell into the hands of a Jewish labour organization and was published abroad as: *Taynaya dokladnaya zapiska Vilenskago gubernatora o polozhenii yevreyev v Rossii. Izdaniye*

While he was serving at Vilno, in 1905, the first Russian Revolution broke out. Pahlen's energetic administration, and his popularity among all classes, made him a target for extremists who felt that such officials weakened their influence on the population. During some of the street troubles in the autumn of 1905 he was wounded by a would-be assassin thought to have been a member of the Bund, a Jewish Socialist organization.

The Vilno post ended Pahlen's career in executive administration. In 1906 he was named Senator of the First Department of the Senate, and the family moved to St. Petersburg, where they lived until the Revolution of October 1917. This post was particularly odious to Pahlen because it had to deal with appeals of the Jewish population against local court decisions. Many of these decisions involved laws of an anti-Semitic nature, and most members of the Department were in agreement with this legislation. His views differed sharply, but he was not in a position to take any effective action.

More agreeable was his work as a lay official of St. Peter's Lutheran Church on the Nevskiy Prospekt. The large parish had some 20,000 members and operated several schools, orphanages, and other institutions. He headed the Council which administered the church and these institutions.

When he received his appointment to head the Senatorial Investigation of Turkestan, Pahlen hastily gathered a staff of young officials, most of them personally known to him. He and his party were on their way to Tashkent, seat of the Governor-Generalship of Turkestan, by late June, 1908.

In Turkestan, every day was made to count. While some of his aides delved into official records in Tashkent, Pahlen and others proceeded to Samarkand, stopping on the way to view the irrigation projects in the Hungry Steppe. In late July, Pahlen made a rapid tour of the Russian settlements in Semirech'ye, looking into the activities of the Colonization Administration and the injustices done

---

Vseobshchago yevreyskago rabochago soyuza v Litve, Pol'she i Rossii (Secret memorandum of the Governor of Vilno on the position of the Jews in Russia. Publication of the General Jewish Labor Union in Lithuania, Poland and Russia). Geneva, 1904. 73 pp. Several years later, at the request of an English friend, he wrote a pamphlet, *New light on the Jewish question in Russia*, published under the pseudonym 'C.A.' (Preface by Samuel Hinds Wilkinson. Published in London, 1908; 67 pp.)

to the nomads. By this time, word that the *revizuyushchiy senator* (inspecting Senator) was coming was enough to cause panic among officials. In August he toured Transcaspia, the centre of administrative corruption, and then, after instituting proceedings against a number of officials and leaving his staff to gather evidence against others, he returned to St. Petersburg to report.

The spring of 1909 found Pahlen again in Tashkent. Convinced that new legislation for the region should take cognizance of Muslim law and local customs, he undertook codification of the scattered and conflicting materials. Seventy mullas were assembled at Tashkent in May, and in the course of three weeks the task was completed.

Following the conference, Pahlen made trips to Bukhara, Khiva and Transcaspia, then toured the cotton-rich Fergana valley and surrounding mountains, viewing some of the incipient attempts to exploit the mineral wealth of the region. After that he returned to St. Petersburg.

The Senatorial investigation lasted from June 1908 until June 1909. During that time Pahlen and his assistants scrutinized nearly every aspect of governmental and economic affairs, including the regional, provincial, district, municipal, rural, and native administrations; and mining, agriculture, colonization, taxation, the police, prisons, courts, and state property. His lengthy reports are the best single source concerning Turkestan in the pre-First World War period.

Pahlen made ample use of his power to suspend and prosecute officials found involved in indiscretions. In the first general housecleaning in Turkestan's administrative history, scores of officials were arrested, tried, and convicted. General P. I. Mishchenko, Governor-General for less than a year, resigned his office because of the investigating body's criticisms and the arrest of some of his most trusted personnel. In Transcaspia *oblast*, Pahlen and his subordinates removed and punished many undesirables who had attained responsible office. Revelations of waste, corruption, and careerism in the Colonization Administration led to still more convictions.

Pahlen opposed further allotment of land to settlers, feeling that this would deprive the native population of its livelihood and would arouse resentment. He urged instead a slower colonization by attracting outside capital and encouraging private enterprise and by freeing Russians residing in the region from previous restrictions on buying and selling land. This would permit Russians to compete with the natives in normal economic processes, which in his opinion would work for the benefit of both.

To set the administration of Turkestan on a correct course, Pahlen felt it time for the military to give way to civilian elements. For Russians and settled natives alike he recommended introduction of the *zemstvo* institutions of rural self-government. On the other hand, feeling self-government for nomads to be premature, he recommended appointment, rather than election, of native officials.

Pahlen's recommendations, and the housecleaning he had instituted among administrative personnel, were widely discussed. A few shared his concept that Russia bore a paternal responsibility toward the native peoples of Turkestan, an obligation to teach them western ways and self-government.

But advocates of colonization wanted no such exalted doctrines. The Prime Minister Peter Stolypin remained firm in his conviction that colonization offered a panacea which would rid central Russia of surplus rural population and russify outlying regions of the Empire. A. I. Krivoshein, influential head of the Main Administration for Land Organization and Agriculture, of which the Colonization Administration was a part, labelled the recommendations premature until additional colonization should have strengthened the Russian hold on border regions.

In the end, nothing was done. The reports of the Pahlen investigation were printed in massive volumes and then, like the reports of many a previous enquiry, were forgotten. Affairs in Turkestan resumed their normal course, unchanged until the revolutionary year of 1917.

Pahlen, meanwhile, occupied himself with his duties in the Senate, and as a *gofmeyster*, or master-at-court. He was more than once offered the position of Assistant Minister but did not wish to enter more active government work, feeling his liberal political attitudes to be out of keeping with those then prevalent. He served as president of the Young Men's Christian Association in Russia, and supported church and philanthropic activities.

At the outbreak of war, in August 1914, Pahlen was at Bad Kissingen, in Germany. There he had a difficult time for two weeks because of anti-Russian hysteria, and was nearly mobbed. Back in Russia, he saw anti-German feeling unleashed against Russian subjects of Baltic German extraction. In 1916 the criticism of Germanophobes and those jealous of his close relationship with the

Imperial family caused the withdrawal of his title of *gofmeyster*, but he was restored to the position two weeks later by order of the Tsar. His family estates were lost early in 1915, when the German army entered the Baltic provinces.

When the Revolution of October 1917 occurred the family fled from Petrograd and took refuge in Finland. At this time all of Pahlen's notes and a large collection of photographs taken during his Turkestan sojourn were lost.

After the conclusion of the Treaty of Brest-Litovsk the family returned to Gross-Autz, but only for a short time. Reluctantly and because he thought it his duty to take part in the anti-Bolshevik struggle, Pahlen associated himself with the 'free corps' of Colonel (and self-styled Prince) Avalov-Bermondt, leader of one of several White counter-revolutionary movements in the Baltic provinces, with the task of forming a civil administration. When this movement collapsed and the Red Army advanced, he joined the flow of refugees to Germany where his family had already taken refuge. Pahlen continued to live in Germany after the emergence of an independent Latvia, accompanied by expropriation of his own and other large holdings.

Pahlen's last three years were spent in Wernigerode, in the Harz Mountains. During that period he was active in the Mission for People of the East, or 'Light in the East', doing educational work among former Russian war prisoners. In 1922, during a short visit to relatives in Finland he dictated from memory the account of his Turkestan mission. He died in Wernigerode on 14 August 1923.

These stark details of Pahlen's life and career suggest many avenues for further investigation. Unfortunately, few if any of these can be followed up. Had he lived somewhat earlier there would have been biographical material, and perhaps memoirs, in the massive Russian historical journals. Had he been more prominent—or notorious—during the war years more might have been written about him then. As it is, there are only passing references in several articles by Germanophobes. The account here has been pieced together chiefly from family recollections.

Pahlen's report,[3] comprising twenty volumes and a lengthy

[3] *Otchet po revizii Turkestanskogo kraya, proizvedennoy po vysochayshemu poveleniyu senatorom gofmeysterom grafom K.K. Palenom* (Report on the investigation of the Turkestan region, carried out by Supreme Command by Senator Gofmeyster Count K.K. Pahlen), St. Petersburg, 1909–1911.

(*1*) *Narodnyye sudy Turkestanskogo kraya* (Native courts of the Turkestan supplement, is a definitive source concerning Russian Turkestan before the First World War, but makes dry reading. His private memoirs of his journeys and experiences in Turkestan are written in another style, with much trenchant criticism of the local administration and the Central Government. Although a loyal subject of the Tsar, Pahlen's cultural background enabled him to take an objective view of Russian methods. The demise of the Imperial régime, five years gone, also gives his account a now-it-can-be-told quality impossible before 1917.

At the same time, unintentionally, the account conveys, today, something of the thought of another era, when the world was younger and its problems—to our eyes at least—less complicated. The century-long contest with Britain over the approaches to India still loomed large in Russian attitudes. Conquest and colonial rule were still normal, and justified by the alleged need for paternal guidance. It was too soon for a man of Pahlen's background to see that this time was over and that many of his views were out of date. Thus he slips again and again into the present tense, when for the peoples of Turkestan much of the way of life he describes was, even in 1922, past and irretrievable. Yet there is a bridge, for it is

---

region). 1909. (*2*) *Gosudarstvennyye imushchestva*. (*Upravleniye. Obrochnyye stat'i. Lesnoye delo. Sel'skokhozyaystvennyye uchrezhdeniya.*) (State property; Administration; Tenancy regulations; Forestry; Agricultural institutions) 1910. (*3*) *Zemskoye Khozyaysto* (Rural economy). 1910. (*4*) *Krayevoye upravleniye* (Regional administration). 1910. (*5*) *Oblastnoye upravleniye* (Provincial administration). 1910. (*6*) *Pravovoy byt tuzemnago naseleniya* (Legal forms of the native population). 1910. (*7*) *Orosheniye v Turkestane* (Irrigation in Turkestan). 1910. (*8*) *Pereselencheskoye delo v Turkestane* (Colonization in Turkestan). 1910. (*9*) *Pozemel'no-podatnoye delo* (Land taxation). 1910. (*10*) *Politsiya bezopasnosti* (Security police). 1910. (*11*) *Sel' skoye upravleniye, russkoye i tuzemnoye* (Russian and native rural administration). 1910. (*12*) *Uyezdnoye upravleniye* (Uyezd (county) administration). 1910. (*13*) *Uchebnoye delo* (Education). 1910. (*14*) *Nalogi i poshliny. Organy finansovogo upravleniya.* (Taxes and duties; Organs of financial administration). 1910. (*15*) *Gornoye delo* (Mining). 1910. (*16*) *Sudebnyya uchrezhdeniya deystvuyushchiye v Turkestane na osnovanii sudebnykh ustavov Imperatora Aleksandra II* (Judicial institutions operative in Turkestan on bases of the judicial codes of Emperor Alexander II) 1910. (*17*) *Tyuremnoye delo* (Prisons) 1910. (*18*) *Gorodskoye upravleniye* (Municipal administration). 1910. (*19*) *Materialy k kharakteristike narodnogo khozyzystva v Turkestane* (Materials on the Turkestan economy). 1910. *Prilozheniye* . . . (Supplement, 3 vols.) 1911. (*20*) *Otchet po revizii v Turkestanskom kraye. Nedostatki upravleniya* (Report on the investigation of the Turkestan region. Administrative shortcomings.) n.d.

the ideals of humanity and justice of that era which today have sanctioned and expedited the attainment of independence by colonial peoples in large parts of the world—though not in Turkestan.

After Count Pahlen's death his Memoirs remained unpublished, in the original German, in the possession of his family. Now translated into English, they are presented here as a lively and colourful account containing matter of great interest not only for specialists in Russian, Central Asian, and colonial history, but also for the general reader. The account throws much new light on the economy and administration of the Russian-administered territories and of the vassal states of Khiva and Bukhara. It also provides a revealing glimpse of a worthy representative of the pre-revolutionary Russian ruling class.

RICHARD A. PIERCE

Queen's University,
Kingston, Ontario
August 1963

ACKNOWLEDGMENTS

I wish to extend thanks to Countess Margaret Pahlen, Mrs. Helen Pahlen Woolley, Mrs. Marie von Kaull, and the late Nicholas Pahlen for their aid in supplying details of their father's career for the introduction to his memoirs. Mr. N. Couriss has been painstaking in providing the translation with not only the letter but the spirit of the original. Lt. Col. G. E. Wheeler, head of the Central Asian Research Centre, read the manuscript and offered many valuable suggestions. Mrs. K. West deserves much credit for her diligence and thoroughness in final preparation of the manuscript for publication.

R.A.P.

PUBLISHER'S NOTE

In preparing the translation of Count Pahlen's Memoirs for the press the primary aim has been to preserve the character and atmosphere of the original German manuscript. It should be remembered that the memoirs were compiled after an interval of thirteen years during which Count Pahlen not only suffered great personal misfortune, but had been deprived of all the notes and memoranda relating to his mission in Turkestan. A narrative written thus from memory must necessarily be incomplete in many details and also may well, as Count Pahlen himself readily admits, contain some inaccuracies in such matters as topography and the description of Islamic practices. Since the value of the memoirs lies mainly in the general impression which they convey, it has seemed preferable not to attempt to improve on the original by the interpolation of notes and commentary.

Place-names

Of the place-names mentioned in the text the following have been changed since the Revolution:

Auliye-Ata	now	Dzhambul
Dzharkent		Panfilov
Nizhniy-Novgorod		Gorkiy
Perovsk		Turtkul
Petro-Alexandrovsk		Kzyl-Orda
Pishpek		Frunze
Samara		Kuybyshev
Vernyy		Alma-Ata

Money

Before 1914 the gold rouble (100 kopecks) was worth 2s. 1½d. in British currency, $0.50 U.S., or 4 German marks.

⚔ I ⚔

TASHKENT

THANKS to its majestic isolation Turkestan has preserved, almost more than any other part of Asia, a character entirely its own. This huge area, as large as Germany, Austria, and France together, is separated from the rest of the world by waterless deserts in the west, by uninhabited deserts in the north, and by the lofty ranges of the Tyan'-Shan', Altay, Pamir, and Hindu Kush in the east, its sole link with civilization consisting of two railways built within the last two decades.

This was the country I visited a few years before the 1914 War as the representative of the Russian Emperor and at his special command on a tour of inspection and study that was to last for over a year, accompanied by a small group of government officials.

In those days it was possible to travel to Central Asia in all the ease and comfort of a first-class carriage on an express train straight from St. Petersburg for a ridiculously small sum, the journey, via Moscow, Samara, and Orenburg, taking six and a half days. The line ended at Andizhan, in Fergana, another two and a half days' train journey farther on.

But I chose a longer route, and by sailing down the Volga between Rybinsk and Samara on one of the luxury river liners we were not only spared the tedium of travel by rail—we were also able from the very beginning of our journey to view some of the most flourishing provinces of Russia.

It was the month of June, and navigation on the Volga was at its height. All day we met enormously long caravans of barges and boats laden with an amazing assortment of cargoes, such as oil, grain, ore, copper, iron, fats, fish, butter, raw hides, meat, etc., floating along the river. We glided past billowing fields, beautiful forests, rich factories, and trading cities; past the old spires of Tatar Kazan and the great flotillas lying in the huge river harbours of Nizhniy-Novgorod and other towns.

In Samara we settled into our railway carriage and were soon rolling over different country: endless cultivated fields of the furrowed steppe, followed by the prairie with its limitless stretches of grassland. Here and there we caught sight of a village surrounded by fields, but once past Orenburg there was nothing but the uninhabited prairie. A day's run from Samara took us into hilly country, quite uninhabited, and we were told that we were crossing the Ural Mountains. We could see no mountains, however, but only rounded hillocks overgrown with yellow burnt grass through which our train wound its monotonous way. Farther east the country looked even more desolate, till at last we were travelling over the hard, salty ground of the desert.

'Have you seen those hares over there?'

My servant had suddenly rushed into my compartment and was excitedly pointing at the window. The 'hares' on the distant horizon turned out to be camels, which my cheerful Kurlander had never seen in his life before. As we rolled through the wayside stations we caught sight of strange-looking, yellow-skinned, sunburnt little men in ankle-length coats and shaggy fur caps. These were Kalmyks. When we alighted our movements were watched by slanted, Chinese-looking eyes holding an expression of apparent contempt, and I had my first glimpse of that peculiar subtlety with which the Asian regards the European. What I believe to be genuine contempt is veiled by an appearance of outward submission that somehow suggests inner awareness of a culture and an outlook on life vastly older than our own. Two thousand years ago these Kalmyks were a great nation. Asia trembled before them, and even the Emperor of China had to pay them tribute. Their cavalry, commanded by chiefs who had mastered the art of leading great masses of horsemen divided into disciplined squadrons and regiments, roamed the earth and like a cloud of locusts laid waste everything in their path. When the Kalmyks moved south they drove the Huns and the Avars from the northern regions of Turkestan and later set the Germanic tribes on the road of the Great Migration. Today the Kalmyks are a poor nomad people, in constant retreat before the advance of European civilization. They roam over the dismal vastness of the steppes that stretch along the Urals from Siberia to the Caspian, a brown and desolate wilderness relieved only by their own occasional winter settlements, or those of their neighbours, the Kirgiz.

When I revisited this region in March of the following year the whole scene was transformed. The earth was still damp from the melting snow and the whole steppe was carpeted with bright red tulips, blue hyacinths, white crocuses, and hundreds of other flowers, all pushing up through the lush green of young grass. Great flocks of sheep, camels, horses, and goats were moving across the land led by shepherds seated on tiny donkeys or, farther north, mounted on bullocks and armed with long lance-like staves. Thus had Jacob watched over the flocks of Laban in the days of long ago.

Today every owner still carefully counts the number of sheep entrusted to his herdsman in the spring, and expects him on his return in the autumn to render account for every animal lost. In the settlements, the unroofed sheep pens provide but scanty shelter from the weather, the beaten clay walls of the fenced enclosures offering at best only a break against the wind. Against these walls the nomads prop their tents, or *yurts*—circular frameworks of willow branches covered with felt and embellished inside with carpets according to the wealth of the owner. Every Kalmyk or Kirgiz family possesses its own yurt, which the womenfolk can assemble and take down in a matter of hours and which makes up one camel load. In the centre of the yurt a hole is scooped out in the ground and in it is laid a fire of saksaul branches (a species of juniper with widely spreading roots which provides a fuel only slightly inferior to coal in calorific value). The head of a family lives apart in his own yurt, the women and children in another, and every time the tribe moves to another site the yurts are taken down and reassembled. The shepherds are the only people who have no yurts because the women do not follow them when they set out for the grazing lands in the spring; they simply sleep out in the open. Later in the summer, when the steppe dries out, the flocks are moved farther north towards the mountains, the shepherds invariably riding at the head of their flocks.

Each tribe owns a well-defined stretch of steppe ranging from 500 to 1000 kilometres in length, running from the Caspian to Siberia. None of these strips has ever been defined or marked out by any authority yet they have been maintained and sanctified by custom over the centuries, though of course, as in the days of Abraham, disputes arise among the shepherds when the grazing tends to run short in the summer. Within the last decades an effort has been made to introduce basic forms of agriculture in the regions where the nomads usually spend their winters, and so gradually prepare them for a more settled way of life. The localities chosen were those where the melting snows form sweet-water lakes in the spring. Though later in the season the water evaporates, enough moisture is retained in the ground to allow for a crop of millet or corn. The example set by the European settlers has also had its effect on the nomads. They have learned, for instance, the value of mowing grass in the early part of the year and of laying in stocks of hay for the winter. Their sheep need no longer starve when fodder runs short and the wretched animals cannot break through the hard icy crust which covers the fields after a frost. Before, they were just turned out and left to provide for themselves as best they could. Bitingly sharp winds from Siberia following a thaw often spread famine and sickness over the steppe, when the sheep, the nomads' only wealth, would perish in thousands. In that land, as I saw it, nothing had changed since the days of the Patriarchs, and the quest for the south and for the lush green pastures of Mesopotamia and southern Palestine was as strong as ever. Indeed, to observe from the window of a comfortable, modern railway carriage these lingering forms of a way of life several thousand years old, was a most singular experience.

Occasionally we saw four-cornered fortress-like structures built of unburnt clay, adorned by spires and having in the centre cupolas of varying height that looked like Italian domes. These were the tombs of sultans and manaps, the tribal chiefs. From a distance they looked most imposing, but closer inspection would reveal that the whole structure was on the point of crumbling from the effects of rain and melting snow.

Even in our modern times the authority these chiefs enjoy is quite astounding. Based upon the principle of seniority within the tribe, it is comparable to the chieftainship of Celtic clans. Within the tribe and the grazing lands owned by it the manap's authority over the economy and over family life is absolute. 'My land' is the term used by the chief in his dealings with European officials when referring to the pastures of his tribe, for to him the conception of landed ownership applies only to the rights of grazing. On the other hand, the right of private property is conceded to the owners of the wretched gardens and bits of tillage scattered round the tribal settlements. For does not the Shariat (the Muslim code based on the Koran) say 'The land that a man has brought to life is his own', and is not this further confirmed by the Adat (the code formed by the customs followed by generations in the steppe)?

Two days out of Orenburg the monotony of our journey was relieved by the unexpected sight of sailing ships apparently floating over the drab brown of the steppe. We had reached the Sea of Aral, an immense expanse of inland water formed by the Jany-Dar'ya river when it could no longer reach the Caspian because of the gradual erosion of the whole Turkestan plain. The two tributaries of the Jany-Dar'ya, the Amu-Dar'ya and the Syr-Dar'ya, the great waterways of Turkestan, then carved out another course and finally joined together in the Aral depression, there to form the Aral Sea. Records of this catastrophe, which drove the Aryan races out of the land and forced them into their great migration to the West, may still be found in some of the old chronicles.

In spite of the unvarying monotony of the landscape, after leaving the station called 'The Sea of Aral' behind us we were cheered by the view of the snow-covered summits of the Kara-Tau gradually rising on the horizon. From this time on I never once, during my entire sojourn in Turkestan, lost sight of mountains in the distance. Relatively, the Kara-Tau range is not high, but as we journeyed farther inland the mountains coming into view grew higher and higher till in Fergana we saw the glistening white of the Pamir— 'The Roof of the World'.

As we approached Tashkent the landscape gradually became more cheerful, though a full day's journey still lay before us. The Syr-Dar'ya, which we first saw as a silvery streak in the distance, had just then played a nasty trick on the engineers who, against the persistent advice of the natives, had laid the railway line at a distance varying from eight to twenty kilometres from its course. Like all other rivers in Turkestan, the Syr-Dar'ya is apt to change its course with very little notice. Large quantities of rubble and loose stones are brought down from the glaciers every year by the mountain torrents which feed the rivers, and gradually a solid dam is built up which forces the water out of the original channel and sets the river meandering over the sands, sometimes miles from its original course. These deposits also account for the water's yellowish-brown appearance.

Some distance from the Russian township of Perovsk the embankment along the Syr-Dar'ya had been partly washed away and we were delayed while a tiresome operation of trolleys and boats was mounted to get us over to the other side, where we were met by a train sent out to take us to the end of our journey at Tashkent. As I went to bed that evening, I heard nothing but laments by the railway personnel over the breach in the embankment and the loss of their houses and belongings. A chocolate-coloured tide of muddy water filled with swirling débris spread over a scene of utter desolation, watched derisively by the native Kirgiz mounted on their shaggy little ponies.

Next morning we awoke to a different world—of gardens and beautifully cultivated green fields surrounded by mulberry trees and slender poplars, with villages scattered here and there. Sunburnt, sinewy natives stripped to the waist and wearing bright red baggy trousers were toiling in the fields, bent over their furrows or wielding the heavy *ketmen*, or Turkestan hoe. At first sight there is something odd about a Turkestan village to a European, the absence of pointed roofs giving the impression of a place destroyed by fire so that only the walls have survived; an impression soon dispelled, however, by the sight of inquisitive women jostling each other on the flat roofs. Though Tashkent lay half a day's journey away we had reached its oasis, turned by irrigation into a blossoming garden. We were met at the station by native deputations of stalwart white-bearded elders robed in velvet mantles and with curved Turkish swords embossed with silver, gold, and precious stones dangling at their sides. An immense green Bukharan silk tent called a *dastarkhan* had been set up on the platform in our honour and tables literally groaning with sweetmeats placed within it.

The fact that we were now well and truly in the East and in the midst of a civilization very different from our own was brought home to us vividly after our meeting with the very first delegation. The contrast between the few Europeans, consisting of the railway personnel, Russian officials and their families, and the motley crowd of natives was most marked, and helped to enhance the oriental flavour of the scene. We were struck by the natives' great dignity of bearing and gesture, the flowery and picturesque language of the welcoming speeches, the respect and awe of the young for their elders, so obvious in every movement; by the pressing, if exaggerated, hospitality and lastly by the notable dignity of their manners, from the proudest mulla or bek down to the poorest shepherd boy. The hour daily set aside to 'politeness' in the *mektebs*, or primary Muslim schools, would account for the extremely good manners of the individual members of the crowd.

An additional touch of the Orient was supplied by the brightly coloured silk and velvet kaftans and the turbans, which were white if the wearer could read the Koran in Arabic and green if he had made the pilgrimage to Mecca. All these bright colours and dignified deportment were in such contrast with the drab khaki of the Russian officials and with the hasty, servile running to and fro of their servants. In the dastarkhan to which we were led we were confronted with a spread of sweets, fruit jellies, native and European pastry, and large flat cakes of Indian corn, which taste very good when they are freshly baked. Needless to say, we were pressed to sample every bowl on those overladen tables.

Another twelve hours by train brought us from Turkestan[1] station to Tashkent over country that seemed strikingly beautiful after the monotony of the steppe. The cotton plants in the carefully cultivated fields were in full bloom and, at this stage, looked like the rose bushes we have in our own gardens. The foliage is dark green and shiny and the flowers form lily-shaped chalices, white with a border of delicate pink or mauve. Whole villages lay deep in lush irrigated gardens and orchards, while juicy apricots and spring peaches were sold at the wayside stations.

Towards evening we steamed slowly into Tashkent, where we were once again met by delegations and where an official reception had been staged in our honour. The white, flat-roofed railway stations of Central Asia, with their platforms (the width of a fair-sized city street) packed tight with a surging crowd of natives from every Asiatic tribe and race, are a singular sight. No limitations are placed on the numbers on the platform and the whole seething mass of humanity spills over the lines, avoiding death by a miracle as the train pulls into the station. As we moved up to the dastarkhan over magnificent oriental carpets spread out on the platform we noticed grey-clad, mummy-like figures in the crowd, veiled to the eyes and moving furtively in the wake of their men: the timid daughters of Eve had come to have a look at the distinguished strangers.

The deputations were, of course, more numerous here than at Turkestan. First came the Governor and his officials, followed by the European colony, foreign consuls, the Sart notables, the local *Kadi* (judge), the Kirgiz, the Jews, the Afghans, and the Persians. Then there was the traditional presentation of bread and salt, and the inevitable speeches and expressions of gratitude. All this under the

[1] This refers to the *town* of that name, 150 miles from Tashkent.

blinding sun of Central Asia, with the temperature somewhere in
the one-hundred and thirties. But I must add that on the Tashkent
plateau the air is so light that the heat, overpowering on the plain,
causes no discomfort.

Well, we were in Tashkent at last, and in the centre of Turkestan.
That night, as I lay in bed reviewing in my mind the events of the
day I was unexpectedly reminded of home by the earthy smell that
came in through my window, in spite of the strangeness of my
surroundings. The muezzins were calling from the tops of the minarets, there was the gentle murmur of water trickling down the
irrigation runnels, and an all-pervading din of thousands of crickets.
A cloudless sky spread its black mantle over the earth, and millions
of stars in the Milky Way twinkled overhead with unusual brightness.
In the garden, rows of peach, apricot and mulberry trees interlaced
by the delicate tracery of tamarisk branches stood out against the
darker green of cypresses and poplars. Farther off I could see the
lights of the town, where life was throbbing after the heat of the day,
and I could hear the dull rumble of the heavy two-wheeled *arabas*
and the unmelodious intermittent braying of donkeys, ironically
dubbed 'the nightingales of Turkestan' for lack of feathered com-
petitors. It was a night like any other summer night until the rains
should come in October.

After the Russian conquest, Tashkent was made the capital of
the whole Turkestan region. For hundreds of years this part of
Central Asia has been the scene of repeated invasions, of wars,
turmoil, and wanton destruction. The fact that it is still inhabited or
that rudimentary forms of civilization somehow managed to survive
can only be explained by the natural wealth of its soil. What was
once a civilized and flourishing country has been gradually turned
into a desert, fit only for nomads and the exercise of unbridled
despotism by unscrupulous and cruel overlords. A Danish engineer
who accompanied me on my journeys told me that a geological
survey he had made of the main canal supplying Tashkent with water
from the hills proved that it was at least 3000 years old. In those days,
according to chronicles found in Peking, the country was owned by
the Chinese, who brought their engineering skill to the construction,
by native labourers, of an extensive system of irrigation canals.
Traces of these canals may be seen in many parts of the desert and,

thanks to an increased supply of water, some of them have in fact been again brought into use. In Fergana, at about 7000 feet above sea level, there must have been a flourishing mining industry, to judge by the traces I found of expertly laid out galleries and shafts, where the Chinese extracted uranium ore more than 2000 years ago.

The Chinese were succeeded by the Huns, who at one time had a great empire in Central Asia. A Chinese chronicle tells us of the plight of the daughter of one of their emperors, who was forced to marry a king of the Huns in order to seal a peace treaty, and of all the indignities she suffered as the barely-tolerated fourth wife instead of enjoying exalted privileges as she had been promised. Her letters to her father are filled with complaints about the Huns and their way of life, about the freezing cold of their felt tents in winter and their long wanderings from place to place in summer. However, the lady seems to have redeemed her fortunes after the death of her husband, for she contrived to seize the reins of power and then to place them in the hands of her son. Her grandson was a renowned ruler, who from Samarkand reigned over a realm lying to the south of the original territories of the Huns and was probably an ancestor of the great Tamerlane.

The conflicts and battles of many races and peoples have left their trace all over this highway of human civilization, lying at the foot of the Pamir. To the north of Tashkent, in the region of the Seven Rivers, now lost in the sands, or *Semirech'ye* as it is called in Russian, I visited a number of ruins which, judging by their extent, must have encompassed cities of 100,000 inhabitants. The fertility of the soil is everywhere so great that civilization was able to spread very rapidly in periods of tranquillity. But, alas, prolonged peace and ordered government were the things most denied this land of strife. In a land where water spells life, all a conqueror needed to do to ensure victory was to break down the dams and destroy the canals. Only nomads could survive and adapt their life to conditions of perpetual warfare, and therefore, as time went on, what was once a civilized and cultivated country was reduced to the desert we now behold.

Turkish, Arab, and Chinese sources now available to us contain much information concerning the history of Turkestan, but a comprehensive narrative of its troubled past still awaits the historian. Only fragmentary evidence is available locally from the few remaining monuments, as every conqueror in turn sought to destroy the works of his predecessors.

Two historical names, however, are universally encountered in Turkestan: Alexander the Great and Tamerlane, called by his contemporaries 'The Scourge of God'. One meets these names everywhere in Central Asia, and often my questions about the name of a large irrigation canal, a mountain pass or an abundant well, were answered by the words 'Timurlenk' or 'Iskander'.

Under Cyrus and Darius, Turkestan was a rich and fertile province of the Persian Empire and it was in Turkestan that Alexander overtook his opponent, Darius, and himself nearly perished for lack of water. The long trains of water tanks one meets at every station of the Transcaspian Railway bear witness to the tremendous difficulties of water supply even in these days of modern transport. One can but marvel at the feats of endurance performed by Alexander's army, 10,000 strong, or by Tamerlane, who marched 100,000 men across the waterless desert to victory at Bayazit.

After the fall of the Macedonian state the country was ruled for many years by the Parthians, and later was overrun by the hordes of Huns, Avars, Turks, and Kalmyks. From a mixture of all these peoples there emerged a new race, the Sarts, who docilely submitted to and served every succeeding conqueror.[1] In origin they are Aryans, but with a strong admixture of Mongol blood, while their language belongs to the Tatar-Turkic group. They have settled all over Turkestan wherever irrigation makes farming possible, but the majority live round Tashkent, Samarkand and Margelan. In the wake of Islam, which came to Turkestan from the south-west, an Arab invasion penetrated as far as the Amu-Dar'ya. The natives were converted to Islam by fire and sword, and a few Arab settlements may still be found in the vicinity of Bukhara.

Arab domination lasted only a short while and was displaced by that of the Turks in their gradual march south and their victory over Byzantium. The advance of the Turks was, however, temporarily arrested by the emergence of a mighty rival in their rear. He stemmed from a dynasty older than that of the Huns and one which ruled over

---

[1] As was customary during the Tsarist régime Count Pahlen regarded the Sarts as a distinct ethnic group with their own language. Originally, however, the word was applied to the sedentary, and principally to the urban, population of Turkestan without any reference to race or language. A Sart might therefore be of Tadzhik (Iranian), Uzbek (Turkic), or of mixed Iranian and Turkic stock; and he might speak either Tadzhik or Uzbek or be bilingual in both languages. There is no such thing as a Sart language. During the Soviet régime the word acquired a derogatory significance and is now no longer used.

a kingdom situated on the shores of the Golden River, Zeravshan. The ruler and his nobles were all Uzbeks, and the name is still applied to the élite of the Kirgiz. The kingdom included the oasis of Samarkand, the northern and eastern regions of Fergana and Kashgar, and parts of Bukhara. Protected along its frontiers by mountains or the desert it had been ruled for several generations by tough and energetic men when the young Tamerlane was brought to power. He conquered Northern Turkestan and overran the land of the Seven Rivers and the adjoining regions of Siberia. He defeated the Khan of the Golden Horde. After this he set out on the conquest of India and ravaged the land as far as Delhi.

A few years later he led his armies against the Turks in response to a request for help by the Byzantine emperor. Arab chronicles mention the curious fact that about a third of his army was composed of Christians and even included a Russian contingent. This host, after crossing the desert from Samarkand to the Caspian Sea, where it was met by a Russian flotilla of barges with supplies, then swarmed over the Caucasian range into Asia Minor and saved Byzantium by routing the Turks at Angora. Syria and Egypt were conquered in turn, and an empire under one lord now stretched from Mongolia to the Mediterranean. Only death thwarted his plans to invade China.

That Tamerlane's stupendous victories should have impressed the Western world is hardly surprising. He was described as a cruel and ruthless tyrant by his enemies and those who had reason to fear him; his intimates spoke of him as a genius, a supremely talented military leader and an able administrator. This latter description would appear to be nearer the truth if we judge him by the monuments he left behind, by the skill with which he administered his domains, and by the realm he bequeathed to his descendants. The mosques he built and the ruins of the mighty aqueduct which once brought water to Samarkand still stand today, more than five centuries after his death; many of the irrigations still bear the name of 'Timurlenk'.

After his death his huge empire fell apart, like that of his predecessor, Alexander the Great, though his descendant, Babur, seems to have inherited some of his qualities of leadership. From Afghanistan, which was all that was left of Tamerlane's empire, he conquered India, and there founded another empire which was to last until the advent of the British.

After these great events a period of stagnation and progressive decay spread over Turkestan. For a time the south fell to some of the greater shahs of Persia, but slowly civilization was stamped out by plundering Mongol and Turkic nomads. All that was left were a few despots, who used the nomadic tribes to terrorize the population and bolster up their reign of extortion and cruelty.

This state of anarchy prevailed in Central Asia right up to the seventeenth century, when Russia first showed signs of expansion. The Empire, under Peter the Great, tried to put a stop to raids into the region of the Volga and to the destruction of Russian fisheries on the Caspian, two constant causes of strife between the subjects of the White Tsar and the neighbouring tribes of Turkestan. All Peter's efforts, both military and diplomatic, failed; the forces he could assemble locally at that time being far too feeble to break through the bulwark presented by a desert stretching inland for hundreds of miles. In the eighteenth century, however, a chain of small fortifications running from Astrakhan to the Siberian border was built under Elizabeth and Catherine II and we observe a gradual retreat of the nomadic tribes to the south-east of the Russian border. Every attempt by the nomads to break through this line of defence failed and was invariably repulsed. Very soon the Astrakhan, Orenburg, and Siberian Cossacks were the equals of their foes in the art of desert warfare, while pursuit of the enemy often led to deeper penetration and a new line of outposts on the conquered border.

In the course of this gradual penetration from west and north, which progressively brought the area under Russian control, many towns were founded, such as Irgiz, Perovsk, Ili, Vernyy, Auliye-Ata and Pishpek.

At the beginning of the nineteenth century, Turkestan, like Europe at the time of the Napoleonic wars, was in the throes of bloodshed and unrest. A new kingdom, with Kokand as its capital, arose in Fergana and expanded eastward and north, towards China and Kashgar. By the late eighteen-forties, its ruler had gained dominion over a large region extending from the provinces of Kashgar and Kuldzha on the borders of China to the mouth of the Syr-Dar'ya. At Auliye-Ata, in the region of the Seven Rivers, their advance was barred by Russian forces brought from the north and from Siberia. At Pishpek an army of 40,000 Kokand warriors was routed by a detachment of 1500 men under General Kolpakovskiy, later the Governor-General of the Steppe Provinces. The mass tactics of the horde were no match for modern weapons and disciplined troops, and his defeat was so complete that after it the Khan of Kokand never recovered. As a vassal he proved a traitor and subsequently forfeited his kingdom to the Russians.

After Pishpek the Russians took Tashkent. They then crossed the desert in the west and took Holy Samarkand from the Emir of Bukhara, and in 1873 made the Khan of Khiva a Russian vassal. During these grandiose operations, which embraced the whole of that immense region, the Russian troops were led by General Kaufman, a man of outstanding ability. As Governor-General of Turkestan and plenipotentiary of Tsar Alexander he proved a most talented administrator. He was allowed to enjoy virtually unrestricted authority over the newly conquered regions. Legislation, the enforcement of law and order, the right to pardon, of going to war or of signing peace treaties with neighbouring states, were all vested in his person.

In 1880 the whole of the Transcaspian region, then the only remaining territory held by the nomads, was brought under Russian control by General Skobelev's victory over the Turkmens at Geok-Tepe. The entry of Russia into Central Asia, followed by the introduction of European methods and civilization, brought a breath of fresh air to a land despoiled and impoverished by centuries of Asian despotic rule. The reader, accustomed to differentiate between what he has been taught to regard as Western civilization and conditions in Russia, may fail to appreciate the magnitude and effect of the changes wrought in the life of Central Asia by Tsarist and autocratic Russia. Slavery was brought to an end; the arbitrary legislation of the Khans, Emirs, and their puppets, the Beks, who controlled a large part of their masters' wealth, such as their flocks, was superseded by Russian law, under which all the inhabitants, irrespective of their standing, were equal. Hitherto enslaved captives from every race in Asia, emancipated overnight, hastened home to spread the news of these wondrous changes, introduced by a humane administration, upheld by one universal writ, and enforced by Russian arms. Henceforth the verdicts of the Kadis (judges) in the local courts were based on a wise adaptation of the Shariat (the holy law of Islam) to the Russian conception of justice.

The great prestige enjoyed by Russia all over Asia at the end of the nineteenth century was largely due to her moderate and enlightened policy in the conquered regions, for which General Kaufman was directly responsible. It was enhanced by the successes of his armies and, especially, by the victory gained by General Komarov over the Afghans, supported by the British, at Tash-Kepri. This victory dealt a severe blow to Britain's prestige, and her attitude was one of well-nigh overt hostility when Russia advanced her frontiers to Sarakhs on the Persian border, and the Kushka Pass, facing India, on that of Afghanistan. After these campaigns, which ended Russian penetration into Central Asia, an era of peaceful development and progressive improvement in the life of the native population descended upon the land.

Kaufman and Kolpakovskiy were allowed to rule Turkestan with little or no interference by the central government in St. Petersburg. Administratively, Turkestan was divided into the following five provinces with their respective capitals: Amu-Dar'ya (Tashkent); Samarkand (capital of the same name); Fergana (Margelan, later renamed Skobelev); Semirech'ye (Vernyy); and Transcaspia (Ashkhabad). Each province was divided into districts, placed under military commandants and administered by district officers subordinated to them. Tashkent became the capital of the whole region, though at first the two provinces of Semirech'ye and Transcaspia did not come within the jurisdiction of the Governor-General.

At the beginning of this century the original administrative pattern set up by Kaufman was altered by an influx of colonial officials directly responsible to the central government. Administrators of crown lands, internal revenue inspectors, the legal personnel of the newly established courts, the staff of the Tashkent-Orenburg railway under construction, etc., looked for directives to St. Petersburg, not to Tashkent. Even so, when one considers the complexity both of the government machinery so quickly set up and of the huge amount of work it was efficiently accomplishing as compared to the primitive Asian institutions of the neighbouring states, the impact made by Russia on the peoples living round the borders of Turkestan may well be imagined. The thousands of Afghans, Persians, Chinese and Indians who yearly flocked to the bazaars of Tashkent, Samarkand, Ashkhabad, and Margelan to trade or to visit the holy shrines spread the fame of Russia's achievement throughout the length and breadth of Asia.

At the time when the inhabitants of Turkestan were beginning to enjoy the fruits of just government, their brothers in Afghanistan,

Persia, and West China were still lingering under arbitrary forms of despotism, unfettered by any kind of law, and systems which had hardly changed since the days of Tamerlane. The aim of any Afghan bek, Chinese mandarin, or Persian governor was to extract as much money as he could from the province over which he ruled with an utter disregard for the welfare of the population, which he bled in his own interests as well as those of his lord and master. Taxation in those countries was based on the ancient Asian principle of payment in kind equivalent to one-tenth of the owner's income. The taxes were farmed out by the emirs, shahs, or whatever else they were called, against a fixed sum to their satraps, who were then expected to meet the costs of administration and to pay the army in their respective provinces. To bolster up his authority the bek, mandarin, or governor was granted absolute power and was allowed to employ any means he chose, including the death penalty, provided he 'delivered the goods'. In his anxiety to squeeze as much as he could out of the tax-payer, both to line his own pockets and to bribe his master's courtiers, the provincial overlord resorted to every form of pressure. This usually took the form of misinterpreting the Shariat to the detriment of the victim. Since the code requires every owner to surrender a tenth of his harvest or of any other income to the tax collector, the latter, who was as keen as his master to feather his own nest, would, for instance, forbid the peasant at threshing time to remove the harvest, and threaten him with dire penalties such as confiscation, beating, or even death, in the event of disobedience.

The only way out for the unfortunate peasant was to placate the tax collector by paying him in excess of the recognized tithe. This in turn left the door open for denunciations by jealous neighbours, or for concealment of income and further exactions. Reliable witnesses, well acquainted with local conditions, have told me that in Afghanistan, and in west China particularly, landowners and tradesmen were often forced to give up as much as ninety per cent of their incomes instead of the ten per cent prescribed by law. In addition to taxation, other sources of extorted revenue were open to the rulers of these border states, such as the imposition of a monopoly on imports or the fixing of ridiculously low prices on goods saleable exclusively to themselves. The trade in Karakul lamb pelts is an instance of this practice. When I was in Bukhara the inhabitants were compelled to sell these at two roubles to the Emir, who sold them over the border for seven. The same methods were used in Afghanistan in relation to pistachio nuts and almonds. An Afghan farmer told me of an instance when he had set out with a caravan of twelve donkeys laden with almonds which he intended to sell to the Russians at Kushka. He said he was lucky to reach his destination with two donkey-loads, after being forced to part with ten on his way to the tax collector of his provincial lord.

In India at that time the collection of taxes was entrusted by the British to native collectors, and ruthlessly enforced. They in turn worked on the lines common throughout Asia. The unbelievable fertility of the soil and the centuries-old ability of the inhabitants to dispense with the most rudimentary requirements of life, are the reason why conditions such as I have described were able to persist in all these countries.

The reaction of the native population to Russian rule in Turkestan, regarded as something akin to paradise, is easily understood if one remembers that immediately upon their entry the Russians abolished slavery, dismissed the tax collectors of the former rulers, introduced a system of elected courts upheld by District Officers and, most important of all, practically did away with taxation. Isolated cases of corruption cannot, of course, be denied; but what were they compared with the exactions of the past?

In order not to hurt the feelings of the Muslims, to whom the right of the ruler to the tithe was something ordained by the Prophet, the outer form of assessment was preserved. A register of landed property was drawn up and the leviable tax translated into its equivalent in money, based on the cost of production. This assessment was so modest that the tax actually levied seldom exceeded from one to three per cent. A few years later, when expensive cotton replaced corn as the natives' main crop, the burden of taxation was still further lightened by the retention of the tax originally based on corn.

One of the weaker aspects of Russian administration was the comparative modesty of the sums allocated to welfare and to cultural and technical works. It should, however, be noted that the budget of the newly conquered regions barely sufficed to meet the essential needs of administration. The attitude of the Imperial Ministry of Finance in St. Petersburg was one of obstruction, based on the assumption that the conquest of 'the Desert', as it chose to refer to Turkestan, merely added to the Crown's commitments without providing it with new sources of revenue. Nevertheless, for some time after the conquest these shortcomings passed unnoticed. The former Khans and Emirs had maltreated the natives for so long and made so much use of forced labour that the Sarts and Kirgiz, pressed by the Russians into the construction of roads, the building of rows of houses for the Europeans, and the digging of irrigation canals indispensable to the upkeep of their lovely gardens, neither showed resentment nor thought this work particularly irksome. Indeed, they considered they were being very well treated, as compared with their condition under their former masters.

The popularity of the Russian régime in Turkestan lasted for many years, and was expressed in respect and veneration for the distant fountain-head of 'the Russian ideal', the 'White Tsar', 'the Ak-Padishah'. Russia's frontiers could have been extended farther east if the Ministry of Foreign Affairs had appreciated the significance of Kaufman's, Skobelev's, and Kolpakovskiy's achievements early enough. If, instead of deferring to the arrogance of the all-knowing and all-wise diplomats of foreign embassies it had abandoned its policy of the 'worthless desert', the rich provinces of Kashgar and Kuldzha, with their industrious Sart and Tatar population, need not have been unprofitably surrendered to China in order to secure the good graces of so weak a neighbour.

Russia's prestige in Asia was great. It was due to the incompetence of Kaufman's successors that the foundations which he had laid so well were afterwards weakened. Indeed, his conquest of Turkestan is comparable to the conquests of Mexico by Cortez. The troops under his command never numbered more than 5000 men, while the size of the country he brought under control can be gauged by the size of the smallest district which was 500 square miles, later to be administered by some modest lieutenant with a dozen troopers to enforce his authority.

I was able to interview a few of the early pioneers who had served under Kaufman's military administration and to record their impressions. Some of them were highly educated men who spoke two or three native languages—Kirgiz, Sart, Turkmen, or Arabic—and were the authors of learned works. In the early days, when the colony was largely cut off from the home country both by desert and distance, a whole-hearted devotion to its interests was the dominating force in the lives of the settlers, while Europe and all it meant was allowed to recede into the background. By contemporary standards the Russian colonial officials were extremely well-paid, their salaries far exceeding the pay of frontline officers of the army; in addition, they were provided with excellent living quarters and servants. Thus there was no lack of candidates to fill the administrative posts from the material at hand, and Kaufman followed the practice of selecting provincial and district officers from the pick of his battalion and company commanders.

Unfortunately, the few black sheep among them gave the administration a bad name at home when they returned with well-lined pockets. Here I must bear witness to the very high standard of efficiency of the early government officials, who were the true first settlers, to their work and to the civilizing influence they exercised. They maintained peace and order in the land, while immense enterprises such as dairying, fruit-farming, and cotton growing on a huge scale were developed on their initiative. Their work became an integral part of their lives, and to them the native and his welfare were nearer than were their kinsmen in distant Europe.

This feeling of oneness with the land of their adoption was demonstrated at the beginning of the century when Turkestan was invaded by a wave of immigrants from Russia. Their arrival was welcomed by the Central Administration, but the District Officers treated them as intruders, and contemptuously compared what they called their 'barbarous' way of life with the time-honoured customs of the native population. This attitude, it must be admitted, was not wholly unjustified, for the choice of immigrants at the time was not a happy one. The majority were neither peasants from the land nor genuine factory workers but belonged to an intermediary class impoverished by circumstances in Russia. Lured by rosy prospects of a 'promised land' they had emigrated to Turkestan and were only too ready to lead an idle life at the expense of the state; they had no wish to work hard, were not interested in improved methods of husbandry, and looked down upon the hardworking and disciplined natives.

During the last decade preceding the 1914 war, instead of being an asset the immigrants were a source of constant worry to the Turkestan authorities and the position was made worse by interference from the Central Government, roused to action by their numbers. While General Kaufman lived, St. Petersburg was content to leave well alone and never ventured to interfere with his administrative measures. After his death things changed. A long line of distinguished generals, brave in war but feeble as administrators,

filled the post of Governor-General. They were used as tools by their
subordinates and, because of their standing with the sovereign, were
able to obstruct attempts to introduce a centralized policy directed
from the capital. On the other hand, in St. Petersburg every interested ministry was engaged in promoting a policy of its own, more
often than not based on the advice of some minor civil servant, and
one probably at variance with the ideas of the Governor-General.

The transition from a policy of firmness and benevolence to one
lacking in sustained directives had a noticeable effect on the natives.
Hitherto so contented and friendly, they resented the contempt of
the immigrants, were angered by the spate of regulations by which
they were now beset from every quarter, became first restive and then
inimical to Russia. A contributory factor to this change of attitude
was the growth of the Panislamic movement in the Mohammedan
world, to which I shall later return.

Such then, were the conditions prevailing in Turkestan at the time
of my visit. Since then everything has changed. The tide of Bolshevism has swept over the land. Both rulers and ruled have been
indiscriminately slaughtered, and the Asian pattern of despotism,
with its abuses and disregard for the life of the individual, has been
reinstated.

At the time, however—ten years ago—the trend of local life was
geared to 'Europeanization'. The railway engine pulling into a
station symbolized victory over the desert. Cleanly-dressed Russian
railway porters wearing the trade mark of their calling, a white
apron, greeted the weary traveller at the station and conducted him
to a comfortable *drozhki* or cab, generally drawn by two horses.
He was then driven to the European quarter at a spanking trot along
straight wide avenues lined by a double row of trees through which
he glimpsed the *aryks*, or irrigation canals, running parallel to the
street; past one-storied flat-roofed houses and at last brought to a
spacious hotel with spotless rooms, bathrooms, and modern furnishings. The cool of the nights is heavenly after the great heat of the
day, and is the reason why life becomes so intensive after dark. In
the morning, however, great care is taken to shut out the heat. A
house boy, a white-robed, silent Sart in high, soft, white leather
boots, with a white skull cap perched on his head, quietly does the
rounds of the rooms, carefully closing any window accidentally left
open and drawing heavy oriental carpets over them to keep the
bedrooms cool all day. Everyone takes a siesta lasting from three to

four hours but goes to bed very late, so that often at sunrise one is still enjoying the company of one's friends. At night the temperature varies from 49° to 63° Fahrenheit, but during the day it seldom falls below 77° or 82°.

Life in government and business circles in those days was quite European. Soon after my arrival I attended a banquet given by the Governor-General. Most of the men were in khaki battledress (it was summer, and the troops were on manoeuvres) but wearing stars and decorations; the women were in low-cut evening gowns with sparkling jewels and flowers in their hair. One would have found the same setting anywhere in St. Petersburg, Berlin, Vienna, or Paris. Even the flowers on the dining table—roses, white acacia, violets, lovely tulips and daffodils, were reminiscent of home. The fare we were offered, too, was anything but oriental. There was of course the obligatory Russian *zakuska* of caviare, pickled mushrooms and a variety of small pies; and even a *pâté de Strasbourg* tasted remarkably good washed down with the traditional vodka. The menus, printed in French, informed us that we were to be served with a dinner of six or seven courses equal to anything we could have expected at home, while the champagne and other wines were all imported from Europe.

But when, after dinner, we moved into the garden where coffee was served, we were at once back in Asia, with its pitch-black night and the myriad stars of the Milky Way, with the all-pervading din of crickets, the murmuring water in the canals, the bitter taste of the scent-laden desert air which makes the heart beat faster, although it seems so light, since Tashkent lies 600 metres above sea level.

The grounds of the Governor-General's residence were very well cared for at that time and abundantly supplied with the water so precious in Central Asia. The shady leaves of the beautiful trees formed a canopy over our heads, and the coloured lanterns and candles turned the scene into fairyland as we sat sipping our coffee at little tables placed on the lawns. An enchanting spring gurgled at our feet. Coffee was served by native Sarts in ceremonial national dress, with skull caps embroidered in gold and bright silk sashes wound round their waists over white kaftans. The formal black of European evening dress and even the pretty gowns of the ladies seemed somehow out of place in this oriental setting.

As I looked around at the assembled guests I found myself wondering what we Europeans had brought this land, apart from perhaps a little ease and a few technical means of livelihood. Were the people happier before the Europeans stepped in? Was the advent of the soldier, the European engineer and technician to engender a ferment of disintegration destined eventually to destroy the souls of the people together with their ethical and moral standards?

In the course of my tour of inspection I pondered much over this problem. I felt that in addition to my other duties I ought to try to understand the basic principles of the native's outlook on life, study the workings of his mind, and assess the changes which this contact with another civilization had brought about. In turn I was brought to examine the whole problem of Mohammedanism in Central Asia. Unfortunately, I no longer possess the extensive material I collected in those days. It was destroyed by the Red hordes together with my library, the whole classified as 'counter-revolutionary nonsense'. I can therefore only outline the problem as I understand it and as far as memory permits.

❧ II ❧

SAMARKAND

VISIT to Samarkand with its holy places and its beautiful mosques, built by Tamerlane, and some acquaintance with the *medresehs* of Bukhara are essential to the study of Islam in Central Asia. Here one is at once brought face to face with the strange and mysterious world that governs the minds of millions in Asia, generating the mystical force by which they are driven and guided far beyond the frontiers of Russia. It is in this region that the mainspring of this force is to be sought.

For some time after we had begun our journey from Tashkent to Samarkand by rail we continued to travel through the Tashkent oasis. Cotton fields, bordered by irrigation canals with mulberry trees along their banks, were visible everywhere. On our way to the Syr-Dar'ya which we crossed by means of a splendid modern bridge we passed numerous *kishlaks*, or long native villages, set deep in lovely orchards. Then we found ourselves in the desert once more, though it was now less dreary than on the stretch from Orenburg to Tashkent. In the distance the summits of the Alai mountains rose above the horizon. The landscape was dotted with tamarisk bushes and frequent small oases, each surrounded by beautifully green and fertile fields. In the morning we left the Tashkent–Fergana–Andizhan line and branched off into the 'Hungry Steppe'.[1] This is a 200 kilometre stretch of country devoid of water both in winter and summer and universally feared. Before the Revolution the Russian Government had been developing a project which was intended to bring 400,000 acres of desert under cultivation by leading the waters of the Syr-Dar'ya along a broad canal 30 kilometres long and about 40 metres wide. When I visited the works the scheme was still in its initial stages, the canal only half completed and therefore dry.

[1] This 'Hungry Steppe', lying between Dzhizak and the Syr-Dar'ya, should not be confused with the larger 'Hungry Steppe', to the west of Lake Balkash.

In days gone by, the great caravan route to Samarkand and thence through Afghanistan to India lay across the Hungry Steppe. I, too, travelled along this route, but in the comfort of a victoria mounted on rubber tyres and drawn by a troika. Never shall I forget that drive across the desert on a sweltering day in July. We set out in the cool of early morning after a sumptuous breakfast served in our saloon car. Though the country round Khilkovo station was watered by the Syr-Dar'ya all signs of affluence and indeed of civilization seemed to vanish when we left the last irrigation canal behind us. On reaching the ancient route we simply followed the long line of skeletons of camels, donkeys and horses that had perished while crossing the desert. Human skulls and bones too, remains of the prey of jackal and vulture, lie unburied with the bones of beasts under a layer of greyish yellow dust all along this route, followed by caravans for thousands of years, and presenting an endless vista of death.

As the sun rose in the sky it grew hotter and hotter till at 10 o'clock we were forced to halt, and take refuge in the earth hut of a foreman on the banks of the canal. A thermometer on an outside wall registered 162° Fahrenheit, so that at 110° inside the cabin it was pleasantly cool. Here we stayed for a few hours, rested our sturdy Persian ponies, and then resumed our drive across an endless wilderness where the spring grass had long since withered to dust. The soil is a yellowish grey marl, or loess, formed by the disintegration of porphyry rock; carried by the wind off the surrounding mountains in the form of a very fine dust, it gradually settled and built up the Central Asian Plateau. The fertility of the soil as soon as it is given any moisture is incredible; it will produce marvellous harvests all the year round with no manuring at all, thus reducing the problem of cultivation and tillage exclusively to one of water supply.

In the Hungry Steppe, experimental irrigation carried out by the Grand Duke Nicholas, son of the Grand Duke Constantine, has given excellent results, and in this respect he may well be called the pioneer of irrigation in Turkestan. During the course of our drive we were able to see some of the work accomplished by him. After a journey of several hours I caught sight of some trees in the distance and was informed by one of the escort that we were about to approach a village of Russian settlers which was watered by a canal excavated on the instructions of the Grand Duke. As we drew nearer a most amazing figure appeared on the horizon. It was a Russian peasant in the typical dress of the Volga regions (blue cotton shirt, wide trousers, thick white wrappings round his legs, lime bark sandals and a pointed, broad-brimmed straw hat on his head) mounted, of all things, on a bicycle and pedalling toward us for all he was worth. It transpired that he was a messenger sent by the villagers to bid us welcome and invite us to visit them. When we left we had been given a guard of honour of mounted Kirgiz;[1] nothing could have been more incongruous and have more strongly underlined the contrast between Asia and Europe than the sight of this peasant in his Russian dress riding a bicycle ahead of the natives in their parade-dress kaftans embellished with precious stones, festooned with weapons and astride their small, sturdy ponies. We were soon joined by other Russian peasants mounted on tall trotters and thus we proceeded through the Hungry Steppe, convoyed by a brightly coloured escort of Kirgiz and peasants, with the cyclist well ahead of the horsemen!

The village had been founded only ten years before by some industrious Russian peasants, the majority of them Stundists (a Lutheran religious sect), who had settled here after the exiled Grand Duke had brought water to this part of the desert by canal from the Syr-Dar'ya. When the settlers first arrived the place was as barren as the country we had just crossed; now, ten years later, the village was ringed by fertile fields that yielded bumper harvests. If they were spared by the locusts, that is. Near the village we were shown the trap trenches which the peasants dig in the spring during their annual battle with this plague. In these the young locusts, as yet unable to fly, are caught and destroyed. We were also shown an ingenious invention that was claimed to be most successful: a few years later, in the World War, it was known as a flame-thrower, and was extensively used as a weapon. The trees round the village, as tall as thirty year old trees in western Europe, bore witness to the extreme fertility of the soil when properly watered.

A very friendly and hearty welcome was given us by the villagers. Judging by the fact that each of them possessed a minimum of three horses and three cows they seemed to have prospered exceedingly well in those ten years. I noticed that they were raising Asian agricultural crops, for in addition to cotton (*der Geldfrucht*) they were growing *jugara* (sorghum), and winter barley. This

---

[1] During the Tsarist régime the word Kirgiz, or sometimes Kaisak-Kirgiz, was habitually used to refer to the Kazakhs, the real Kirgiz being called Kara-Kirgiz. Where Count Pahlen uses Kirgiz he usually means Kazakh.

exclusively Russian settlement of ten villages covered an area of 40,000 acres.

The canal which had made it arable and was originally traced by the Grand Duke had been planned, dug, and completed by the Sarts alone without the aid of any European technicians.

The success of the scheme immediately aroused the jealousy of the lazy officials in Tashkent responsible for the administration of land owned by the Crown, and a plan was forthwith produced for the overall irrigation of the Hungry Steppe. The preliminary work alone cost more than the Grand Duke's entire canal had done. Blue-prints shuttled back and forth between St. Petersburg and Tashkent and it took five years for the final plans to be approved and the necessary funds allocated. When at last the work was put in hand the plans were once again revised, whole mountains of sand were shifted and several engineers were sent abroad (at the expense of the project) to study Western irrigation schemes. Ten years later the Hungry Steppe was still arid with the exception of the water brought to it by the Grand Duke's canal. As a result of a report I submitted the work was accelerated; some of the engineers were dismissed, and a few were committed for trial. Shortly before the 1914 war water at last began to flow into the desert land and reports pronounced the cultivation of cotton on a large scale to be feasible.

Some distance from Khilkovo station the line branches south. At Dzhizak deputations if anything more colourful than on previous occasions were again assembled to greet our arrival. Government officials and high-ranking military officers stood in the front rows, headed of course by the Chief District Officer (a colonel), his deputies, a few interpreters and *jigits* (mounted police). This group also included the garrison officers, their wives, the judiciary, the local school teachers, etc. In fact quite a crowd, when all the relatives come to see the show are taken into account. Protocol demanded that every member be greeted with a handshake and a few polite words. Next came the delegates of the Russian civilian population, consisting of small craftsmen and traders, with the traditional bread and salt. Their spokesman, a pettifogging lawyer, unburdened himself of a very long and pompous speech which apparently greatly displeased the Chief District Officer. On the whole I thought it rather inoffensive. Apart from expressing the desire of the business community for more self-administration and a curtailment of the District Officer's powers it was exaggeratedly chauvinistic in tone.

The dastarkhan table, laden on this occasion with lovely peaches, was set just behind the deputations. The Russians were followed by rows of natives. There were white-bearded Sarts in white or green turbans and nomad Kirgiz in their shaggy caps. Then came the Jews, three deputations of them. First the Oriental Jews, in brightly coloured kaftans with a silken cord in lieu of sash (a relic of Bukharan times when they were forbidden to wear ceremonial sashes like the Sarts). Next to them the Russo-Polish Jews of the west, regarded by the former as a sect, in their best European clothes, headed by their rabbi carrying the Torah. Lastly the Marans of the east, Jews who were at one time compelled outwardly to embrace Islam but who retained their faith in secret. They are distinguished by the observance both of the Mohammedan Friday and the Jewish Sabbath and are universally despised by every class of the rest of the population. Their occupation is usury, and jobbing in the varied and perpetually fluctuating Asian currencies. (In Turkestan, in addition to the Russian rouble, the Persian kran and the Indian rupee as well as Turkish and French coins are legal tender. All these specie are used, more often than not, by the Jews to cheat the natives.) In addition to the three Jewish deputations there were others of Tadzhiks, Hindus, Afghans, and even Persians, who had come with a present of bread and salt. In the circumstances it was not surprising that we were held up much longer than was originally planned, while the deputations were being dealt with and dispatched.

After Dzhizak the train headed south for a range of mountains, and on leaving the desert curved upward through a valley along the banks of a small river. In crossing the range the railway runs through a narrow pass,[1] once the greatest obstacle encountered by caravans on their way to India. Railroad engineers have blasted away the steep rocks which at one time came so close together that there was barely room for the road. The face of a tall cliff to the right of the pass bears an inscription in Arabic visible from a great distance. The text, in lettering as high as a wall, informs the traveller in glowing terms that Tamerlane conquered the world and led many hundreds of thousands of warriors, camels, and horses across this pass, something no one had dared to attempt before him. For centuries the message stood, a witness to the might of the greatest ruler in Asia, till the day when the servants of the White Tsar were able with the aid of modern technical equipment to overcome this

[1] The Sanzar Pass.

apparently insuperable obstacle. Dynamite, steam, and electricity pushed aside the mighty walls of porphyry, and now trains run proudly on their journey south. Slavonic lettering just as tall and a gilded imperial eagle carved in the face of the rock by Russian engineers over Tamerlane's inscription proclaim that: 'In the year 1895, His Majesty Emperor Nicholas II was graciously pleased to order the construction of this railway. Order carried out, 1898.'

After the Russian conquest the province of Samarkand, formerly part of Bukhara, had the good fortune to be excellently administered by able governors. Among the many things to their credit are the splendid roads, lined two and three deep on either side with beautiful trees providing welcome shade to the traveller. The average Westerner, while enjoying this relief, hardly appreciates the foresight and drive required to obtain such results in Central Asia. No trees grow unless they are artificially watered, and in Samarkand this entails the construction of a complex system of canals parallel with road building. Thanks to these provisions long stretches of the highways are lined by lovely gardens with enough water to allow for the growing of mulberries, essential to the Samarkand silk industry. One of the governors, towards the close of the last century, was a passionate gardener, and had gardens laid out all over the province. In Samarkand I was taken to visit the College of Fruit and Vine Growing, which at one time must have presented a remarkable sight. The grounds were originally planned by a German and contained many rare species of trees and vines. Unfortunately, by the time of my visit the place was like a wilderness because the effect of a lavish supply of water—at that time the governor's hobby—on the phenomenally fertile native loess was something the European gardener had not foreseen. The result was a crop of savage weeds by which he was utterly routed. By contrast the gardens of the local Persians, who knew how to utilize every drop of water to the best advantage, were as neat and tidy as could be.

An enterprising Russian named Filatov, who had arrived in Samarkand together with the occupying Russian battalions, had at once laid out some vineyards. He planted most of them with vines from the Rhine and the Neckar, and trained them along bent willow branches to form arched alleys according to the method employed in Central Asia. As soon as he could he started pressing his grapes. To his amazement, in this area the vines imported from the Rhine produced a sweet, heavy, and fiery wine, very much like Tokay, which Filatov sold to the Orthodox Churches as Communion wine. Particularly interesting was the construction of his cellars. Long tree trunks were sunk into the ground and placed four storeys high on top of each other. No arches or props were used to support the wall and ceiling. The loess in which the cellars are excavated is so plastic that it has half the strength of concrete, and deep holes dug into the ground will not cave in. In the centre of the cellars Filatov installed a great hall, at least thirty feet high, where he decanted his wines and sampled them together with his friends. These four-storied constructions were never damaged by the frequent earthquakes in spite of their having no technical means of support or reinforcement.

Samarkand oasis is irrigated by the Zeravshan. A large catchment area in the region ducts water along two arterial canals, one of which supplies Samarkand while the other is placed at the disposal of the Emir of Bukhara in compliance with the terms of a treaty of friendship between his country and Russia. After the conquest of Turkestan by the Russians the great dam serving both Samarkand and Bukhara was found in exactly the state in which Tamerlane's engineers had left it. Had it been built of local loess it would obviously have been washed away long ago, so some other kind of material must have been used. In Merv, for example, the great curved Sultan Dam on the Murgab river is built of special bricks, presumably imported from afar, because up to the present no clay has been found locally from which those delf-like bricks could be made.

Up to the beginning of the century the dam on the Zeravshan was a most primitive affair, built of dung and earth held together by bushes, reeds, straw, and crooked thorn branches. This construction was reinforced by piles tied together in the shape of a pyramid, weighed down with stones and driven into the river bed. At flood time, when the level of the water had to be lowered, the whole edifice was pulled down and later laboriously rebuilt with fresh material, since all the old stuff had of course been washed away.

Naturally, these cumbersome methods made a heavy demand on the available manpower, very often at times when it was most desperately needed in the fields. The ordinances requiring the population to supply an unlimited number of labourers for work on the dams, made in the days of Bukharan rule, were maintained by the Russians, who exercised little or no control over the whole system of impressed labour. Every year thousands of men were dispatched to the catchment areas where, particularly round the dams when the river was in flood, they worked for days on end waist-deep in icy cold water. The engineers who were supposed to pay these unfortunate fellows a daily wage usually pocketed the money and did nothing to improve the condition of the dams.

However, soon after the turn of the century an active governor of Samarkand took matters in hand on the advice of an honest engineer and replaced the existing installations at the main dams by modern concrete structures with hydraulically-operated, corrugated-iron sluice gates. A network of telephones was also installed, linking the larger and smaller dams so that the amount of water required at any time in a given arterial canal could be regulated and controlled. Though the native population was undoubtedly immensely impressed, the authorities and employees who administered the supply of water must have worried not a little at the threat to their incomes.

As I have said, the waters of the Zeravshan were used to irrigate both Samarkand and Bukhara. Before the construction of the new system the dam regulating the supply of water to both these regions was in Russian-controlled territory and supervised by a Russian water *aksakal* (supervisor), which meant that the latter was in a position to arbitrarily withhold or increase the requisite supply of water merely by making a slight alteration to the angle of flow. An alteration of a few inches was very often all that was needed to augment or diminish a supply of water to a particular parcel of land. This opportunity for graft by a minor government employee was removed when the old practice of tearing down the dams each year was abolished. The new concrete dams, and a water supply controlled through corrugated iron sluices, enabled the chief engineer to control by telephone the level of water in any canal down to a millimetre. The power held by a Chief Engineer able at will to raise or lower the level of the water by deftly operating the sluices in a country where no rain falls between March and November, and water is synonymous with life, can be clearly appreciated.

At that time the annual salary of a chief engineer amounted to 4,000 roubles including his living quarters, which were provided by the State. The temptation placed in his path, particularly in the orient where since time immemorial no one has ever obtained anything from an official without some form of a gift, is obvious. When the Engineer in Chief in control of irrigation in Samarkand was presented to me I was amazed at the collection of Bukharan decorations, all studded with diamonds, proudly displayed on his chest;

they were worth a fortune. When later I expressed surprise I was
told: 'You should see his wife's jewellery, all of it presented by the
Emir of Bukhara. Don't forget that in Bukhara a good or bad
harvest depends entirely on the goodwill of the Engineer in Chief.'
Yet this man was considered relatively honest, for he refused to be
bribed. To turn down a Bukharan diamond star, however, was
apparently not so easy. As a result Bukhara got much more water for
her fields than she had a right to ask, whereas the Governor of
Samarkand was obliged to submit to restricted irrigation. The
particular governor I met was also smothered in sparkling Bukharan
decorations, as were his subordinates.

This plethora of diamond stars helps to explain why government
officials often kept one eye, if not both, conveniently closed. But in
spite of all these defects, and judging by the city's lovely shady
gardens, the luxuriantly sprouting cotton, ears of rice, panicles of
sorghum and sturdy clover I saw during my stay in Samarkand, there
was plenty of water left over. The population was well fed and content. The opulence of the brightly coloured kaftans one saw was
arresting and in great contrast to the downtrodden appearance and
tattered clothing of the natives of Bukhara. There, it was obvious
that the beks and valis of the Emir were sucking the population dry
and successfully diverting the revenue brought in by the waters of
the Zeravshan into their own and the Emir's pockets.

At a short distance from Samarkand we passed by the ruins of an
aqueduct consisting of two tall, pointed arches set at an angle to
each other. A third arch was said to have been standing until
fifteen years before, when it was destroyed by one of the frequent
earthquakes. In days gone by this was the main artery of Samarkand:
fresh, glacier water from the hills, brought by Tamerlane to his
favourite city. Tradition has it that it was built by some of the
foremost engineers of the West, which would explain its similarity
to Roman aqueducts. Now, unfortunately, the city drinks the dirty
water of the Zeravshan.

At the station, the usual officials were assembled to greet us
(the menagerie of fawning officials, I inwardly called them). A shady
avenue two miles long, lined on both sides with four rows of plane
trees, leads from the station to the town; the surface is perfect and it
had been sprinkled with costly water in our honour. As usual I was
greeted as the ambassador of the Ak-Padishah, the White Tsar, and
was even addressed by the title of Yarim Padishah (half of the Tsar).

After a visit to the Orthodox Church—an obligatory call for a Russian official—we drove accompanied by the Governor down to the main square of old Samarkand, the Registan, the former seat of judgment of its rulers. Seated in a troika we proceeded at walking pace through the narrow streets escorted by horsemen who, mounted on ceremonial chargers, acted as outriders. They were the notables of the town, clad in gold-embroidered velvet kaftans and belted with handsome old yatagans, all studded with precious stones; the bridles and saddles of the chargers were of silver, the saddle cloths embroidered in gold. Two troops of Cossacks rode in front of our procession to clear the way; occasionally they were compelled to push the crowd somewhat rudely aside but nobody seemed to mind and we progressed slowly for fear of hurting anybody. Thousands of people were massed on the roof tops; it was a miracle that these did not cave in under the weight.

The sheer beauty of the overall colouring was literally breathtaking. Everyone was dressed in their best, wearing silk kaftans mostly striped in beautifully blended colours: red and green, yellow and black, white and lilac, white and black, orange and white, etc. The turbans, called *chalma* here, were just as colourful, though white, showing that the owner could read the Koran in Arabic, seemed to predominate. There were also many natives from parts of Asia beyond the borders of the Russian Empire: Hindus, Afghans, Chinese, Persians, and Turks, dressed quite as picturesquely, their garb contrasting with the long kaftans of the Turkestanis.

We were now slowly approaching the Registan. It consists of a huge courtyard paved in squares of alabaster with four lofty minarets at the corners. Constructed of glazed bricks in a pattern of alternating turquoise blue and white the buildings glowed in the shimmering rays of the Central Asian sun, an enchanting sight, while in the background the distant snow-covered foothills of the Pamirs lent an extra touch of beauty to the scene. On one side of the courtyard a tall building with an open cloistered hall of pointed arches, common to all the mosques in Turkestan, and surmounted by a dome very much like the one in Florence, blazed richly in white and blue. An immense terrace runs the whole length of the building, with an imposing flight of steps leading down to the courtyard. Six hundred years ago Tamerlane stood on these steps to judge the misdeeds of the subjects of his far flung empire, and here, at a nod from him, thousands—nay, tens of thousands—of heads rolled in the dust, and thousands of

other trembling human beings were dismissed with a blessing. Here
the most wretched of defendants and the proudest of plaintiffs
crawled prostrate to the feet of the greatest ruler the world has ever
known to solicit the grace of his attention.

As I proceeded to the Registan, seated in my troika, the crowd
parted and bowed in deep respect to me, the ambassador of the
White Tsar, and then stood in silence according to oriental custom
while I slowly mounted the steps of the terrace. There, almost un-
attended, I stood and surveyed the kind of scene Tamerlane must
have witnessed from this very spot, and these involuntary thoughts
came to my mind: how patient were these people, enslaved for
thousands of years, how lacking in will power, how unassertive,
how dependent for the fulfilment of their needs on the mercy of a
transitory despot. They had abided in meekness like this under
Tamerlane and Alexander the Great; like this they had trembled
before many smaller tyrants, emirs, sheikhs, and khans, and like this
they now stood bowed before the remote and distant figure of the Ak-
Padishah, the White Tsar, to them a gigantic, imperial symbol of
might, who had vouchsafed them peace, well-being and order after
an eternity of extortion and petty tyranny.

The reasons for all this festivity and rejoicing were patent: they
had decided that their needs were going to be placed by me, his
envoy, before the Ak-Padishah. Even today I can still feel the sense
of expectation that ran through the dense crowd at my feet. How
easy it would have been at that time to give these industrious people
the leadership they needed, and gradually introduce them to civilization, instead of allowing this wonderful opportunity to founder on
the rocks of bureaucracy and idleness in the chancelleries of St.
Petersburg and Tashkent. Suggestions and reports submitted by the
most competent officials or others acquainted with local conditions
were all either turned down, filed, or bitterly resisted. Thus, yet
another part of Russia was allowed to fall into the hands of a fistful
of resolute bandits and to revert to barbarism and a rule of tyranny.
What is Bolshevism, after all, but a resurrected form of Asian
despotism?

The symbol of Tamerlane's secular power, and the Mohammedan
and Asian foundations of the way of life he established throughout
his world, became clear to me in the Registan and its *medreseh* and I
marvelled at the fact that identical concepts should now have been
accepted as an ideal by Bolshevism and put into practice.

These concepts are founded on the absolute negation of the individual as a member of human society. Man's work and time, his very life, counted for nothing to Tamerlane. In his state there was but one will, his own. He justified this premise by a deep conviction that he was the interpreter of God's will, wholly directed towards the ultimate good of humanity, as revealed to him by Mohammed. For the masses to be brought to a state of complete submission to his will this truth required to be daily and hourly demonstrated to the people, while the diversity of the methods he employed to indoctrinate the masses with his concept of an Asian world order was indeed astounding.

Considered from a psychological point of view these concepts lack one of the basic fundamentals of the western way of life, that of the family, which in Asia simply does not exist. This is immediately apparent in the planning of Mohammedan living quarters and houses. I have visited many of them, and everywhere I have noticed the same uniformity of structure and division. From the street all one sees of a house is a blank wall with a door to one side marking the entrance. When this is opened in response to vigorous knocking one enters a long, covered passage flanked by two high walls, usually with a built-in door-keeper's niche. At the end of the passage is another door, leading into a spacious courtyard that contains the men's quarters and stables. A ledge or bank of beaten clay, lying well in the shade of the overhanging roofs, runs round the courtyard like a gallery in front of the buildings surrounding it. This ledge is about two feet high and three to four feet broad; access to the individual rooms, each with its own door, can be gained only by stepping over it. Generally there are a few carpets lying on the ledge in place of furniture. When callers arrive cushions are fetched and visitors and hosts sit or lie on the ledge gossiping, eating and visiting. The rooms are very small and are used only for sleeping, as the day to day life of the family is centred in the courtyard. Another passage leads into a second courtyard, built on the same lines as the first though somewhat smaller, reserved for the womenfolk.

Only women and the master of the house are permitted to enter this inner courtyard. The Shariat lays down that no other men may ever come here except the closest of blood relations, and then only if the law forbids them to marry the woman they will meet. This limits the men visitors to brothers, fathers and uncles, and even they have first to obtain permission from the husband.

The Shariat also rules that every woman is entitled to a room of her own and that she may refuse entry to any person except her husband. Each woman is responsible for the furnishing of her room, which often leads to jealous quarrels between the occupants. Beautiful embroidery and carpets, mostly the handiwork of their owners, adorn the walls. Dresses and jewellery are kept in brightly-coloured chests, for there are no cupboards in Oriental houses. If a woman wishes to go out to visit her father or relations she must first obtain the permission of her husband or, if she is unmarried, her father. Then she must draw a grey dressing-gown over her head (this is supposed to represent an old, discarded dressing-gown of her husband's) and in addition wear a black or red horsehair veil over her face. I need hardly add that these mummy-like figures in the street look exceedingly ugly.

Usually the women's courtyard opens on to a garden, with a vineyard where the women spend most of their day enjoying the shade. In the evening they retire to the flat roofs of the houses, where they sleep at night.

At the age of two, boys are usually removed to the men's quarters and from then on are cared for and educated by their fathers. Like their western brothers they love running about the streets and, outside, are allowed to mix and play with girls, provided the latter are of unmarriageable age. Owing to climatic conditions girls reach puberty very young, often at ten, and then they must go about veiled and are taken into the women's part of the house.

From their earliest childhood the little girls are taught complete submissiveness to men and no girl would ever dare to lift a hand against a boy, even in play. I once watched a boy of six soundly belabouring a girl at least three years older than himself with a stick. She was in tears, yet did nothing to wrench the stick from the boy's hand though he was so much smaller. Nor did her companions do anything to help her. On another occasion, in Khodzhent, when I was showing my camera to a crowd of jolly children, a little girl of six who was greatly interested suddenly began to cry, and I saw large tears rolling down her cheeks. The boys next to her were pinching and beating her so as to shove her out of the way and get nearer my carriage themselves. When I grabbed one of the boys and gave him a piece of my mind I noticed that the onlookers were most astonished, as according to their ideas the girl should have immediately made room for the boys.

The Mohammedans believe that women, like animals, have no

souls, and treat them accordingly. The Shariat authorizes the woman's husband, or her guardian, to strike her at will, while if she so much as dares to lift her hand against him she is punishable by death. This was the law before the Russians came. Just imagine a woman's life under these conditions! To begin with she is not even allowed to enjoy her children for any length of time. The boys are taken over by the fathers at the age of two; the little girls, though staying with their mothers until they are marriageable, i.e. ten or twelve, have to work and play with the children of other wives, or, like the boys, spend much of their time in the streets. Thus, women are reduced to spending their days either embroidering *suzane* (embroidered silk coverlets for the walls) or making carpets, but mostly killing time by gossiping. I once met the wife of a Russian Chief District Officer, a well educated woman with a university degree, who because she spoke Sart and Kirgiz fluently was able to visit the homes of many native women and had in consequence gained a thorough insight into their way of life. Her descriptions of these women were shattering. According to Madame Medyanetskiy their main topic of conversation consisted of spicy stories of a Boccaccio nature, while their mental level was far too low to enable them to apprehend the inferior status they were allotted in life.

Two factors contributing to the inferior position of women were the customary early marriages and the existing rules of divorce. For a girl to be married and a mother at nine is nothing unusual, while the husband, more often than not, may be a very old man. The generally demoralizing effect of customs like these, the moral anguish suffered in the harems, and the prevalence of venereal disease among women can well be imagined. The Shariat permits a man to divorce his wife at any time and the procedure adopted is as simple as possible. All he has to do is to repeat '*Talaq, Talaq, Talaq*' three times in the presence of his wife for the divorce to become absolute, when it is there and then registered by the Kadi. At the end of three months the man is at liberty to remarry and the woman to take another husband. As a man is restricted by the Shariat to four wives and eight concubines, the informality of divorce proceedings places no bounds on the widespread practice of polygamy. Should a man, for instance, wish to marry a fifth, legitimate wife, all he need do is divorce one of the preceding four. Indeed this is quite a common occurrence, especially if the intention is to get rid of an aged wife and acquire a younger one. Withal, the divorced wife remains in the harem as a sort of servant and looks after her own children and those of the other women.

Of course, these rules mostly apply to the well-to-do classes, but when I was in Turkestan the majority of the Sarts were well off according to their standards, as living was extraordinarily cheap. It was explained to me at an assembly of mullas, which I attended for a month to examine with them certain portions of the Shariat I had had translated into Russian, that it was advisable and, in fact, a good thing to deny the women luxuries in dress and food and thus keep them from 'being as immoral as the wives of the Christians'. As it was, the mullas complained about the intrusion of luxury into the life of the harems now that rich and educated Mohammedans were able to get themselves wives in Constantinople and Alexandria, though 'our own wives don't cost us much', they added.

This attitude explains the great simplicity of women's dress in rigid Muslim circles. I once visited a mulla in the company of a Russian woman of Tashkent society. We were most hospitably received and offered the traditional rice pilau and the excellencies of a well-laid dastarkhan. As an exception we were entertained close to the women's quarters, gazed at by the wives of our host, who granted them permission to look at us from a safe distance of twenty feet 'for the sake of peace and quiet', as he said. The wives were dressed very simply in long chemise-like smocks reaching down to their ankles, bright baggy trousers and embroidered leather boots. My companion was allowed to visit the harem and was there told that fresh smocks had been donned that day in honour of the occasion. This referred to the garments I have just mentioned, which were worn, so my friend said, with nothing else underneath. I noticed the same kind of dress on yet another occasion, when I was present at a wedding and had lent my camera to friends who were visiting the harem. The picture of the bride and her friends showed the same poverty and simplicity of dress.

I mention these details only to show how little there is in common between family life as we understand it and that of a native household such as I have described. Nothing ever varies year in and year out for the unfortunate women where everything in life depends on the mood of the master. As Madame Medyanetskiy said: 'They rapidly become dull-witted, and fade at an early age.' The children grow up like a pack of animals, quite deprived of any effective motherly influence.

From infancy a boy born into such a household accompanies his father on his travels abroad and it is quite usual to meet father and son riding the same horse a great distance from home. Another kind of life, however, shorn of any family influence, starts for the boy at the age of six when he first goes to school (the mekteb), which is obligatory for every young Mohammedan. In these schools the spiritual foundations of the Mohammedan religion, its ethics and its relation to secular life, are taught in a form common to the entire Muslim world, with the result that the young Mohammedan is moulded into a well-defined type, everywhere the same. Thus the formative influence of the mektebs over the youth of a large portion of the human race cannot be sufficiently stressed. When a young Mohammedan first comes to the mekteb his mind is a *tabula rasa*. He leaves as a conscious member of a human society where such notions as family tradition, racial origins, geographical boundaries— in fact all the things indispensable to the cultural development of man as we see it—mean nothing at all, his own interpretation of life being based on concepts ceaselessly repeated in school which he continues to cherish in after years. This is the way ordained by God's prophet and this is the way it must forever remain.

The 'new boy' is put into a room with a lot of others who may have been there for several years and who sit there monotonously repeat- ing the precepts they must know by heart, set down in the Shariat, the Holy Law of the Prophet. When I was in Turkestan all the mektebs I saw were exactly alike—generally a room in the mosque building, the floor on which the pupils sat brightly carpeted, and the teacher, usually an old man, perched on a cushion in one of the corners. In his hand he held a scroll or an old book, or sometimes a cane with which he pointed at the boy due to recite the lesson set for the day. The curriculum was supposed to embrace 'all know- ledge', for all wisdom is contained in the Shariat. A boy begins by learning the Arabic alphabet, and then goes on to memorize Arabic prayers and a multitude of the Prophet's sayings, which of course he fails to understand at the time.

The impression produced both by the drone of the boys' voices reciting their lessons and the sight of them seated cross-legged on the floor is most peculiar. They are all dressed in the habitual oriental kaftan, locally called *khalat* (a long smock like a dressing gown, reaching down to the ankles), and have small round skull caps of satin or silk on their heads. Bent over their books, each with a

flask of Indian ink beside him, they are busily engaged in tracing
Arabic letters with reed pens while they repeat half aloud the lesson
they are learning by heart. From time to time the teacher points his
cane at one of the boys, who then starts mumbling a little louder
than the others. And so it goes on for practically the whole day.
How children can stand this mode of teaching and not become
utterly dull-witted in the process is something to wonder at.

'But what is it the children are learning by heart?'

'Oh! Mohammedan prayers', was the answer given by the
majority of the officials accompanying me, if they were unacquainted
with local languages. The representatives of the Russian Ministry of
Cults were equally vague on the subject, though the inspection of
these schools came within their authority. Not satisfied with these
answers I asked for a collection of the books, mostly old scrolls of
parchment, used by the teachers at their lessons and had them
translated. Unfortunately this was among my material destroyed by
the Bolsheviks, so I must now rely on my memory.

From the material collected the main impression I gathered concerning the mektebs, which was confirmed by experts on local
conditions, was the universal character of the instruction given to the
boys. Everything they were expected to know was taught in these
schools. The method of instruction was academic, the subjects
being presented as God's revelations to the Prophet and the natural
sciences being treated unsystematically and in a manner that was
quite obsolete. Nevertheless, when the extent of that field of knowledge is taken into consideration, and also the number of years spent
on it, it must be frankly admitted that by the age of fifteen a boy
could not have but amassed a great deal of knowledge, and would
take away, stored in his mind, a collection of fundamental proposi-
tions and a ready-made outlook on life.

Take for instance as an illustration the rules of politeness, taught
almost daily and all the year round. The boy learns them by heart
and keeps on reciting them from the age of six to fifteen. Gradually
and unconsciously he conforms his behaviour to these rules and in
this way they govern the manners of the entire population. Naturally,
the rules of politeness in East and West differ greatly and are typical
of their respective cultures. In the East they are founded on respect
of the young for the old, whereas our Western ideas of chivalry are
unknown. They teach the art of self-restraint, a valuable asset in a
world where tempers are quick.

The effectiveness of the lessons taught in the mektebs becomes apparent when one observes the behaviour of any gathering, or the conduct of the crowds in the streets. There is none of the crudeness so typical of the lower classes in the West, or of the vulgar self-assertiveness of its élite; instead, there is a calmness and self-confidence which gives the people an appearance of dignity. Young men stand aside to let an older man pass; they are silent when their elders speak; dignitaries are greeted respectfully in the street. It is bad manners either to use bad language or raise one's voice.

I was also struck by the willing obedience of the population to some given sign. Mass discipline like this is something we do not meet in the West, but it is not the result of any outward form of coercion such as barrack-room discipline; it is the natural outcome of youthful years spent in the mekteb absorbing the reiterated precepts of the Mohammedan outlook on life. I met this form of discipline everywhere in Central Asia, whether I was visiting the tyrants of Bukhara and China or moving among the hustling crowds of Taskhent, Samarkand and Margelan. I found it among the merchants in the bazaars, and at public meetings which I addressed. The rules of good behaviour, learnt by heart, contain a large measure of sophistry, as any and every eventuality of daily life is met by a precept suitable to the occasion; for answering questions when visiting, for the street and the bazaar, for commerce and the courts, for travelling, for the garden, the fields or one's home, for feasts, for mourning and for fasting and for a gay time. These rules explain why the impression conveyed by the Asian is one of self-possessed dignity, devoid of affectation or timidity, and why he is never impetuous nor ever sheds the restraint he has imposed on the exhibition of his feelings. The same attitude was noticeable among prisoners in jail or other places of detention, and I attribute it all to the schooling of the mektebs.

The science of politeness was treated in the mektebs as a secondary subject and was described as the science of human relations. The main subject was ethics, i.e. religious instruction. The knowledge that was imparted to the student, or to be precise was dinned into him, embraced a variety of subjects. The concepts of the Mohammedan religion, its foundations and content were naturally allotted pride of place, and particular attention was paid to stressing the basic concept of monotheism: 'There is but one God and Muhammad is His Prophet'; or, 'God is the All highest and His representative on earth is the Caliph'. The tenets are contained in the 'Sayings of the Prophet', and the pupil is required to learn them in Arabic by heart, parrot-fashion, without as much as understanding a single word at first. Constantly repeated and adapted they run like a thread through all the boy's learning, and gradually, in the course of the years he spends at school, they become part and parcel of his life, dominating his soul and spirit. He is taught that strict adherence to custom is the most important prerequisite of bliss demanded by God of Man.

We Europeans may be inclined to regard the precepts which govern the life of a Muslim at every step as nothing but a collection of meaningless rules, but a little reflection will show that every one of these rules is founded on an essentially Mohammedan conception and the application of Mohammedan ethics. Take, for instance, the most striking of them, that of obligatory prayer, regulated both by the time of day and the day itself in words that every Mohammedan knows by heart. At the appropriate hour, regardless of place and surroundings, he will spread his prayer carpet before him, reverently kneel down and pray. The prayers themselves are typical. In the main they exalt the concept that there is but one God, and the interpreters of His will on earth the Prophet Mohammed and the Caliphs.

Next in importance is the obligation to fast at certain times of the year which must be known by every boy who wishes to escape heavy punishment. This obligation is also an exercise in self-discipline and has been advanced as a reason for the successes of Mohammedan armies in the field, enabling them to withstand the rigours of prolonged hunger. The daily reading of the Koran is yet another obligation taught the boys in the mektebs.

All these things added together train the boy's mind to move within the confines of an entirely Mohammedan world and help gradually to influence his political convictions. A Mohammedan's sense of nationality is blunted by the absence of a sense of family, whilst qualities that can attract a Muslim boy, youth or man to the rest of humanity (or, conversely, repel him), are closely linked with his adherence to the followers of the Great Prophet. Only problems connected with his religion are of any interest to him; everything else in the world is a matter of either indifference or contempt. For him the infidel world, the whole of Western civilization, is of no importance; not being compatible with his own outlook on life, it must be regarded as the enemy which he must oppose, and both inwardly and outwardly keep at a distance. The spiritual union between the individual and the rest of the faithful stretches over all the Mohammedan world like a net, while the measure of its effective reality is revealed by a cursory study of the Press in the main strongholds of Mohammedanism, like Alexandria, Constantinople, Algiers, or any Mohammedan city of India. In point of fact, when I was studying this problem in the heart of Central Asia I learnt more about the happenings in the Muslim circles of Turkestan from the Cairo papers than I did from official reports in Tashkent or the local press.

Because the political structure of the state was laid down by Allah, and defined by his mouthpiece the Prophet, politics, of course, was one of the subjects taught in the mektebs. The course was a very simple one and could be condensed into a single sentence: 'The will of the Caliph or of his representative is the will of Allah'. The extent to which the whole political thinking of a Mohammedan is dominated by the acceptance of this concept is little short of amazing, as is also his ability to parry any obvious contradictions by advancing a suitable counter argument. In consequence, I have often been presented with assurances of loyalty to Russia both written and oral in which the White Tsar was regarded in the light of a friend or even a vassal of the Caliph of Constantinople. 'Ak-Padishah' was the accepted title of the Emperor of Russia. Since, under his rule, peace and law reigned in the land and ancient Muslim customs were left untouched a ready explanation for the title was available: 'It is the will of the Caliph; he has entrusted the Muslim subjects of Russia to the keeping of the Tsar'. For the inhabitants of Central Asia the wars between Russia and Turkey were nothing but a long drawn out misunderstanding between friends. Even the Emir of Bukhara stressed to me the 'friendly' character of his relations with the Emperor of Russia, though in fact they were those of a small vassal with his liege lord. An unswerving allegiance to the leadership of Constantinople was so firmly rooted in the Mohammedan mind that all attempts by the Russian government to impose its own influence invariably failed. This is a subject I shall presently examine in greater detail.

History and geography as taught in the mektebs were also made to conform to Mohammedan conceptions. History was restricted to a detailed account of the life of Allah, to the spread of his teaching and the growth of his empire. In this connection some quite astounding ideas were expressed in the textbooks, as for instance that the whole world belonged to Allah and his Caliphs. The alleged fact that the King of England was often compelled to lend the Caliph his soldiers, or had on more than one occasion assured him of his loyalty, was used to prove that England was a vassal of the Caliph. The German Emperor, too, had visited him in Constantinople and paid him homage. (The Franks were less favourably mentioned.) Facts and events were not connected in any way and were mentioned only in order to illustrate or prove a given theme. A description of lands inhabited by the faithful and of the roads leading to Mecca and other pilgrim cities in Asia, Africa, and Europe was all that was learnt in geography. A little mathematics, algebra, astronomy, natural science and medicine completed the course.

Rules governing the personal life of the individual are set down in texts and are learnt by heart, like everything else in the mektebs. The problem of sex is thoroughly explained to boys only eight years old, who are also taught the rules of married life, warned of possible diseases and instructed in preventive and curative measures in explanations as detailed as any to be found in specialized and scientific works on the subject in the West. It is at this stage that the all-prevailing attitude of contempt for women is particularly emphasized.

The facts I have mentioned should help to show how the young Mohammedan mind is gradually moulded into accepting and later adopting a way of life and an outlook based exclusively on the teachings of the Koran, and also the ensuing influence and impact of this religious philosophy on the desert world of Central Asia. I must, however, add that the conflict between Mohammedanism and the Christian way of life, founded on the free development of the individual and his critical faculties, has without any doubt also left its mark upon this world.

The gradual loss of political power by the Caliphate has had a profound effect on all Muslim countries, but the turmoil caused in the inner circles of Mohammedanism by this diminution of its influence was largely unappreciated by the West except in the case of individual manifestations of this unrest such as the annihilation of the janissaries in Constantinople, the struggle between Egypt and Turkey or the Mahdi movement. It was, however, made evident by the revolution in Constantinople and the seizure of power by the reforming group. The causes of the revolution were deemed by the

inner circles to lie in the inability of the ethical concepts of Mohammedanism to stand up to the damaging critical spirit introduced by
Western civilization. A new bulwark was needed; there had to be a
rejuvenation at the very fountain head of the Mohammedan outlook
on life, the school; and a demand for the radical reform and moder-
nization of the mektebs.

The means that were adopted to achieve the reform are not easy
to appreciate without some insight into the political education of the
leading Mohammedan circles, and for an infidel, a *kafir*, to penetrate
this inner sanctum is a difficult task. When I first approached the
subject I had very little material at my disposal and had to be content with a collection of miscellaneous information brought to my
notice. However, little by little a definite pattern began to emerge.
Thus, during the year I was in the country I learned from a report
by the Turkestan Political Police that a certain mulla from Mecca
who had been travelling round the district for two years and had
then disappeared was no less a person than an aide-de-camp of the
Sultan. Some time later a member of my staff reported meeting a
strange mulla in the Kirgiz steppes in the far north of Turkestan,
who passed himself off as an emissary of Constantinople and whom
the inhabitants greatly honoured.

A number of similar instances led to the impression that many of
the higher schools, like the *medresehs* (theological schools situated
within a mosque where student mullas are trained), were being
visited by envoys who urged the necessity of reforming both these
and the primary schools, the mektebs. It was emphasized that they
were 'transmitting an order', and the information that the reform
had already taken place in European Russia and Turkey was
frequently joined to the demand.

Further instances came from a number of other sources: from two
judicial enquiries, one in Kazan, on the Volga, the other in Katta-
Kurgan, in Turkestan; from the Egyptian and Turkish press, and
from one of my staff who had been instructed to investigate the
matter and collect as much relevant data as he could. In order to
gain access to the more exclusive Mohammedan circles he let a room
to one of the medresehs. A fluent oriental linguist, he was able to
converse with the students and their teachers and was in addition
allowed the use of their library. Soon he came upon an astonishing
fact: in spite of the Russian customs and censorship a collection of
new textbooks, mostly printed in Constantinople and Cairo, had

found their way into Turkestan within the previous two years. He also obtained details of the new educational programme which had been drawn up, if I am not mistaken, at a conference in Cairo, subsequently elaborated, and was now ready to be taught in the mektebs throughout the whole Mohammedan world in Asia, Africa and Europe. It transpired that the reform had already been put into effect in some countries, though because of its remoteness the change-over had only begun in Turkestan at the time of my visit.

The reform[1] demanded the Europeanization of the mektebs. The first step to be taken was the alteration of the outward appearance of the schools with a view to abolishing the old system of teaching by rote and introducing a method of applied instruction. The picturesque carpeted room with its kneeling boys was to be abolished and replaced by benches, rostrum and blackboard. Nor was that all. Maps and pictures were to be hung on the walls. Anyone acquainted with the revulsion felt by the Mohammedan for any picture, as a possible representation of foreign gods, will realize the magnitude of the upheaval caused by the reform in the minds and outlook of the faithful. However, a simple statement such as: 'We have been ordered to do this by our elders', or, 'the wise mullas and the Sheikh ul Islam surrounding the Caliph have given their approval', were apparently sufficient to stem opposition and get the changes accepted throughout the Mohammedan world.

When I compared the old and the new school textbooks I found that in the main the difference was rather one of form than of substance, a uniform language being used and the subjects differently presented. All the old basic concepts were retained, however, as was also the precept of submission to the authority of the Caliph as Mohammed's representative on earth, the latter tenet being particularly stressed in Central Asia by a fanciful extension of the frontiers of his empire to include the whole of Russia, half Austria, Spain, Africa, and the whole of Asia. In the new books the medieval interpretation of natural history and historical subjects was replaced by a description of the achievements of modern science, and the subjects taught were translated under their appropriate western headings: arithmetic, algebra, geometry, history, literature, etc. In addition, an entirely new item was introduced; a grammar of the

[1] The reform was known as the *Usul-i-jadid* or New Method (of Education) and was initiated by Gasprinskiy, a Crimean Tatar, at the turn of the century.

modern Muslim language. More resembling a modernized form of Turkish than Arabic, it was a living language that had evolved largely as a result of the requirements of expanding intercourse and modern life. In my dealings with the natives a request for an interpreter was often met by the statement 'I understand Muslim'— not Sart, Kirgiz, Tatar, or Turkic. The term was also currently used by the Russian officials, and if any order to a native was not promptly obeyed one might often hear: 'Are you deaf, or don't you understand when I speak to you in Muslim?' A Muslim language common to the whole of Asia was what the Panislamic circles wanted to achieve, and the form of modernized Turkish they introduced was rapidly grasped and even spoken by all the Sunni (Muslim Orthodox) peoples of Asia.

A number of newspapers using the new idiom soon made their appearance, such as the *Interpreter*, the popular organ of the Crimean Tatars, edited by Gasprinskiy, who was a prominent exponent of the Panislamic idea in Russia. The new language was now the only one taught in the mektebs, and because it was so closely related to the local dialects the problem of adopting it in the schools was easily overcome. The reform was of course opposed in some quarters, mostly those dominated by the older mullas, who wanted to cling to the ancient methods. But on the whole the reform was successful and in some countries, like European Russia, it was put through in two years, while even in Turkestan I watched the new form of teaching being applied in one mekteb after another.

My attention was drawn to the eager acceptance of this modernizing trend in countries as far distant as Morocco, and I was told that the influence apparently wielded by its leaders was a symptom which Russian state policy could not afford to underestimate and which it needed to watch with great care.

Who were the intellectual leaders so willingly followed by this great mass of humanity? How were they picked from the vast multitude of the Prophet's followers and placed at the head of the movement? These were the questions to which I sought an answer.

I got no satisfaction from the local Turkestan officials in the chancery of the Governor-General other than the usual 'Oh! its the influence of the mullas over the masses'. The Governor-General himself, a grey-haired, energetic soldier who was content to leave the direction of affairs to his Chief of Staff, was greatly startled by my quest for this kind of information. He could do no better than hand me over to his Chief of Staff, who in turn passed me on to a Secretary, a former land surveyor who usually dealt with the more ponderous correspondence between Tashkent and St. Petersburg and who possessed the happy faculty of couching his efforts in the best of official styles. As the files contained no information on the subject a circular questionnaire was rapidly drafted and launched on a round of provincial governors. These gentlemen, following the rules of the game, fell back on their own staffs, who then passed the question-naire on to the Chief District Officers and so on until at last it reached the bottom rung of the Russian administrative ladder, the young lieutenants in the districts. The latter handed the question-naire to their interpreters, who were mostly uneducated natives, with an order to read it and draft a reply. Later I came across some of the completed forms, and in view of the circumstances was not surprised by the naïve tenor of the answers. The interpreters were of course Muslims, and in no time the leading Mohammedan circles of Turkestan and, incidentally, the rest of the world, were aware that the Russian Government was closely, or in official parlance 'un-officially', watching the movement. The majority of the question-naires returned by the District Officers merely stated that in their districts all was quiet, including the Muslims. In due course the questionnaires reached the chanceries, the various Heads of Depart-ment were summoned and the Governor-General proudly informed me that he now had a fat 'secret' file on the Panislamic movement. In actual fact the contents of the reports were both deplorable and biased, as the interpreters had been at pains to conceal as much of the truth as possible.

Meanwhile the political police, working independently of the Governor-General and dealing directly with the Imperial Ministry in St. Petersburg, had in the course of enquiries into the activities of revolutionary organizations quite accidentally discovered, in Katta-Kurgan, a district centre of Samarkand Province, a group of young men who were apparently affiliated to a secret society. The material seized was not, as a matter of fact, particularly revealing, consisting mainly of photographs of friends assembled together, a programme for the reformed mektebs and some letters pointing to an academic interest of the society in the Panislamic movement. Later there was evidence showing that the district had been visited by an envoy of Abd ul Hamid and that a voluminous written exchange of ideas be-tween Constantinople, Cairo, and the group in Katta-Kurgan had taken place. To prove his zeal the local agent of the Okhrana promptly dispatched all the material collected to St. Petersburg. It was found that the members of the society were mostly young local mullas and a few students from the Samarkand medreseh, who had joined a movement directed from Constantinople by a party called 'Union and Progress'—later the party of Enver Pasha.

It should be noted that the medresehs are higher seats of learning, the Mohammedan equivalent of what we would call theological colleges, where the young mullas—the future Mohammedan divines, if they may be so called—receive instruction. Every mosque tries to maintain a medreseh, if it has the funds. These funds, called *waqf*, come from varying sources, but usually from legacies bequeathed to charitable causes. Tamerlane was very generous to the Samarkand medresehs, and thanks to their wealth they soon became famous throughout the Mohammedan world; the importance of Samarkand in Central Asia equalled that of Rome in the West, while its reputation of possessing the best theological college in the world continued to prevail under Russian rule.

In the initial stages of occupation the Russian authorities showed little interest in matters concerning the religious life of the Muslims, with the result that corruption gradually crept into the administration of the waqfs. The supposed administrators of these charitable funds were quick to take advantage of this Russian indifference and laid claims to the endowments as their rightful owners. The general position was something like this: an estate was recognized by the Russian administration as a waqf on production of documents proving that it was a genuine bequest and if the deeds bore the seal of some former ruler, Emir or Khan. In the majority of cases this evidence was not forthcoming, and General Kaufman adopted the practice of either having the funds collected or, and this was the usual procedure, recognizing the claims to ownership of the administrators.

The complexity of the waqf problem prevents me from going into it as thoroughly as I should like. However, it must be understood that the term waqf was used very broadly and was not restricted to funds or property held by the mosques but applied equally to any charitable bequest, including forms of revenue from chattels and real estate. For instance, the rent money of a room might be bequeathed in a will to the maintenance of a road on the land of the testator, an object pleasing to God according to the Shariat, with the result that

5

the whole house containing the room became a waqf and was consequently exempt from confiscation by some Mohammedan despot.

This privilege attached to the waqfs incidentally explains their prevalence in Central Asia before the entry of Russia; the placing of hard won possessions under the protection of Allah was the only means of safeguarding them against arbitrary confiscation by petty tyrants. Quite unintentionally as far as the Russians were concerned the revenues of the Samarkand medresehs, which were mainly composed of such bequests, supplied the mullas and students with a handsome income. The inner life of the so-called Mohammedan clergy being of no concern to the Russians, it was allowed to proceed quite unhindered. Following oriental custom the thousands of pilgrims to the holy cities of Samarkand made presents to the mullas every year, of money and gifts in kind. These donations were obviously free from any sort of official control and went into the pockets of the mullas, some of whom were very wealthy men, often owning flourishing businesses. The Russians also took the view that the repair and upkeep of the mosques and medresehs was nothing to do with them but was entirely the responsibility of the mullas, to be defrayed out of their revenues; and they left things as they were. This attitude was, as a matter of fact, accepted practice in the days of the Emirs and their Beks, but with the difference that they effectively controlled the takings of the medresehs and mosques. Now, with no control being exercised, many buildings were in a very bad state of repair and the mullas, pointing to the crumbling shrines, claimed this to be a direct result of Russian rule.

In general, the status of the mullas had much declined under the new masters of the land. When Bukhara and Kokand ruled Turkestan many of the really lucrative posts were filled by nominees of the Emir, and the social standing of the mulla class was very high. As a result of new conditions and a certain amount of gerrymandering with elections the mullas were now reduced to witnessing the rise to positions of importance, like those of Kadi, of persons who were in their opinion either uneducated or unworthy, and had to suffer the indignity of being obliged to stand shoulder to shoulder with the much despised Jewish rabbis at official receptions. Thus it came about that the class which felt itself entitled to the spiritual leadership of the people by reason of tradition and a profound knowledge of the Koran and other holy books, was led to adopt an attitude inimical to Russia, intensified by a drastic cut in its legal, and not so legal, sources of income.

It must be borne in mind also, that the medresehs served as a rallying point for the ablest, most ambitious, and strong-willed elements of Mohammedanism, mostly young men who had spent their lives absorbing the spirit of the Sunna and the Shariat and were filled with a burning zeal to serve in the cause of Allah's Prophet. It is not surprising that their sympathies and aspirations were directed to the West, to Constantinople and Mecca, nor that they were angered by the rule of the infidel, the kafir. Consequently, when Abd ul Hamid lent his support both openly and in secret to a wave of religious fervour and rekindled fanaticism which swept over the Mohammedan world at the end of the last century (incidentally costing him his throne), it was only natural that this movement should provoke a strong emotional reaction in Central Asia. A number of political groups, among which was that tracked down by the gendarmerie in Katta-Kurgan, were founded as part of a well-planned organization which began to spread over Asia and other lands with a Muslim population, while the school reform already mentioned was used as a stage on the road leading to the main objective—the restoration to its former brilliance of the Caliphate. The movement was headed by scholars from the medresehs, the product of a centuries-old tradition who had been taught to regard the Mohammedan faith as a national religion and were in constant touch with each other through the pilgrimages which they made in droves to Mecca, Egypt, and Constantinople.

Typical of Mohammedanism is the absence of an organized body of clergy or some form of hierarchy as understood in the West. Religious influence in the Mohammedan world is exercised by the mulla not as such, but rather because he is an able exponent of the Mohammedan doctrine, well versed in knowledge and orthodox in his views. The universally acknowledged and unquestioned head of Mohammedanism is the Caliph, the representative of Mohammed on earth; the rest of the faithful are equal in his sight and answerable to him alone. The collegiate principle is as contrary to the spirit of Mohammedanism as would be an hierarchy of the clergy. At one time an attempt was made by the Russian Government for the benefit of its Muslim subjects to create an institution modelled on the organization of the Christian Church. Under Catherine II a mulla was appointed to every mosque and placed under the authority of a bishop, called *mufti* by the Empress. Three such Muftis were nominated, the one in Orenburg by tacit consent being given precedence over the other two. These dignitaries maintained the most friendly relations with the authorities and, indeed, very worthily represented Russia's Mohammedan subjects. Attached to each was an elected consistory, which dealt with matters concerning the faith and helped in the settling of family problems. However, the Mohammedans outside Russia refused to recognize the religious authority of these officially appointed ecclesiastics; to them they were nothing but Russian civil servants. In Turkestan the influence of the Muftis was negligible and General Kaufman, its conqueror, at once recognized the futility of the whole scheme. He substituted instead the authority of the Russian Emperor, declaring him Supreme Lord appointed by Allah to rule over his Mohammedan subjects and endowing him and his temporal representative, i.e. the Governor-General, with the prerogative previously enjoyed by the Caliphs—of settling all religious problems and disputes.

During the first few years after the conquest this arrangement worked extremely well and very conveniently for the Russian authorities, but it gradually dawned on the leaders of Mohammedan thought in Central Asia that an infidel Governor-General was not the person best suited to interpret the Shariat. Gradually, too, the young students of the medresehs showed a tendency to accept the guidance offered by Constantinople, while those of them who wished subsequently to teach in the medresehs of Samarkand were increasingly constrained to do their post-graduate course in the renowned universities of Turkey and were thus withdrawn from Russian influence. The lofty reputation of Samarkand's medresehs was noticeably on the decline and the leadership they had for so long exerted was being assumed by Bukhara, where an orthodox ruler, in the person of the Emir, both controlled and led his mullas as in the days of old.

The foregoing is a brief description of the Panislamic movement, of its gradual increase of influence in Central Asia and the methods adopted by it to gain adherents to its cause. In the forefront of the movement stood the ardent young students of the medresehs. It was young men of this type, inspired by the ideology of the 'Union and Progress' party in Constantinople, who formed the group in Katta-Kurgan already mentioned. The dossier on the case, which I studied, conveyed an impression of political immaturity. The formation of this particular group in Katta-Kurgan was a consequence of the prolonged isolation of Turkestan, which on the whole was rather indifferent to the interests of other parts of the Mohammedan world and was inclined to concentrate on problems of purely local importance, these being at the time concerned with the restoration of the erstwhile glory of the medresehs. The immediate objective of some of the groups was very often local, but the root cause of all this unrest was rebellion against the pernicious influence of the infidels, the kafirs. The re-introduction of the waqfs and reversion to the days of the *reis* were widely preached and put forward as the best means of salvation. The reis were censors who, prior to the conquest, enforced adherence to established custom, had the right to enter any house at will and, in the pursuance of their duties, might even violate the sanctum of the *haremlik*, the women's quarters. They were also empowered to inflict corporal punishment on anyone found working at the time of prayer, irrespective of rank. The proper observation of fasts, the style of women's dress and a host of other matters came under their jurisdiction. Needless to say they were abolished by the Russian administration.

In Turkestan at the time of my visit the majority of these Panislamic organizations had as yet no definite political objectives, though they were much valued by the movement because of the intimate ties they maintained with Constantinople. Thanks to this connection other parallel organizations came into being which, though largely independent of the centre in Constantinople, and firmly founded on a Central Asian ethnographical basis, nevertheless acted as a leaven in bringing together and uniting all the Mohammedans of Asia.

These latter organizations were directed by the so-called *Ishan* movement. We shall better understand the spiritual factors which lay behind Ishanism[1] if we consider those characteristics, predominantly Semitic and theocratic, which marked the origin of Mohammedanism and its subsequent development throughout the world; for mysticism, in the Aryan sense of the word, was utterly foreign to the followers of Mohammed. However, during the process of its expansion, Mohammedanism was increasingly influenced by the racial characteristics of the peoples it absorbed and converted;

---

[1] What the author calls a movement was simply the practice of the tenets of Sufiism. *Ishan* was an honorific term in the esoteric language of the Sufis. It is the 3rd person plural of the Persian personal pronoun meaning 'they'.

such as Hamitic fetishism, mainly manifest in Africa, and the inclination of the conquered and converted Aryans, mostly Persian and Indian, towards external forms of ascetism and the mystical interpretation of the Koran. Indeed, the schism which led to the cleavage of Islam into Sunnites and Shiites was caused by the opposing ideologies of these two tendencies. Even among the Sunnites the religious life of the Aryans possesses an undertone of mysticism, and differs from that of their Semitic brethren. The Turks and the Mongols, converted to Islam at a later stage, stand nearer to the Sunnites, in spite of a taint of fetishism. The Sarts, on the other hand, tend to interpret Mohammed's teaching symbolically, and disclose a leaning to mystical ascetism, monasticism, and the formation of sects and associations.

It would take too long to examine the practical expression given to all these multiple tendencies, but one of their characteristics is important; namely, their clandestine organizations, reminiscent of medieval knightly orders, and the large following they command. Their origin lies in the desire to develop the inner ethical life of the individual, as propounded by the Shariat and presented as the highest ideal to the followers of Islam.

The desire for self-improvement is the force which lies behind all these brotherhoods. It is essentially Aryan in origin and an expression of Aryan thinking. A group of followers and acolytes might gather round some idealist, often a celebrated mulla of one of the medresehs, probably a man of great religious zeal, a mystic, well versed in theology. After a while this group would bind itself into an association, governed by a set of rules and united by a form of oath. The members would then be known as *murids*, and the mulla as the *Ishan*. At the beginning the Ishan would act as the spiritual adviser of his murids but, as time went on and they progressively imbibed the Fire and Sword spirit of Islam, the association would gradually degenerate into a fighting organization in the cause of Mohammedanism. Absolute obedience to Islam was demanded of the murid, who was further bound to follow its every injunction, to accept and apply its every interpretation. When I was in Turkestan Russia's prestige was still great and her far-reaching power had a halo around it. The individual *Ishans* were afraid to show their hostility to the rule of the unbeliever, and they limited their activities to recruiting followers for the Panislamic movement.

The inner structure of Ishanism was organized down to the smallest

detail. A group's Ishan was its commander; his oldest and most able
murids acted as section leaders under him; in turn, the sections were
split up into smaller units, each commanded by an appointed chief.
The organization was spread over the entire region, though apart
from its ultimate aim, which was the world domination of Islam, it
was not connected with the essentially political associations of the
Young Islamic Movement, which stemmed from Constantinople.
The motivating forces of Ishanism were ethics and mysticism,
whereas the other organizations were inspired by politics and red hot
political passion. Though the Ishan organization had branches
throughout the whole of Turkestan the leaders concealed their
activities so skilfully that the Russian authorities were hardly aware
of their existence. In cases where a fanatical Ishan had ventured too
far into the open it was usually the local Russian authorities who
played down the facts brought to light by inquiries into a puzzling
situation. A typical example is the so-called 'revolt' in Andizhan,
which occurred at the end of the last century.

In Tashkent I examined the dossier of a pardoned German Mennonite who at the demand of the Russian Chief District Officer in
Andizhan had been sentenced to three years' imprisonment with
hard labour for libel. Like many of his brother sectarians he had been
exempted from military service and given a government job instead
—in this case that of state forester in the Andizhan district. The
Mennonites were quite justly renowned throughout the Empire for
their honesty, trustworthiness, and obedience to the laws of the
realm, which none of them had ever broken. The case was, therefore,
somewhat unique in the annals of Russian justice. It started over a
report the Mennonite had submitted to his immediate superior, the
Domain Head Forester. In this he stated that he had learnt, from
perfectly reliable sources which however he could not reveal, that a
rising of Muslims in the Andizhan district and surrounding region
was being actively prepared. It happened that the Chief District
Officer in Andizhan at the time was a jovial, kindhearted colonel
possessed of a blind faith in the integrity of his subordinates. When
he had read the Mennonite's report, which had been passed to him by
the Head Forester, he asked his District Officer how much of it he
thought was true and was reassured by the latter's assurance that
the whole thing was a tissue of lies and an infamous libel. By now
the report had reached the Governor-General and was provoking
quite a stir in high administrative circles. This prompted the

District Officer to stage exemplary proceedings against its author. As the Mennonite was holding a government job in lieu of military service he was subject to military jurisdiction. He was in consequence tried by a military court and sentenced to three years' hard labour. By the time he had served half his sentence an astounding event occurred in Andizhan District.

In one of its most fertile regions, about thirty miles from the town of Andizhan, there lived a rich Uzbek locally held in the greatest esteem. He owned extensive gardens and rice fields and was renowned for his devoutness and the charity he bestowed. He was also in good standing with the Russian authorities. The District Officer of Andizhan was often his guest, and he was an influential patron in the offices of the Chief District Officer, for he paid many generous fees.

The District Officer, a captain from the Caucasus and himself a Mohammedan, was much loved by his Russian comrades and had at least twenty-five years of service behind him. He had been the main force responsible for the sentencing of the Mennonite.

One fine day the above-mentioned Uzbek invited the Chief District Officer and the District Officer to a splendid feast. The two high dignitaries spent several days as guests of the Sart, then one evening went gaily home. After only a few hours they were awakened by shots. Soon the Chief District Officer received word from the commander of the local Russian garrison that a great mass of armed natives had attacked the barracks. One company had been surprised while asleep, and wiped out, and only through the presence of mind of the sergeant of the second company had this one been saved, the attack repulsed, and the enemy put to flight. In the pursuit the green banner of the leader had been seized and he himself taken prisoner.

It was this leader who had played host to the Chief District Officer. He was the local Ishan, and in a seizure of fanaticism after an exciting gathering in the mosque where he lived he had proclaimed a *ghazavat*, or holy war, against the infidels. He had assembled his 400 murids, marched the whole night, everywhere preaching rebellion, and, drawing the population with him, had suddenly fallen upon the Russian garrison. I visited the barracks and saw the traces of this attack.

The barracks, covered with corrugated iron, were half below the surface of the ground, in long trenches. Here the garrison, consisting of two companies each eighty men strong, was quartered, sleeping on bunks placed in two rows along the length of the trench. This contingent was the only armed force in the whole of Andizhan. The garrison's rifles were stacked at one end of the room, while ammunition was stored in an armoury between the two barracks.

The Ishan's plan was based on the soundest of logic. He justly calculated that if he succeeded in wiping out these two companies the entire region up to Margelan, where there was only one battalion, would be in his hands and there would be nothing left to stop his victorious advance on Tashkent. He therefore stormed the barracks under cover of night and succeeded in rushing one of the two buildings, where he and his murids, armed with yatagans and antiquated muskets, butchered those of the soldiers who were not lucky enough to escape through the door. Fortunately, however, the regimental sergeant major had his quarters in the armoury. He promptly seized two boxes of ammunition, rushed with them to the second barracks and distributed the contents to his men, the door meanwhile being defended with bayonets against the attacking natives. The first few shots were enough to sow panic among the rebels. The loyal murids stood by their leader, but the local inhabitants whom he had collected on his way lost no time in getting out of the fight. The eighty survivors of the garrison, led by the regimental sergeant major and an orderly officer, quickly disposed of the murids and captured the Ishan, who accepted defeat with true oriental fatalism.

The Mennonite who had given advance information of the Ishan's intentions was of course pardoned, and was granted a large indemnity in compensation for the wrongs he had suffered. However, the real culprit, the District Officer who had lulled his chief into a sense of false security and who was, as it subsequently turned out, one of the Ishan's murids, was neither punished nor brought to justice. He was merely transferred from Andizhan, though his name continued to figure on the lists of the Turkestan Military Administration as I was able to see for myself.

The revolt caused quite a commotion in St. Petersburg, exposing as it did the lethargic methods of the Turkestan Central Administration. Naturally, the government officers in Turkestan tried to minimize the real extent of the movement and dispatched a stream of reports to the capital playing down the events and purporting to show that the entire episode was nothing more than an isolated manifestation of political unrest. The Ishan was sent to Siberia and his estates were confiscated.

The first official reaction from above to the revolt was an order issued by General Kuropatkin, then Minister of Defence, requiring the Governor-General of Turkestan to exact retribution on a scale worthy of Tamerlane. A strip of land five kilometres wide and stretching from the boundaries of the Ishan's estates as far as Andizhan, thirty kilometres away, was to be confiscated from the local inhabitants and handed over to Russian settlers. This, the order maintained, would show the whole of Asia the kind of punishment any future rebels against the might of the White Tsar might expect. It also stated that the action proposed was motivated in part by the alleged fact that the Ishan on his march had been joined by large numbers of natives and that this was not reported to the authorities.

In Turkestan the order produced the greatest consternation, placing the authorities as it did in an impossible situation. The land in question was recognized as one of the most fertile areas in the region. It was more densely populated than Belgium, and was so parcelled out in allotments that its confiscation would entail the dispossession of thousands of law-abiding smallholders, all of whom cared nothing for politics and were solely interested in paying their taxes and doing their work. The strip consisted of large meadows and splendid orchards of the loveliest peaches, apricots, and many other fruits, and of tilled fields bearing gigantic crops of rice, sorghum, maize, millet, and wheat. General Kuropatkin's order now required the gentlemen of Tashkent to hand over this wealthy region to Russian peasants for whom they had no sympathy; a pack of lazy, idle fellows who still clung to their obsolete methods of tillage with a three-yearly rotation of crops, who would produce nothing but rye and oats, who stubbornly refused to organize their lives and who were, in consequence, perpetually on the verge of destitution. In addition, the petty bureaucrats faced the prospect of losing many a cosy income earned on the quiet.

This sort of thing could not be countenanced, and Tashkent, Margelan, and Andizhan jointly moved heaven and earth to have Kuropatkin's order revoked. Eventually, a heavy fine in cash was imposed on the native population of the thirty-kilometre strip and only the unlucky village which housed the barracks attacked by the rebels had its inhabitants removed and its land confiscated in favour of the military authorities, or, to be precise, taken away and presented to the parent battalion of the butchered company.

The battalion, in the person of its Commanding Officer, promptly leased the land for a large sum to its former owners; the houses in the immediate vicinity of the barracks were pulled down, but the land on which they had once stood was all ploughed up and, at the time of my visit, was producing an excellent crop of cotton. Half the revenue from the crop went to the battalion, while the other half was given to the natives in payment for their labour. As I have said, the District Officer, a Muslim captain, was never brought to trial for fear of implicating the whole administration of the district. The documents I examined revealed very plainly the culpable negligence of the authorities, who should have been fully aware of the existing state of affairs from the many reports of its minor officials concerning the extent and general trend of the Ishan movement. I ascertained further that the District Officer had been in the habit of making gifts to his superiors who, though aware of his dishonesty, dared not proceed against him. The whole unfortunate episode revealed how much deterioration there had been in the superb administrative machinery originally set up by General Kaufman. That General Kuropatkin's order was modified on this occasion was fortunate for the prestige of Russia in Asia, as otherwise too many innocent lives would have been affected.

The revolt in Andizhan was the first open manifestation of the Ishan movement, though even in the last century it had made itself felt during the conquest of the Caucasus in areas inhabited by Muslims of Aryan origin as can be seen by the number of years it took to subdue Shamil, the legendary Ishan of the Caucasus.

The quelling of the revolt did not, however, put an end to the movement in Turkestan. During my visit there I met a delightful mulla, attached to one of the Tashkent medresehs. He was an extremely gifted man. Well educated, even when judged by European standards, and widely travelled, he had been to Paris, Algiers, Morocco and, of course, Constantinople. He was the Ishan of about 400 to 1,000 murids dispersed over the whole region of the Amu-Dar'ya. Outwardly there was nothing distinctive about this middle-aged man who received his visitors garbed in the prescribed black khalat and green turban of a pilgrim to Mecca. His Russian was fluent. And yet I had definite information both from my own staff and from the Okhrana that here was a powerful Ishan, commanding the obedience of a vast army of murids who, at a sign from him, were prepared to lay down their lives for the faith of Allah. Unaware of the extent of my knowledge about his political background he never, in the many engrossing conversations we had together, concealed his ardent loyalty to the cause of a Mohammedan empire. He bitterly deplored the falling off of moral standards among his countrymen, their addiction to drink (beer), their dishonest methods of trading and the decline of morality among their women. All this he blamed on the infidels, the kafirs, without, however, showing any particular animosity to Russia. He was also an enthusiastic supporter of the school reform, and the mekteb of his medreseh was one of the first to adopt the methods, benches, and text books prescribed by Constantinople. His conception of faith in God contained a profound yearning for purity, for spiritual serenity and the loosening of the ties of evil in this world. His whole approach to life strikingly illustrated the Aryan trend in the Sart interpretation of Mohammedanism.

The dossier on a sect of orthodox Muslims of Tatar extraction drawn up by the gendarmerie of Kazan in European Russia revealed a totally different approach to Ishanism by Muslims of Mongolian origin. Although the relationship between the Ishan and his murids remained unaltered, the aims of the organizations and the methods they pursued to achieve them differed considerably. There is no longer the slightest trace of that urge toward the moral and ethical improvement of the individual; the numerous associations present nothing but combat groups moved solely by political ideals. The documents relating to the Kazan sect plainly revealed the existence of a spirit of political fanaticism verging on hysteria joined to the practice of conspiratorial devices and plain murder, the whole inextricably mixed up with the crudest of barbaric superstitions. In fact, a typical example of the way in which the teaching of the Koran was interpreted by the Tatars. Not without significance, too, was the influence in Central Asia of Dervishism in the forms in which it is practised by the Arabs and Indians.

The papers dealing with the abortive rebellion of the Andizhan Ishan, and the report on his trial, throw an interesting light on the reasons which prompted him to adopt so desperate a course. I quote verbatim: 'I witnessed the gradual deterioration of the people, how they were abandoning the true religion and forsaking the paths traced by the Prophet of God. Fasts were no longer observed, women were living in sin and taking lovers. The holy places were neglected and were crumbling away; the people had somehow to be forcibly brought back to the Faith, and the infidels, who were responsible for breeding this spirit of unbelief in the country, evicted.'

The Ishan's followers, banished with him to Siberia, eventually all returned after a few years thanks to sundry amnesties. However, their lands, once so flourishing and now confiscated and handed to Russian settlers, had turned into a wild morass of reeds as a result of inept husbandry. Their endless complaints about lack of water prompted the aksakals, who were terrified of them, to give them more than they needed, and soon the entire region was smothered. As soon as they had returned, the former owners hastened to rent their fields from the Russians and painstakingly brought them back to their original state of cultivation. The settlers on their part migrated to the towns, set themselves up in trade and there proceeded to enjoy the incomes derived from the lease of their allotments.

The reform and Ishan movements in the Mohammedan world of Central Asia were of immense significance to the state in so far as they affected, in one form or another, the life of the entire population of the region. This significance was enhanced by the fact that the majority of the mullas and students in the medresehs were Sarts. Here I should add that in Turkestan, apart from the Sarts, a large section of the population was composed of natives variously described as Mohammedans, such as the Kirgiz, Turkmens, Uzbeks, and Tadzhiks. In addition there was a balance of Arabs, Chinese, Dungans, Kalmyks, Afghans, and Persians which with the exception of the Jews consisted of wanderers or temporary settlers, divided among the two main stems, the Sarts and the Kirgiz.

Although the Kirgiz are termed Mohammedans, this definition would have been incorrect a century ago. A nomad people, wholly devoted to cattle-breeding on a large scale, they followed no particular form of religion in the past, and even today they still show no pronounced signs of religious awareness. A hundred years ago, at the time of the conquest, they were dubbed Muslims by the Russians in official reports and registers because of certain Mohammedan customs they had adopted such as polygamy, and prayers at certain set times of the day. As applied to the Kirgiz chiefs and their immediate entourage the definition was in part correct, as most of them were in fact Mohammedans. Among them, even before the Russian conquest, it had been considered the right thing for anyone pretending to a higher cultural level to pose as a Mohammedan, and all of their sultans and manaps outwardly professed Mohammedanism. They kept Sart or Tatar mullas in their settlements, and while praying to the God of Mohammed they continued to observe a form of religious ritual influenced by fetishism. In addition they possessed a holy law of their own, the Adat, whose tenets often differed widely from those of the Shariat and, consequently, from Mohammed's Koran. Within the last century, however, Mohammedanism gained much ground among the Kirgiz, thanks largely to the policy of the Russian authorities, who supported the mosques and their dependent medresehs and virtually barred the message of Christ from reaching the people. Missionaries were required to obtain official permission for their work and even so, were restricted to the Orthodox clergy by a decree of the Holy Synod. Unfortunately the Orthodox church was no longer imbued with a missionary spirit because of its long subservience to the state, and its obstructive attitude to any form of initiative. This is why the process of conversion to Mohammedanism of the nomads in Turkestan was expanding under Russian domination and proceeding apace even at the time of my visit.

The contrast between the family life of the Sarts and the Kirgiz was of particular interest. The former meticulously obeyed the tenets of the Shariat and had in consequence reduced the status of the woman and mother to the level of a soulless being. The Kirgiz, on the other hand, were inclined to monogamy, if simply for the reason that wealthy tribesmen were the exception rather than the rule. While a bride might still have to be bought by the groom (payment was usually by instalments) and the *kalym*, or post-marriage morning gift, have to be laboriously collected and paid to her father; whilst the widow might be regarded as a chattel to be inherited, and be forced to marry the heir in line; whilst the wife might be expected to saddle her husband's horse and hold his stirrup as he mounted, or was barred from sitting at meals with the men and must meekly stand by her husband and hand him his food, gratefully accepting a juicy bone as a token of his goodwill—nevertheless a nomadic life of wandering across the desert made the woman so important to the welfare of the household that her position as mistress and mother of the children, whom she and not the father reared, was firmly assured.

The whole structure of Kirgiz life was founded upon race and tribe. The elders of the tribe were its masters, and it was precisely in the sphere of tribal life that the influence of the woman was most felt. Numerous indeed were the agreements, measures, disputes, and decisions that the Russians were able either to conclude, adopt or avoid thanks to the influence exercised by the Kirgiz women. The outward appearance of a Kirgiz woman immediately reveals the difference between her status and that of her Sart sister. She never veils her face, and she is free to talk to and deal with strangers; her spiritual independence is shown by the temerity with which she frequently refuses to follow an unloved husband to whom she has been sold by father or brother, by the dignity of her bearing, and by her forthrightness in a court of law. The Kirgiz way of life, based as it is upon the family, involuntarily gives Kirgiz Mohammedanism a distinctive imprint of its own, and one which differs strikingly from the Sart interpretation. Nevertheless the teaching of the Shariat is slowly spreading throughout the Kirgiz steppes, mainly owing to the influence of the mullas. The wealthier tribesmen are adopting Sart customs, the mullas are preaching the desirability of relegating the women to the harem, and the sense of oneness of tribe and family is being superseded by a feeling of religious community with the rest of the Mohammedan world—a realization of its solidarity and power.

Under Russian rule it was the medresehs of Samarkand that were largely instrumental in awakening the people to the reality of Panislam. They helped to restore the ruptured connection between the Caliphate in Constantinople and Central Asia, which had previously been dominated by petty tyrants each posing as a Caliph of the Prophet, and they marked out the channels along which this kinship of spirit might develop. In fact, they were responsible for the reform in the Mohammedan way of life and general outlook.

What, one may ask, will be the fate of the movement now that an essentially Russian national domination has been replaced by Communist rule? Of one thing I am sure, namely that the hopes of a spiritual revolution entertained by the originators of the Islamic reform movement were never fulfilled. When all is said and done the old mektebs were better suited to the psychology of the people, and their powerful organization was able to influence the development among the masses of that cult of authority which results in blind obedience. The new schools aimed at eliminating Western influence by introducing a Western spirit of criticism and Western methods. Yet it was this spirit which eventually destroyed the ancient concept of Mohammedanism, as was proved by the downfall of Turkey and other Mohammedan states. Attempts to found a state solely on political or party dogma such as were made by the reformers in

Constantinople and Egypt proved futile. To weld the masses into unity a world concept is required, like that adopted originally by Mohammedanism and daily proclaimed by the muezzins from the heights of the minarets: 'There is no God but God and Mohammed is his Prophet.' *La ilaha il Allah wa Muhammad rasul Allah*!

I ought to add that this concept has retained more of its original vitality in those parts of Turkestan such as Khiva and Bukhara which are still ruled by independent Mohammedan overlords, for during my tours of inspection I was able to observe the conditions prevailing in these regions and could assess the significance of a political entity based entirely on the application of the ancient Mohammedan way of life.

⚔ III ⚔

BUKHARA

THE conservative teachers of the mektebs I visited in Samarkand and Tashkent always referred to Bukhara as their Alma Mater. On my first visit there I had in due course met the Emir, who was accompanied by an impressive retinue, at his summer residence of Kermine; had duly conveyed to him a message of goodwill from the Emperor of Russia, and in turn been most regally entertained. Because of all the court festivities I did not see much of the country, an omission I was fortunately able to repair later. But however cursory my impressions it was obvious that the population of Bukhara was much poorer, in appearance at least, than that on the Russian side of the border. The kaftans of the simple people were less gaily coloured than in Turkestan, looked shabby, and indeed were often tattered. By contrast, those of the well-to-do were covered with gold embroidery and positively sparkled with diamonds. The labourers one saw, whether working in the towns or toiling in the fields, appeared pale and undernourished compared with the natives of the Russian provinces, and wore a look of fear. Yet this was a land ruled by a Muslim prince who was praised to the skies by every medreseh in Turkestan and represented as one of the greatest scholars of the Shariat.

In the course of my tour of inspection I visited Bukhara twice more with the special objective of studying conditions in a country that was allegedly governed by a system founded directly on the most orthodox of Mohammedan principles. The first of these two journeys took me to the capital, where I visited the mosques and medresehs. During the second I went to Chardzhou, a Russian settlement on Bukharan soil. Favoured by the railways, it had mushroomed from nothing and grown quickly. It was administered by a Russo-Bukharan council and was inhabited by Europeans well acquainted with local conditions.

One of my commissions was to investigate the extent to which the

6 63

ties between Russia and Bukhara could be freed from governmental control and profitably developed, with particular stress on the civilizing aspect of any such policy. The ruling Emir was of course aware of this part of my mission, and in consequence endeavoured as far as lay within his power to conceal from me the true state of affairs in his country, doing his best to depict everything in the rosiest of colours.

At Kermine station I was met with the customary oriental pomp, greeted by the heir apparent (the present Emir), decorated by him with the insignia of the Order of Iskander, the highest decoration in Bukhara, and driven in his company along the eight kilometre stretch of road to the Emir's residence. We proceeded in a landau presented at some time to the Emir by the Emperor of Russia. Before reaching the Emir's residence, which consisted of palace and gardens laid out in the centre of a typically Asian city, we traversed a long, arid stretch of steppe. As we bowled along in our closed landau under a scorching sun I was all but stifled by the heat. Only the window curtains were raised in response to a request by the heir, who was anxious to exhibit himself seated beside me, dressed up as I was in all the finery of my gold-embroidered court dress. Our escort was composed of Bukharan 'Cossacks' wearing picturesque uniforms of bright orange kaftans and shaggy white Persian fur caps, and festooned all over with weapons in silver scabbards studded with precious stones. The riders' mounts were all Arab bred. (What a pity that in Bukhara these handsome horses are so grossly overfed and that a fat neck is supposed to enhance their beauty.) These 'Cossacks', incidentally, were the only regular troops the Emir possessed; they looked well disciplined, and were at that time commanded by a Russian officer. A few individuals in tattered Russian uniforms and dirty turbans—supposed to be soldiers—lolled about the streets and presented arms as we drove past. None of them, I noticed, had modern rifles, and the muskets they wielded were of the flint-lock type.

At last, after a drive of seven kilometres, we reached Kermine and then proceeded along a street flanked on both sides by mud brick walls fronting beautiful gardens. The streets in this old Asian township were so narrow that our carriage, drawn by three horses Russian-fashion, barely managed to squeeze through in spite of the vigorous work of the jigit who rode in front to clear the way. The carts and caravans we met coming in our direction were forced to turn into side streets narrower than the one we were following, and it is no easy matter to halt and turn a caravan of fifty camels. Whenever this happened we were obliged to watch patiently as the jigits cleared the way with the aid of *kamchis*, or whips, like the Russian *nagaika*.

The Emir's residence, surrounded by irrigated gardens, was built on a slight rise and approached by a narrow lane which led up to a high gate surmounted by the Emir's arms: a kamchi more than four yards long around which were hung the skulls and trophies of his enemies. Here we were greeted by his Ministers and court dignitaries and escorted to another gate consisting of two massive double doors of plane timber most beautifully carved. Inside these stood the Emir, waiting to receive me, the envoy of the Ak-Padishah, and to extend his greetings, couched in flowery Asian terms and interpreted by his personal doctor, a Russian. I made a suitable reply, and transmitted the Emperor's greetings.

After I had presented the members of my suite to the Emir he led us to his room in the men's quarter of the palace, which had originally been built by his father and selected as a summer residence because of Kermine's elevation above sea level. The rooms of the palace were well proportioned and about the size of those in an average city flat. There were none of the customary long enfilades, and the total number of rooms did not appear to be great. If I remember correctly there were only three reception rooms, connected by single doors, while the rest all led into a kind of covered cloister in accordance with the usual Sart custom.

A remarkable feature of the reception rooms was the threshold of each connecting door, twelve inches high and made of beautifully carved ebony, over which the Emir lifted his gouty foot laboriously. The walls were faced with beautiful alabaster, the work of Arab masons as the Emir told me later, and white Moorish stalactites hung from the ceilings. The wood of window frames, doors, and much of the panelling was of ebony (or, to be more precise, of black plane-wood long immersed in water), beautifully carved. A modern note was struck by the electric light and hideous brass candelabra (a cheap product of Moscow) adorned with glass tulips for lampshades. Wonderful old Bukharan carpets, either in the typical brown colour or woven in the famous Kaaba pattern, were strewn over the floors, one such carpet covering an entire room. On top of these lay a few of the red and white Turkmen runners so prized in Central Asia.

(At that time a runner of this sort, 75 centimetres wide, cost up to 100 roubles per metre.)

The Emir's private room, to which he now conducted us, was somewhat smaller than the others but was hung from ceiling to floor with the most magnificent carpets the local industry could produce. He seated himself in a deep armchair and had another brought in for me and our retinues moved away to a respectful distance, with the exception of two interpreters who placed themselves behind the Emir's chair. The Emir wore the habitual khalat, made in this case of ivory satin and hemmed with gold. The epaulettes of a Russian Lieutenant-General glittered on his shoulders; across his chest he wore the ribbon of the Order of Alexander Nevskiy, while the diamond-studded star of the Order itself as well as numerous other Russian decorations, all heavily jewelled, were pinned to his khalat. The customary dastarkhan was served to us on silver trays, together with glasses of tea. This was followed by an exchange of courtesies which lasted well over half an hour. The Emir enquired about the state of the Emperor's health and I responded by enquiring about his own and that of his children; we discussed the journey, the weather and the probable yield of the next cotton crop. When the subject of water was mentioned I felt that we were at last about to broach the one problem of vital interest to Bukhara, namely the supply of water from the Zeravshan, the construction of dams, etc.

At the beginning of our interview the Emir had spoken to me via his interpreters; as our conversation progressed he became more and more vivacious, no longer waiting for my answers to be translated, for of course he understood Russian perfectly, and at last he came to the point by frankly asking me to state the real significance of my visit. I evaded the question, saying that it was only the vastness of his domains that prevented the Emperor from personally visiting all his subjects and that he had dispatched me as his representative. The Emir expressed his gratification, and expatiated upon the satisfaction he derived from the ties of sincere friendship which united Bukhara and Russia. After half an hour he rose and conducted me to the rooms reserved for my use, enjoined me to rest and requested the honour of my presence at a state banquet one hour later.

Mercifully it had become a little cooler by then, and the long table laid for eighty to one hundred guests was set in the gallery surrounding the courtyard. It was prettily decorated with flowers, fine cut glass and a handsome centre-piece, but the lavishness of the setting diminished in proportion to the distance from the centre, where the Emir and I were seated. We were flanked to the right and left by alternating members of my suite and Bukharan notables, while opposite us sat the Chancellor of Bukhara, the Kush-Begi, an imposing figure, obviously of Persian descent, clad in a ceremonial khalat of gold brocade sprinkled with diamonds. Seated to his right and left were my Bukharan officials, the Russian Diplomatic Agent (our representative at the Emir's court), and his secretaries.

A Bukharan band was assembled in the courtyard and I was informed by the Emir that it performed 'as well as the Imperial band, and played without the use of any scores'. This, indeed, required no emphasizing, as every bandsman rendered selections of his own choosing by ear, the united efforts resulting in the most dreadful of cacophonies. The Russian national anthem, as played by the band when the Emir toasted his friend the Russian Emperor was quite unrecognizable. It was then my turn to drink to the health of the Emir and his son, and altogether it took us over two hours to get through the banquet. The fare was a mixture of Russian and Bukharan culinary art. We started off with a rich assortment of hors d'oeuvres, with caviare served in little tubs and all kinds of tasty preserves: pepper in olive oil, pickled melons, smoked fish, and German sausages in tomato sauce. There followed the twelve main courses and sundry intermediary dishes, all nicely identified in French and Russian on our menu cards, and accompanied by copious libations of wine.

I must frankly admit that this particular meal presented one of the hardest tasks I ever faced in the course of my onerous duties in Turkestan. While making diplomatic political exchanges with the Emir, who considered this an appropriate time to get down to fundamentals and who was now making no use at all of his interpreter, I was expected to partake of every dish, in order not to give offence to my host, and empty glass after glass of every wine. The banquet provided a good illustration of the craftiness of the Asian mind, and an experience to be repeated later in Khiva, for time and again the Emir brought up the ticklish questions of water supply and of the tax he was trying to impose on the profits earned by Russian merchants. Several times during the meal the favourite dish of the Turkestanians was served, pilau, or plov, as it is called in Tatar and Turkish. Bukharan pilau, Caucasian pilau, Persian pilau,

Tatar pilau, they are all varieties of rice steeped in fat mixed either with roasted quails, sugared eggs, or with raisins and roasted lamb. We wound up with a selection of melons, peaches, apricots, etc., mixed, spiced, and frozen, followed by Turkish coffee and a battery of liqueurs.

I was somewhat concerned about my retinue who, I had noticed, were paying due tribute to the iced champagne, so very welcome in the overpowering heat. I therefore gave the signal to depart as soon as the meal was over, and we set off for the station in a long caravan of vehicles, escorted by the heir apparent. The Emir's high-ranking courtiers rode beside our carriage with flaming torches, while the bodyguard of Bukharan Cossacks cantered in front and behind our procession. The event was, unfortunately, marred by an accident; the Emir's chief equerry, Azim Beg, was thrown violently by his horse and was left behind, lying prone on the road with a broken collar bone and a few broken ribs. My retinue were all very pleased with the day and were in the highest of spirits owing to the golden stars with which they all, including my valet, were plastered. I, personally, was disappointed. I had had no opportunity to study the workings of the Bukharan machinery of state, nor had I been able to glean any useful information about the state of the country or its people.

The Emir's reputation among the Mohammedan spiritual leaders was, as I have said, very high. Like many other oriental rulers he was an autocrat, and he was considered an authority on the Shariat by those well versed in Mohammedan law. On certain days of the week he dispensed justice in person; his donations to the mosques were generous and he did much to restore them to their former splendour. He had given millions toward the restoration of the crumbling mosque in St. Petersburg, which was a copy of the surrounding Orthodox churches. (The work took several years and was finished just before the 1914 war.)

My own impression of the Emir was that of a cunning and acquisitive personality. The oriental splendour of his palace contrasted badly with the frightened appearance of the Bukharan natives we met on our journey. I could not but feel that all this magnificence and generosity was only a façade. Small things seemed to corroborate this impression. For instance, I noticed at table that only about a dozen guests were given silver knives, spoons, and forks; the less important had to make do with plain metal ones, while the minor courtiers were supplied only with spoons or had to eat with their bare hands. Again, during the hour preceding the official banquet, when we were supposed to be resting in our rooms, some members of my suite had taken a stroll in the courtyard. There they met the Emir's falconer, who, it appeared, had lived in Russia and was delighted to air his Russian. They were amazed at his contempt and positive hatred for the Emir, which he made no effort to disguise. 'Look at this bird to which I am chained,' he said, pointing to his falcon. 'It is just like my master, unloving and selfish, and it gorges itself on flesh; I don't know how many times I have been beaten on this wretched bird's account, and if it should ail I'll be thrown into prison, where a man dies like a beast. The Emir is a wicked fellow.' The man was quite frank, and spoke out openly in the certainty that none of the natives present understood any Russian.

When his words were reported to me I paid little attention to them because at the time I knew nothing of the conditions that prevailed in Bukharan jails, but they came to my mind six months later when I visited the prisons of the capital. These conditions I shall now describe.

Imagine a deep depression at the foot of the citadel, surrounded by high, grim-looking walls and towers. At the bottom of the depression a few parallel trenches have been excavated, each about 18 feet across and 120 feet long, and between 42 and 48 feet in depth, so that looking down one has the impression of gazing into a well. Stretched over the trenches on a level with the ground is an iron grating. Emaciated, listless human beings are discernible in the depths, moving about like animals in some menagerie or lying stretched out on the filthy straw matting, 'waiting to be remembered by the Emir', as I was told by the Bukharan notable who accompanied me. At the citadel's outer gate street vendors had urged us to buy flat barley cakes and large loaves, the Russian Diplomatic Agent hastening to explain that it was customary to distribute this bread among the prisoners as one of the good deeds prescribed by the Shariat. I purchased a few basketfuls, but when I saw the look of awful greed with which the prisoners watched me I quickly had more of them fetched. The bread was then thrown down to them, and I was horribly reminded of the bears' feeding time in a zoo. But even in these foul surroundings the oriental upbringing was never forsaken. There was no stampede, no rush for the bread. Instead, every one of those wretched human beings stretched out a limp hand to pick up the bit that was nearest, then rose, and with hands crossed on his breast and his gaze upon us, murmured 'rahmat' (thank you), before sinking down exhausted.

What a contrast to the behaviour of prisoners in our European jails! In the course of my career as a civil servant I have visited many prisons, and have everywhere observed a uniform spirit of outward discipline and concealed defiance among the inmates. Everyone of them knows, of course, for what reason and for how long he has been sentenced, yet, if you ask, you are overwhelmed by excuses and proofs of alleged innocence. When there are several prisoners in a cell together the weak will certainly be robbed of their food by the strong unless watched by extra guards. In Bukhara it was all very different. Here the old were served by the young, and none knew how long they would have to languish in jail. The customary: 'Until the Emir in his mercy deigns to remember him' took one back to the days of Jacob and Pharaoh.

When a prisoner was being jailed, several bars of the iron grating were moved aside and the wretch was then lowered by a rope. My wish to go down and talk with the prisoners and my efforts to do so were balked by difficulties put in my way such as the time it would take to open up the grating, the difficulty of obtaining a ladder, etc., and on that occasion my time was indeed limited by a very full list of engagements. Moreover, my escorting officials were profoundly shocked at the idea and added the weight of their own arguments to those of the Emir's servants, doing their best to frighten me off with lurid descriptions of vermin and the risk of infection. Even so, I did succeed in exchanging a few words with the prisoners through my interpreter and was thus able to gain some idea of the Emir's conception of justice, though in the majority of cases it was well nigh impossible to get a definite reply to my questions. The usual answer was: 'I don't know'; or 'according to the Shariat' or simply 'such is my fate'. Eventually my interpreter, a Russian lieutenant from the Caucasus, got the prison overseer to show me a few prisoners who he thought would soon be released, as the amounts of their ransom had been recently fixed by the Emir. One of them was supposed to be among the richest merchants in Bukhara; he, it appeared, was being mulcted for money because he had fallen foul of the Emir's finance minister, the almighty Kush-Begi. (A few years later the latter's extortions caused such a riot that he was forced to flee and seek refuge in Persia.) When I asked the Russian Diplomatic Agent why he had not attempted to enforce better treatment of the prisoners, and had allowed conditions to prevail which were quite incompatible with the civilizing influence Russia was trying to exert, he proudly pointed to a contraption of reeds stretched over the open grating. This, he said was a measure he had caused to be put through during his tenure of office. Previously, the prisoners had either been stifled by the merciless rays of the sun as it beat down upon them, or had been frozen and half drowned by the rain and snow in winter.

One shuddered at the mere thought of what those unfortunate beings had to endure. It was obvious that a few days as the Emir's prisoner were worse than any length of confinement in our jails.

When at last I had myself driven away, feeling much oppressed by all that I had seen, the Diplomatic Agent told me that explicit orders from St. Petersburg strictly limited the scope of his interference in the internal administration of Bukhara. The Ministry of Foreign Affairs in the capital had given me to understand that the government's attitude to Bukhara was based on the recognition of its complete independence and right to self-government, and that our influence was conditioned by the geographical position of the country. The Ministry of War, which I learnt was responsible for the actual administration of the entire region, took a different view, and chose to treat the Emir as a vassal of Russia. This was also the view of the Governor-General, or rather of his staff; but locally, of course, the Emir's diamonds and presents did much to allay any desire to interfere in the internal affairs of the Emirate. On the other hand, some of the older officials saw no particular need to improve conditions in Bukhara and held that, on the whole, it was quite salutary for the natives to compare the tyrannical conditions in China, Afghanistan, Persia and India with those in Russian-ruled Turkestan. This I thought a curious argument, though not devoid of some logic.

When General Kaufman ruled the region things were of course different, since the merest wish of the mighty Governor-General was law to the Emir. His successors, however, had their wings drastically clipped. The change of policy coincided with a period when the Ministry of Foreign Affairs was much preoccupied with England's complaints and even threats concerning the policy of expansion and alleged annexation in Central Asia that was being conducted by Russia's generals. The undesirability of allowing an administrative head to solve the problems of Central Asian external policy was strongly represented to the Emperor, and soon afterwards an Imperial Decree banned any interference in the internal affairs of

Bukhara and limited the duties of the diplomatic agent in that country to safeguarding the interests of its Russian residents, thus giving the Emir a chance to shake off the tutelage of Tashkent. A very able diplomat, the Emir frequently visited St. Petersburg, where he was received at court by the Emperor with all the honours due to the ruler of an independent state. A judicious distribution of diamonds, decorations, and other bounties generally resulted in some form of material advantage to Bukhara. At first the Emir had been placated by decorations, but when he had collected all the stars that Russia could bestow upon him, the Ministry of Foreign Affairs had to resort to other marks of distinction. A start was made by progressively adding to the grandeur of his title. General Kaufman, when dealing with the Emir, had addressed him as 'Sir,' (*Vashe Stepenstvo*); after one of the Emir's journeys to the capital this was raised to 'Honourable Sir', and subsequently to 'Count,' 'Excellency', 'High Excellency' and finally to 'Highness'. In the eyes of the natives he now ranked higher than the Governor. As a token of gratitude for a torpedo-boat destroyer built at his own expense which he donated to the Emperor during the Russo-Japanese war, he was enrolled in the Cossack regiment of the Guards and permitted to wear the epaulettes of a full General of the Russian Army. The local population of Turkestan no longer had any doubts but that he outranked the Governor-General in Tashkent and could do as he pleased in Bukhara.

As I have said, the Ministry of Foreign Affairs on the banks of the Neva persisted in regarding the conquest of Turkestan as a military adventure. It refused to recognize the value of this region to Russia and deprecatingly termed it 'the Desert'. apparently having eyes only for Constantinople, distant Vladivostok, and Korea. This was the attitude that lay behind the return of the rich province of Kuldzha to China, the abandonment of the natural frontier line of the Tyan'-Shan' in exchange for some paltry concessions on the Amur river, and the cession of the wealthy Karakul district to the Emir of Bukhara. This last step was taken in opposition to the expressed wish of its Sart and Chinese inhabitants to be placed under Russian rule, and despite the fact that it had never formed part of the Emirate and was originally owned by Kashgar.

On his return from the coronation of Tsar Nicholas II in Moscow the Emir was able to boast that he had sat at the Imperial table, while the Governor-General of Turkestan was not deemed worthy of this honour. Apart from the policy pursued by the Government, the aforementioned lavish distribution of diamond-studded decorations in the right quarters contributed not a little to loosening Russia's hold on Bukhara.

Rumours of the sums that had been donated by the Emir to the medresehs in Constantinople and to some of the influential mullas in order to gain their good graces prompted me to ask experts on local conditions about the sources of his wealth and the lavish amounts bestowed so freely on those he considered useful. Then, for the first time, the known size of his income was revealed to me: a deposit of 40 million roubles in shares and securities in the Tashkent branch of the State Bank, huge accounts in the banks of Moscow and St. Petersburg, and cases full of gold and silver in his Treasury in Bukhara. In addition there was the revenue, quite impossible to check, from loans advanced at exorbitant rates of interest to his Bukharan merchants, and even abroad. (Turkey was mentioned in this connexion.) The Emir was credited with being one of the best judges of diamonds and turquoise in the world. Quite obviously he was one of the world's richest men, and one of its greatest capitalists. This wealth was all of fairly recent origin, and had been amassed after the Russian occupation of Turkestan and because of the protection he had gained as the result of our orderly administration.

In the past the Emirs of Bukhara, while recognized as great rulers, were no more important than the Khans of Kashgar, the Emirs of Afghanistan, or the Khans of Khiva, who were considered equal to them both in birth and rank. The Khans of Khiva, in particular, were acknowledged to be of nobler descent and were certainly wealthier.

Under Russian rule a rural economy based on barter was replaced by one founded on the value of money, and the Emir's father was the first of these rulers to appreciate the power it would afford him. Among his subjects there was no lack of able and crafty business men, especially among the Jews, accustomed for centuries to handling finance. (These were the descendants of the Babylonian captives who had not returned to Palestine.) With their aid he set about founding a system of taxation equivalent to a series of financial and trade operations. For instance, a concession, sold at an arbitrary price by the Emir, was henceforth required for any form of trade. This was followed by monopolies in his favour of certain kinds of merchandise. Next, he imposed fixed prices on articles of local produce such as silk, satin, copperware, wool, and hides of every description, and banned their export. Thus he was able to buy up these goods at prices he himself had fixed, and sell them abroad at an enormous profit. His trade ordinances were a source of constant friction between him and the Russian merchants trading in Bukhara, particularly after the building of the railway by the Russian government. The Emir insisted on his right to levy the same taxes from the Russians, a claim which was in many cases disputed both by the merchants and by the Russian administration across the border.

As I mentioned earlier, the taxes were farmed out to provincial governors, who were then required to defray all the expenses connected with the administration of their respective provinces and, in addition, to contribute handsomely toward swelling the Emir's exchequer. Thus a continuous flow of money kept pouring into the treasury, where it stayed, as there was virtually no state expenditure, the only drain upon it being occasioned by the ruler's withdrawals to meet his personal requirements. These devices for extorting money from the population were complemented by a flourishing rural economy; all in all, the Emir's yearly income and the volume of his amassed and hoarded wealth ensured a total of fantastic proportion, to be arbitrarily used in the promotion of his devious policies. In order further to perfect his tax-impressing machinery he surrounded himself with a bevy of Shi'i Persians whom he had enrolled because of their renowned ability to squeeze money out of the population. If this lessened his popularity among the orthodox Sunni theologians it did nothing to alter their conviction that his was a power it would be just as well to placate, having regard to the sums he distributed to the mosques, the medresehs, and the Mohammedan ecclesiastics. For those of them who had within the last few years adopted a hostile attitude to Russia, the Emir stood forth as the noble, unimpeachably orthodox Mohammedan ruler, while the mullas from Constantinople whom he had bribed with Bukharan money stood solidly behind him and encouraged his every move.

The 'Young Turk' Party and the reforms sponsored by it were unpopular with the Emir and he gave them no support within the confines of his state, so the mektebs in Bukhara continued to teach along the old-fashioned and traditional lines. This was in contrast to that part of Bukhara which had passed under Russian rule, where the new text books extolling Panislamism were either printed or copied on parchment and were brought to the attention of the Central Asian subjects of the White Tsar. The reis still functioned in

Bukhara and assiduously reported to the Emir any suspected infringement of the Islamic law. Within his realm the mullas were orthodox men of God, properly appointed by the representative of the Caliph (the Emir) and holding their offices at his pleasure, not half-laymen crookedly elected to office for a term of three years, as was the case in Russian Turkestan. There, the mulla was forced to devote the first year of his tenure to paying off the Kadi for his intervention at the election, the second to securing an income for himself, and the third to securing the good offices of voters likely to be influential in the next round.

During my second visit I spent two days in Old Bukhara. I had hoped to see something more of the government of the country, for the Emir was at that time in the Crimea, where he had an estate, but even so too much time was passed in official receptions, dinners, and visits. Here I will describe a court session held by the high Kadi, which admittedly had in my honour somewhat more pomp than usual. A handsome carpet had been laid over the open space in front of the mosque. Perched on a cushion to one side of the carpet was the Kadi, an impressive white-turbaned figure in a velvet khalat, and beside him my followers and I were seated on cushions and carpets which had been brought specially for the occasion. The plaintiffs and the defendants, accompanied by their families and counsels, stood some distance away and the scene was ringed by a dense crowd of spectators, respectfully silent and overawed by the presence of the Kadi. In case of need a few of the Emir's soldiers, in tattered uniforms, had been posted here and there. At a sign from the Kadi the litigants approached, and with arms folded across their breasts knelt down before him. Their chosen representative, a well-dressed, handsome, long-bearded Sart, then stepped forward and bowing deeply laid a scroll setting out the complaint before the judge. He was at once followed by one of his assistants, who placed another scroll, less lengthy, called a *rivayet* (quotation from the Shariat) beside the first. The same procedure was followed by the defendant's counsels. All this was repeated several times, in dead silence. Meanwhile, sheets containing rivayets, filled in by scribes versed in the law and from time to time shown to the judge, were rapidly piling up at his feet. Presently he selected one of them and showed it to an assistant standing behind him. It was then passed to the clerk of the court. The latter, who knelt beside the judge with reed pen and ink at the ready, scrawled some letters on a piece of paper and handed it to the disputing parties, who then rose, bowed respectively to the judge, and slowly withdrew, still facing him. The scrawls on the piece of paper were the verdict, which when translated appeared to have no bearing on the case. I was however assured by experts that the meaning was quite plain to everyone concerned.

When I asked who paid the judge's fees, I was told it was the litigants. The Emir, it appeared, contributed nothing to the maintenance of justice in his realm. Further enquiries showed that the income of a Kadi was considerable, judging by the sums quoted to me. Once I had met such a Kadi, in Tashkent; I had visited his house, and on another occasion had attended the marriage of his daughter. This man owned several wives, kept up an elaborate establishment and could afford to marry off his daughter at the ripe age of fifteen. (Usually the daughters are given away in marriage as young as possible, both to obtain the *mahr*, the portion paid the day following the ceremony, and to relieve the parents of the expense of their maintenance.) According to rumour this particular Kadi earned 60,000 roubles a year. As incomes of this order could be obtained only by deliberately tipping the scale of justice in favour of the rich rather than the innocent I was not surprised to hear that the natives preferred to withhold their cases from the local courts and have recourse to Russian justice, which enjoyed an Empire-wide reputation of incorruptibility. One of the methods adopted was to hire a Russian to act as proxy; moreover, many Bukharans were Russian subjects, there being a pronounced desire among the natives to seek Russian nationality just as in the days of Rome when its alien subjects often sought the status of Roman citizens. This ambition resulted in a pile of applications to the Russian Diplomatic Agent and repeated complaints from the Emir about the loss of his subjects.

In spite of its centuries-old hold over the minds of its followers the implementation of Islamic law had brought Bukhara nothing but slavery, despotism, poverty and every form of restriction on the cultural and spiritual life of the individual. Now, for the first time in history, Western ethical and civic concepts of freedom, work, civilization and the right of the individual to recognition had penetrated the country to a certain extent, thanks to Russia's conquest of Central Asia. That the introduction of these concepts should have coincided with the growing malaise of the West, as exemplified by the waning of ancient forms of life and tradition— both powerful factors for stability—was unfortunate, and a fact no impartial observer could ignore. In the Mohammedan world it led to the cleavage of communities into two diametrically opposed factions. The one, which was passionately devoted to Islam, was sustained by the Shariat and Sunna-minded or orthodox mullas anxious to retain their domination over the masses and intent on fighting Christian civilization by fostering the dawning consciousness of Islam all over Europe, Africa, and Asia. The other was fully aware of all the advantages conferred by freedom, a political structure founded on law, and the security of the individual and his possessions from arbitrary assault.

This latter function leaned increasingly towards the régime established by Russia, for this was without doubt a political system which had applied these principles in the East more realistically than any other power, the British in India included. The tradesmen, businessmen, and craftsmen of which it was mainly composed, habitually withdrew their children from the local mektebs and sent them to Russian schools. Here their whole outlook on life was changed and many were the young men who earned their officers' commission in the Russian Army, to which in those days they had full freedom of access. In Tashkent, the capital of the region, one half of the members elected to the Town Council (the Duma) were, according to the provisions of Russian law, native-born Asians, generally prominent merchants, manufacturers, or employers. It was obvious that the influence of a class working and trained in the European tradition, and ready to accept Western ideas, was bound to increase. These consciously civilized natives were the object of envy to men of equal status in Bukhara, who did all they could to gain similar standing and who swelled the number of applicants for Russian nationality. The privileged position of Russian subjects in Bukhara and other parts of Central Asia was, of course, a contributory factor, while the contrast between conditions in Bukhara and Russian-controlled territory was so great that I have many times been asked why we allowed these conditions to persist.

A striking example of the profound gratitude shown by the population for any Russian-administered branch of social welfare was afforded me when I visited the hospital built by the Emir at the suggestion of the Russian authorities. The action was prompted by the abysmally insanitary conditions in the city of Bukhara and the danger of infection to the Russian residents. The provision of funds for public welfare is not one of the charities named in the Shariat, and the Emir parted with his money with little or no grace. However, part with it he did, and the hospital was quickly built by Russian engineers. Some consolation was afforded the Emir by an elaborate opening ceremony at which he dispatched a lengthy telegram to the Emperor, thus advertising his generosity to both his subjects and his sovereign. The hospital was a handsome one-storied building, painted white, large enough to house between 150 and 200 patients. It had large windows, something previously unseen in Bukhara, and the equipment was as up-to-date as was possible at the time, baths and plumbing having been installed with much trouble since Bukhara possessed neither mains nor sewerage. The medical staff consisted of a very pleasant Jewish couple, man and wife, the Diplomatic Agent explaining that they had been specially appointed since it was easier for people of their nationality to gain the confidence of Moham- medans. On the day I visited the hospital the husband was ill, and his wife was coping with all the work with the assistance of a few nurses and medical orderlies. 'A chronic case; it could so easily have been avoided if he or she had attended a doctor in time', was the sentence I heard repeatedly as we went on our round of the patients, stretched out in spotless beds. The doctor told me that the number attending the daily clinic was very large, most of them suffering from various kinds of eye infection, especially the trachoma which is so terribly prevalent in the East.

When we entered the women's wards the patients hastily drew their blankets over their faces and timorously answered our ques- tions only after lengthy persuasion by the lady doctor. Some of the cases were heartrending, especially the nine-year-old mothers, tiny and sickly-looking, holding their puny babies in emaciated little hands with henna-stained nails. According to the doctor, the life these girls are compelled to lead with their husbands defies descrip- tion.

Tuberculosis, syphilis, and trachoma were as rampant among the women as among the men; I also noticed numerous cases of specifi- cally Central Asian diseases, such as pendeh, boils, etc. The doctor told me that during her husband's illness she had had to abandon, temporarily, the practice of visiting ailing women in the harems, but that as soon as he recovered she would start again. She had received an impression of unspeakable suffering, depravity, and dirt resulting from a way of life imposed by the laws of the harem. Worst of all were the conditions of child-birth and care for the newly-born, which were responsible for the deaths of innumerable mothers and babies, or the cause of life-long suffering, maiming, and blindness.

The woman doctor was particularly distressed about the evil custom of child marriage, and indeed one could not but recoil at the idea of such children as the wives of some sixty-year-old merchant or mulla. They looked so innocent, despite their painted eyebrows stencilled into a straight black line.

The men's section of the hospital contained an extraordinary medley of types representative of all Asia, from dark-skinned Hindus, Aryan Afghans with the distinguished deportment of Spanish grandees, handsome Turkmens and long-bearded Sarts, to diminutive beady-eyed Kirgizes, Kalmyks, and Chinese. In the wards one missed the gay colouring of native kaftan and turban, for the patients, all looking somewhat sheepish, were attired in the drab hospital garb customary in Europe of striped dressing gown and white skull cap. This was the only hospital in the city, and in fact the only one in the world of the Emir's possessions. Despite all its shortcomings, public welfare in Russian Turkestan had at least provided every region and district with a barrack-like hospital; there were in addition many doctors scattered over the country who were ready to supply a medical service free of charge to the local population, thus ensuring at least a supply of drugs in cases of urgent need.

The number of patients in the Bukhara State Hospital was considerable, and even the fanatical mullas were not averse to availing themselves of its services. A particular source of comfort was the knowledge that one of the women doctors attached to the hospital was an eye specialist. Incidentally, I learnt from her that on one occasion a leper had applied for admission, but she had of course been obliged to turn him down.

I commissioned a Russian doctor, a graduate of the St. Petersburg Military Medical Academy attached to my staff, to draw up a report on the public health institutions in the region and the preventative measures in force against the spread of disease. In consequence, I received a shattering account of numerous forms of infection, epidemics, and diseases prevailing in the area, especially in the vassal states of Khiva and Bukhara, where health conditions beggared description. Bubonic plague, cholera, and influenza were rampant, and the threat of infection from these scourges hung like a sword of Damocles over Russian Turkestan. Everything was regulated by the tenets of the Shariat and these, apparently, were

7

adequately met if a leper was banished to the desert. The population of the villages and towns still flocked to the local miracle
workers to be treated by magical formulae, incantations, and herb
concoctions.

Certain localities, alleged to possess some particular form of
curative properties, were held in great esteem and became centres of
pilgrimage. Thus, in the courtyard of a mosque in Kokand I was
shown a withered tree ten inches across, which had a long branch
projecting at right angles to the trunk about two feet from the
ground. The bough was supposed to possess the miraculous power
of helping barren women. All they had to do was to come to this
particular tree as pilgrims, seat themselves astride the bough and
slither down its length as far as the trunk. The tree was an ancient
plane tree, some 400 years old, and its timber, hard as iron and
further hardened by the hot rays of the sun, was absolutely polished
by the thighs of the countless women who had slid down its length,
handsomely contributing to the revenue of the mosque in their zeal.
Many other mosques owned similar fetishes; for instance, a hair from
the Prophet's beard, or from the tail of his horse, both of which were
considered objects of exceptional veneration, while a detailed story
of how this or that relic came into the possession of the mosque was
always forthcoming from the mulla in charge.

On one occasion at breakfast-time I was greeted in a mosque with
an exceptionally lavishly spread dastarkhan. The table was set in full
view of the public on a terrace under one of the arches which often
mark the approach to a mosque. To decline this token of oriental
hospitality in so sacred a place was out of the question, so we sat
down and got ready to face the food which was being brought in.
As a matter of fact we were all very hungry on that particular morning and I frankly admit that the rich pilau of rice, raisins and lamb
tasted wonderfully good. If only we had stopped there! Unfortunately for us, however, the pilau was followed by *shashlyk* with
kavardak sauce and *kumys*. Kavardak is a thick sauce made of goat's
milk, vinegar, mustard, slices of cucumber, raisins, sheep's kidney
fat, pepper, spices, apricots and peaches; in fact a mixture of things
both possible and quite impossible to digest. Kumys is fermented
mare's milk, usually served from a *kurdyuk*, a sheepskin used in the
desert as a container for liquids. To wash down this feast we, the
kafirs, were even treated to a libation of French champagne. Towards the end of the meal I took out my cigarette case, but **was**

politely requested by the mulla to refrain for a while from smoking. He then proceeded to open a small glass door fitted into a recess in the wall by which we were seated, and, having covered his head with a silk kerchief, he brought out a small casket. Then, turning to me he said: 'Please, smoke now; I am removing the hair of the Prophet to an inner chamber.' It appeared that although eating and drinking (even champagne-drinking by infidels) in the presence of the Prophet's hair were acts considered particularly blessed, smoking was tabu; why, I failed to understand.

In the courtyard of yet another mosque, a few dead trees were festooned with the ribs and skulls of horses. They were holy trees beneath which missionaries, the messengers of Allah, had preached, and the bones were those of their battle chargers. Pilgrims to these holy places believed that when the trees once again burst into leaf this would herald the dawn of Mohammed's kingdom on earth and the resurrection of the holy men, seated on their chargers. In other places rebirth of trees was linked with the end of the world. The origin of many of these fetishes can be traced to the days of Arab or Mongol domination, though some are even more ancient, dating back to heathen times. However, these saintly relics are by no means the sole source of attraction and do not explain why some mosques in particular become the centres of pilgrimage.

The answer is, I think, to be found in the immense influence of the medresehs over both young and older students and the sermons preached by learned and reputedly holy mullas. This was strikingly revealed to me in the course of the three-week conference later held in Tashkent, to which I had invited a group of learned mullas with the object of studying and editing a Russian translation of rules based on the Shariat which I had had prepared.

The main regulations under review were those applying to the family, to inheritance and tutelage, as well as definitions concerning ownership and grazing rights. I had found supporting material for the Russian text in French codified collections from Tunis and Algiers, and in compendiums and digests by English magistrates on cases where the litigants were Mohammedan. The total text comprised some 500 paragraphs, each translated into Sart, and was printed on loose sheets. These were distributed to the most eminent mullas in Turkestan with a request that they examine and annotate the individual paragraphs. When this work was done and the conference convened, we carefully examined the draft paragraph by paragraph, amending the Russian wording in the light of the mullas' remarks. The agreed text was later published as an unofficial collection of laws and appeared in several successive editions.

Two things were thus achieved. First, the Russian courts which controlled native courts, had at their disposal henceforth a systematically tabulated collection of regulations of the Shariat in Russian; second, thanks to the Sart translation the local population was given access to what had previously been the guarded secret of native jurists. The fact that the Hanafite sect (followers of the great Mohammedan jurist Abu-Hanafa), ruled the medresehs both in India and Turkestan, so that the same interpretation of the Mohammedan faith was practised in both places, was of very great assistance in this task. I must here place on record how immensely impressed I was by the earnest work of the mullas, many of them regarded as all but holy, during the whole period of our deliberations. An apparently insignificant word, or perhaps a paragraph heading, was considered a matter of the greatest importance since in their view we were dealing with the laws of God, and these were not to be lightly treated. Sometimes the position was made rather difficult by the lack of a Russian term which would express some well-defined Muslim juridical concept. Thus, I particularly recall the meetings dealing with the *mahr*, or after-marriage-morning gift. In Mohammedan law the mahr clearly contained two concepts of guardianship: the *vali* and the *vasi*, both of which deal with the rights of the individual but which differ in their approach to the ward.

The term vali was, I believe, applied to someone exercising a kind of *manus* over the person and property of the ward. As opposed to this, vasi expressed the idea of guardianship, both of the person and the property, as it is understood in European civil law. Vali rights were exercised by a ruler over his subjects or by a father over his children, and a vali nominated by a father had authority over a woman even if she were married and the owner of a vasi over her own estate. Any further examination of the finer points of Mohammedan law would, I feel, take us too far at this point. Moreover, without the help of my notes and papers I cannot be sure of the accuracy of my terms and definitions.

The assembly of mullas was most imposing. We met three times a day in an atmosphere of collected repose and thought. All these distinguished men, who when they appeared outside were the object of the deepest regard and even veneration, applied themselves with the greatest zeal to their task and never allowed their attention to flag during the debates. We adjourned at the hour of prayer, when the mullas trooped out into the garden, unfolded their prayer carpets and knelt down to pray, utterly indifferent to the inquisitive gaze of European passers-by. The behaviour of these seventy most eminent men in the whole of Turkestan was truly remarkable. Not once did I hear a dissenting opinion expressed aloud, and no younger member dared to contradict or even to interrupt a speech by someone older than himself. Later, perhaps, I might be discreetly drawn aside and given a different opinion. These asides, when they accrued, plainly showed the rift between the two schools of thought, conservative and progressive; but the rigid rules of the Shariat were maintained, and respect to the opinion of one's elders was duly observed.

I was astonished at the peaceful atmosphere of the assembly, and at the diligence with which it pursued its labours. Never had it been my privilege to preside over a gathering so keen to accomplish the task set before it. At the same time, I was alive to the fact that among the assembled mullas were at least ten or twenty Ishans any one of whom had the power to unleash a wave of rebellion over the land by a mere gesture. However, in these particular circumstances they chose to see in me an envoy of the White Padishah, who had expressed concern for their religion and who desired to establish order and justice in his domains. The results of this attitude were translated into pleasant and fruitful collaboration.

Later, in Samarkand, I met some of these mullas again and was conducted by them round their mosques with every sign of friendship. They even bestowed upon me an honour very rarely vouchsafed to an infidel. The covering of the great carpet at the tomb of Tamerlane, which dates back to the days of the conqueror himself, was removed, the carpet was spread out at full length, and I was invited to walk across this priceless treasure without removing my shoes.

There is no need, I feel, to dwell upon the beauty of the mosques in Samarkand, which have been described by so many travellers. They are, in any case, all very much alike. The impression made by the mosques upon the thousands of pilgrims and embassies which streamed to Samarkand from all the corners of Tamerlane's empire in the days before they were ruined by earthquakes and wars was probably only rivalled by the effect produced upon the subjects of the White Tsar by the golden cupolas of Moscow. Today, however, it is not the mosques but the crypt where Tamerlane lies buried which is the centre of attraction in Samarkand. This crypt is situated within the confines of the mosque called *Gur-Emir* ('The Tomb of the Lord'), and is reached by a long flight of steps leading up to the building through a grove of cypress trees. I was ceremoniously met by the mullas at the foot of the steps, and slowly led up to the top, supported under the elbows. Access to the tomb is gained through a small door surrounded by the most beautiful arabesques, then through a dimly lit passage, and finally through another, darker room.

The mausoleum proper is a dome-shaped room, at first glance rather unimpressive both in size and ornateness, in marked contrast to so many of Tamerlane's other works. Closer inspection, however, reveals the costliness of the materials of which it is built. The walls are lined with onyx or some similar stone, and the dome, of Moorish design, is decorated with alabaster stalactites, obviously the work of Spanish and Arabian craftsmen. In the centre lies a solid slab of polished nephrite three metres long, engraved with Arabic lettering. Both the mausoleum and crypt were built, on Tamerlane's orders, during his lifetime; the nephrite block, according to legend, being carried from China by thousands of men. How they succeeded in bringing it through the passes of the Tyan'-Shan' and the desert is hard to imagine. This species of rock is exceptionally hard; it must have taken years to chisel out the lettering. The onyx lining of the walls is of foreign origin and reputed to have come from Tibet.

The floor of the mausoleum is covered by a thick carpet designed in such a way as to leave a space in the middle for the green-veined tombstone. It is unique in that it fits the circular building exactly, and is not four-cornered like other Oriental carpets. It must have taken years to weave, and it is quite impossible to guess how many women laboured over it, or where they came from. The design is strikingly original, following none of the usual oriental patterns— neither the Kaaba lines of Turkmen and Bukharan ornamental rugs nor the floral designs of Persian and Smyrna carpets. This 600-year-old treasure is protected by a linen cover over its entire surface, and it is on this cover that the mullas tread when they go back and forth to their prayers, tourists being allowed to approach the tombstone only after they have put on slippers made of felt. The cover having been removed in my honour I was able to admire the lovely ancient design of arabesques and flowers, woven into a white background. The achievement of an evenly-shaded white background is much prized even at the present time, because only naturally bleached wool is used and this requires perfect matching if a blotchy effect is to be avoided.

A narrow flight of steps leads from the mausoleum to the crypt, where Tamerlane lies buried exactly beneath the nephrite stone. According to tradition some of his friends and contemporaries are also buried in the crypt. The grave of the mighty conqueror, shorn of any splendour of the golden ornaments or precious stones so favoured in the East, is as unpretentious and simple as was his personal life. Yet, centuries later, this very simplicity produced an immense effect.

All the work that this man accomplished, all that he tried to achieve, is in process of decay. His mighty empire exists no longer, his buildings lie in ruins. The limpid waters he brought to Samarkand no longer flow, the arches of his aqueducts lie broken. The irrigation canals he traced in fields and garden are but arid ditches, and the despised kafir reigns in his beloved city. The faith for which he fought, and which was carried to lands where his dreaded name was but a rumour, now faces extinction, because the concepts upon which it was based have proved barren and have brought to the world nothing but misery and ruin. In the end, enforced conversion, hatred of the infidel deliberately fostered in order to create a state of religious awareness, a general massing of humanity under the Creator of the World, and the welding of all true believers into a solid phalanx of fighters against sin and injustice failed. Life made a mockery of these exalted ideals because the chief attributes of godliness—love, compassion and the exercise of free will toward good—were plucked from the human breast.

Nevertheless, we do sometimes glimpse something of the lofty ideals which Tamerlane pursued, and see how he applied them to his personal life. There was the day he halted his armies during a victorious campaign and retreated to Samarkand simply because no man, as he said, should hold too exalted an opinion either of himself or of his aims. His tombstone, by his own order, was cleft in two, to show that nothing created by man is ever perfect. Again, we read that it was his custom on the eve of battle to listen to a recital of a defeat suffered by one of his forebears as a result of self-satisfaction and lack of preparation.

These traits explain the preservation in Central Asia even today of the memory of Tamerlane's ideals, of the great tasks he strove to accomplish and the results he achieved, coupled with memories of his mighty feats of war, his astounding victories and the enormous booties he levied. In this part of the world any evidence of the great and the sublime, be it the remains of a perfect irrigation system, the ruins of some splendid bridge spanning a raging torrent, or something exalting the Mohammedan faith in manuscript or work of art, is invariably associated with the name of Tamerlane.

✣ IV ✣

FERGANA

RICHES and treasure characteristic of the whole of Central Asia are to be found in the lovely valley which lies at the foot of the Pamir and Alai mountains. But there also are to be found many of the economic problems which beset the entire East.

When I visited this region the journey to it was fairly simple. At first we followed the main railway line to Samarkand and Bukhara as far as Chernyayev Station and then branched off to the east, heading straight for a line of mountains. When at last we reached Andizhan we had the impression of facing a gigantic wall of stone, topped by a massive white roof. Its height is so enormous that the summit is invisible if you look straight before you at the horizon; you have to crane your neck to get a view of it. This is the Pamir, 'The Roof of the World'.

These mountains have a contour quite unlike that of the Alps with their easily distinguishable peaks presenting a profile of serrated mountain tops. In the Pamir, and in the Alai range which lies at right angles to it, the mountains are too huge and the distances too great for individual heights to be picked out. The Pamir is 10,000 feet higher than Mont Blanc, and most of its peaks are about the same height. Standing at the foot of this gigantic mountain mass one sees in the foreground a chain of small hills (or so they seem), partly cultivated. Farther back is a second chain, sparsely wooded, its upper slopes covered by emerald green fields and pasture. This particular chain, which stands out very vividly against a darker background of higher mountains, holds most of the many ores buried in the soil of Fergana. Another range, snow-capped in places, can be seen farther back still, and beyond are the eternal snow-covered peaks of the main mass of mountains. Behind the Pamirs and concealed by them lie the Himalayas, and the mind of the traveller is involuntarily drawn to tropical India still farther beyond.

If we turn our backs to the Pamir the Alai range is on our left, joined further north by the Tyan'-Shan' mountains which border on China. One of the spurs of the Alai, which run parallel to the Pamir in a westerly direction, bars the entrance to the Fergana valley. A powerful stream, the Kara-Dar'ya, runs down from the mountains and spills its waters over scree and boulders into the valley between two enormous rocks of porphyry. At this point the stream is barred by a very large but primitively constructed dam and directed into two large canals which were cut several thousands of years ago. By following the line of foothills these two canals enclose the entire valley, and by means of smaller canals they supply the water needed for its irrigation. By now the beds of the two main arteries have been so washed away that if it were not for the dam they might be taken for two rivers, each about forty metres wide.

The province owes its wealth to this complex system of irrigation excavated centuries ago, presumably by Chinese and Aryan labourers. There being no rainfall between the months of March and October, the area would otherwise be nothing but desert. In this region water is treated as something holy. Litigation over land rights, political scheming, advance in culture—in fact the whole of man's work and activities centre upon the question of water supply. The soil is the famous loess produced by dust-fine particles of lime, porphyry and other minerals swept down from the mountains by the wind. Yellowish-grey in colour, and in consistency resembling lime, when damp it can be easily moulded into any shape, thereafter setting as hard as gypsum. Mixed with water, it rapidly dissolves into sludge. For five or six hours after flooding, the fields are quite impassable and as yielding as a bog, yet on the following day the upper crust has solidified to a depth of a few inches into a rubbery layer strong enough to support men and horses without caving in. It is into this layer, before it has had time to set hard, that the seed is quickly sown, an operation usually performed with the aid of the ketmen. During the hours of daylight the temperature is at hothouse level, and germination is very rapid. When the young shoots come up they protect the soil from the rays of the sun and draw the moisture necessary for growth from the sub-soil, where it has been stored as in a reservoir.

Every village has its 'water expert', who arbitrates on all matters dealing with irrigation and against whose decisions there is no appeal. Long before the Russian conquest, these officials (the aksakals) were elected by the *kishlaks* or villages, with but rare interference by

Khan or Emir. The whole matter of irrigation is so desperately important that even the enforced labour which it may sometimes entail is willingly accepted by the local population. Indeed, a break in a dam on any given *aryk* is a calamity comparable to a similar event in Holland, with the difference that the resultant losses are caused not by flooding but by the wholesale draining off of precious water into the bed of the Kara-Dar'ya and consequent drought.

A ration of water to any particular farmer is generally spread over several weeks at given intervals, his neighbours and other villages being supplied in rotation. By the time the water reaches the termini of the canals the supply in the upper stretches is probably practically exhausted, and great care must be taken in distributing it between the secondary and smaller canals. The job of inspection and checking is entrusted to head aksakals under a chief aksakal appointed by the Government.

A village usually possesses an aryk of its own, the width and depth at the point where it joins the main canal having been carefully laid down. The angle of flow, on which the rate and volume of water depend, is also carefully fixed. Permission to divert water into this aryk is given for certain days and at set times, the villagers then allocating it among themselves according to old established custom. They apportion the supply by hours, even quarters of an hour, and sometimes even by minutes. At the appropriate time each villager excavates a small aryk from his field or garden and joins up with the main canal serving the village, these smaller ditches being usually sealed off at one end by a diminutive dam of mud. The fields are perfectly flat and about half an acre in size. They are mostly surrounded on all four sides by small dams less than a foot high. The actual amount of water used to flood a given area over a stated period is designated by various names, the one I have heard most commonly used being *su*—the ordinary word for water. The concept of *su* as a precise volume of water has a definite and generally accepted connotation. Thus land owned by a farmer is not reckoned, taxed or evaluated in hectares, desiatins, or any other surface measure, but solely according to the quantity of *su*. The term is in general use, and the value it implies perfectly clear to every native.

The amount of water supplied by the Kara-Dar'ya depends upon the amount of snow which thaws in the mountains. The warmer and dryer the season the more water there is to distribute, and in the event of an overflow the surplus is returned to the Kara-Dar'ya exactly as in our millraces in Europe. When this has to be done, a section of the dam is broken down by great numbers of men impressed from the villages. As yet, no Russian engineer had mastered the intricacies of these operations and when they became necessary had invariably to rely on the advice and help of local experts from among the natives.

The main dam, the 'Kampyr-Aravat', is situated about two kilometres downstream from the porphyry rocks through which the river gushes into the valley. Here I was shown how its waters were diverted into one of the smaller aryks, by a gang of some fifty men who had ridden in from a distant settlement to irrigate their village. When I arrived in the morning the bed of the aryk was still dry and sealed off from the dam. The men, I noticed, had brought large bundles of twigs and reeds, tied to the flanks of their horses. Laden with these, about twenty men forming a chain resolutely stepped into the ice-cold waters of the Kara-Dar'ya, then threw the bundles down and started treading them in, adding to their own weight with stones passed to them by their comrades on the bank. The chain worked at an acute angle to the current, and soon the main stream was being diverted toward the mouth of the aryk by the growing dam of bundles, the strength of which was being continually increased by sand and gravel lodged between twigs and reeds by the rushing waters. The man at the end of the chain kept on adding to the length of the artificial dam by sinking bundles handed down to him from the bank, the aryk was opened with a blow of the ketmen and the waters gushed into the canal.

As far as I remember, this particular village had been allotted six hours within which to flood and irrigate its fields and was then required to remove the temporary dam. This was quickly done by chopping it away with ketmens, all the material, of course, going to loss.

What I had witnessed illustrated the primitive form of economy existing in Fergana, the so-called 'cotton-land of Russia', where every extra drop of water meant a specific extra quantity of precious fibre. But this was the way things had always been done and, according to the natives, there was no sense in adopting new methods. Besides, had not the aksakals from time immemorial made a living out of controlling these operations, with which they were so well acquainted? There were, of course, any number of foreign contractors who could point to dams they had constructed elsewhere by modern methods. None, however, would agree to work except at the price of large concessions in return for the water they could save, and this was contrary to the principles laid down for Turkestan by the old administration of General Kaufman. Backed by Imperial sanction, he had ruled that 'no foreign capital was to be invested in Turkestan and that any undertaking in the region was to be defrayed by Russian State or Provincial funds'. Nevertheless, at the time of my tour of inspection many applications were being submitted. None of them ever came to anything because of the cut-throat competition among the applicants, all of whom were too intent upon getting all they could out of any proposed scheme for an efficient irrigation system. Thus everything remained as it always had been, and cotton, to the satisfaction of our bureaucrats, 'was nevertheless produced'.

When I visited the region in 1908 and 1909 the value of cotton supplied by Turkestan to the spinning mills in Moscow, previously supplied by imports from the United States, amounted to 300 million roubles. Shortly before the 1914 war cotton production in Central Asia was on the increase, the bulk coming from Fergana. In other regions, like Syr-Dar'ya, it had only just started, while in Samarkand it was hindered by the unresponsive attitude of the natives. On the other hand the Turkmens inhabiting the oases of the Transcaspian region had taken up the cultivation of cotton as early as twenty years before the war and were among the keenest producers. The best fibres came from the Khanate of Khiva owing to the exceptional productivity of its loess soil.

The conditions for cotton-growing in Central Asia to a latitude stretching a little north of Fergana are ideal, and the possibilities limitless. Everything here depends upon an adequate supply of water, for any stretch of desert will produce cotton provided it is irrigated. Two large watercourses flow through the region: the Syr-Dar'ya and the Amu-Dar'ya. In addition there are several smaller rivers in Turkestan, which do not reach the sea but peter out in the sands or dry up in the summer through evaporation, such as the Tedzhen and the Murgab in the Transcaspian region and the Zeravshan in Bukhara and Samarkand. The natives also make use of every lake and every mountain stream which comes tumbling down from the hills, and they collect water in wells during the periods of rainfall to irrigate their valleys. The local systems are of course more primitive than the larger ones, and are usually the work either of individual communities or else smaller manaps and sultans, while the material employed to seal off the valleys is very crude and therefore often washed away or destroyed. Moreover, they are not easily adaptable to any form of systematically organized cultivation, relying as they do on the rainfall whereas the only really reliable sources of water supply are the glaciers. This is one of the reasons why Fergana enjoys a privileged position, the level of the Kara-Dar'ya being less subject to variation in the dry season than that of other rivers.

The system of irrigation I have described, which was introduced in the first place by the Chinese several thousand years ago and then taken over and handed down by the Kalmyks, is admirably suited to the peculiar properties of the pliable, loess soil—the collecting and storing of water in its sub-surface. The advantages gained by the terracing of fields, so common in Italy, have never been appreciated by the natives of Central Asia. Water, after it has been utilized, is allowed to drain off into low lying ground which no one takes the trouble to cultivate, where it forms large areas of swamps. Marshy depressions caused by this waste are found in the vicinity of practically every village. The whole of Fergana, in fact, is surrounded by a belt of swamps, which explains the prevalence of malaria in Central Asia.

In the course of my investigations I examined many plans for terracing the fields, for improved drainage and water conservation, but all would have necessitated a prolonged period for the re-education of the population and the abandonment of old established techniques, while the novel methods introduced by Russian irrigation engineers had so far yielded very meagre results. Unfortunately, there was in Russia no establishment of university level where agricultural science was properly taught. General Kaufman had at one time intended to found a technical college at Tashkent for engineers specializing in irrigation, but had to abandon the idea for lack of funds and because of the difficulty of finding a properly qualified teaching staff. In consequence the majority of the Russian aksakals assigned to the region were either former railway and mining engineers who had learnt the science of irrigation *in situ*, or, at best, men with a technical education at secondary school level. Under these conditions mistakes and failures were unavoidable, like the failure of the grandiose Hungry Steppe irrigation scheme in the Samarkand region. The establishment of a correct profile for a main irrigation canal was, apparently, the best our European engineers could achieve. Direction, fall, and the network of distributory canals in relation to the size of the area to be irrigated were matters they did not worry about. It took them years to master the properties of the local soil. Generally, the canal trenches were either too steep, in which case the beds were washed away and blocked the passages lower down, or else they were too shallow and did not provide for a sufficient flow of water and everything got silted up. The native technicians, for their part, simply started their trenches at the point of junction with the main artery and then proceeded, without levelling instruments or mathematics, cunningly to use a trickle of water in a parallel runnel both as a gauge and guide. These men were all self-taught, the art being transmitted from father to son, and in the main their work was faultless. One could not say as much about the efforts of our European engineers, nor could one be surprised at the lack of faith in their work shown by the local inhabitants.

In the eighteen-eighties the late Emperor Alexander III founded an experimental station on 400,000 acres of Crown land in the Transcaspian region, near Merv. It was originally proposed to restore the ancient dams built by Tamerlane and his successors, and to start a school for practical research into modern methods of irrigation. After twenty-five years of work, much of it experimental, and consequently often unrewarding, an efficient system of main irrigation canals was laid out on the estate. New concrete dams were set up, and the flow of water used to generate hydraulic and electric power. The smaller, intermediary canals were all provided with sluices and corrugated iron lock-gates and were interconnected by telephone. Unfortunately, the actual cultivation of the fields as well as the harvesting was left to native share-croppers, who carried on in the old way, following methods with which they were familar. The system of terraced fields was not introduced and the surplus water after irrigation was still drained off onto low-lying ground, where it formed the customary swamps. Though only partially successful, the project nevertheless did serve a useful purpose by furnishing much needed experience to engineering candidates who wished to obtain local appointments. The success or failure of this lofty scheme had little or no bearing on the methods pursued by the local inhabitants; one could hardly hope for better husbandry from the natives without the incentive of proven results and the adaptation of exemplary systems which they could then have been required to follow. At the time of my visit to Fergana this was but a vain hope, as even in Russia the necessary techniques had not yet been evolved.

However, by the adaptation of American strains, the quality and yields of the cotton harvest had been vastly improved since the days of the conquest. When the Russians arrived upon the scene cotton growing in this part of Asia was already very popular, but the quality of the produce was poor, as seed of Asian origin was the only kind used. When ripe, the seeds were contained in a tightly closed pod, in appearance rather like the unopened bud of a large rose. The petals of the pod were brittle and brown and got mixed up with the cotton during harvesting. The fibres of the indigenous plants were short and hard. The American and Egyptian strains had an open pod, about the size of an orange, the ball of cotton in which the seeds were embedded being easily separated from its supporting petals. In America this is done by very practical machines, called gins. Small circular saws separate the cotton from the seeds and thresh the latter. The whole process consists of feeding the pods of raw cotton into the machine, which throws the cotton out at one end and the seeds, resembling coffee beans coated in white velvet, at the other. Hydraulic presses then press the cotton into bales weighing about 3.5 hundredweights each, and the seed is processed by removing any adhering fibres of cotton. Later it is heated and pressed into oil cakes, the residual oil being collected, filtered and used for human consumption.

The economic value of cotton, as a primary factor in the economy of the newly conquered region, was quickly realized by General Kaufman. When numerous attempts to improve the local strain had failed, American seed was imported and thoroughly tested for suitability to climate and soil, and the best kinds retained. The immediate result was a fourfold increase in yield. The natives were ordered to sow nothing but American strains, while the smallholders were given the seed free and granted loans for the provision of working capital. During the next years production rose sharply, every suitable bit of soil being put under cotton, and because cotton crops brought in better returns the cultivation of grain was allowed to decline. The diminution of acreage under cereals in its turn brought about a growing demand for imported grain from Siberia, which travelled to Central Asia overland until it was replaced by cheap grain from the Volga region after the completion of the Orenburg–Tashkent railway and the progress inland of the Transcaspian line built by Annenkov. From then on American cotton became the staple crop in Central Asia, as well as the universally accepted commodity of barter.

From Russian Turkestan its cultivation spread to Afghanistan, Kashgar, and Persia, where it developed into the best money spinner the agrarian population of those countries had ever known. Indeed, so enthusiastic did the Afghans become that they used up all the available water in the upper reaches of the Amu-Dar'ya and the Murgab, greatly to the annoyance of the inhabitants of Russian Turkestan living downstream, who were now deprived of their customary supply.

One great difficulty, however, beset cotton-cultivation; this was efficient marketing of the harvest, hampered by inadequate railway communications, a shortage of rolling stock, and the absence of solid, properly constructed railway bridges. At the time no quick solution of these problems could be found. The peculiar properties of the loess soil rendered the construction and regular functioning of the railways extremely difficult, while the greatest obstacle of all was, of course, the universal shortage of water. To overcome this difficulty it had become accepted practice to lay the lines parallel to the valleys of the larger rivers at a distance of about eight kilometres from the main channels and to pump the water to the stations up pipelines. But because in this part of the country the rivers frequently change course, a pumping station that had been built close to the bank might, the following year, find itself far removed from its original source of supply. The constant shifting of pumping stations to new sites was expensive and laborious, and the engineers thought they could solve the problem by trying to confine the two biggest rivers, the Amu-Dar'ya and the Syr-Dar'ya, to permanent, artificially-created channels. Resort was also had to artesian wells, but these proved a failure, as the soil of the Central Asian plateau, being mainly composed of dust-fine rock particles, either yielded no water at all, or water so salty that it was unfit for operating the railways. The best results were obtained by reverting to the established system of aryks, which rapidly transformed the stations into small, flowering oases wherever they were used. In spite of all the ingenious methods devised, there still remained long stretches of railway which could only be supplied by the system introduced by General Annenkov, which was to haul trains of water-tanks mounted on railway trucks to the stations.

Reverting to the question of soil—this in summer was as hard as iron; in winter, during the rainy season, it was soft and yielding; whole stretches of railway seemed to run over a kind of morass and were sometimes engulfed by the frequent subsidences. During the rainy season the permanent way was in constant need of repair until the later frosts came to the rescue.

The habit of the rivers of changing their course rendered the correct siting of projected crossings unbelievably difficult, and preference was usually given to places where the banks were reinforced by conglomerates. Also, in those days and under the prevailing local conditions the sinking of bridge pylons was an extremely hazardous and complicated business. For instance, during the preliminary work on the bridge over the Amu-Dar'ya at Chardzhou, a solid bed of rock for the caissons was never reached, the laws of friction as applied to the marly soil having mercifully maintained the pylons in position from that day to the present time. The thirty minute crossing by train of the bridge over the Amu-Dar'ya, one of the longest in the world, affords a good opportunity of appreciating the difficulties which faced the engineers in their attempts to curb nature in Turkestan.

When General Annenkov was building the railway, so vital to the strengthening of Russia's hold on the newly-conquered region, he was driven by a compelling sense of urgency. Thus, when he came to the Amu-Dar'ya, the Great River, he wasted no time in building a permanent bridge. Instead, he built a wooden lattice bridge resting upon wooden caissons, much resembling the temporary bridges built during the war. Hailed at the time as a notable engineering feat, the bridge stood for many years and safely carried the trains which crawled cautiously over its enormous length. Only when it was destroyed by fire was it replaced by a permanent steel bridge. The problem of confining the Amu-Dar'ya to one channel was one which had beset the engineers from the early days of the wooden construction. The waters were constantly breaking through the banks either east or west of the bridge and leaving it standing high and dry. Continuous strengthening of the banks proved unavailing; finally a row of dams in a fourteen-kilometre stretch near Chardzhou solved the difficulty by ensuring the river's even flow.

No sooner had this obstacle been overcome than a new one arose. Previously, nobody had worried about the drifting sands of the desert. Now it was found that they were piling up against the railway and river embankments and threatening to wreck the laborious work of the engineers. An attempt was made to stop the sand drifts by planting trees and bushes along the embankments, but with limited success. More practical results were obtained with a kind of desert herb. When this was sown it quickly produced strong roots which gripped the dry loamy soil and held it fast. Within a few years a firm swarth of green ran parallel to the embankments, in which trees could safely be planted.

Fuel was yet another difficulty. Though the coal fields in Turkestan, and especially those of Fergana, produced coal of good quality, at the time of my visit they had only just commenced operating and the best of the seams were still untouched. As the quality of the coal locally produced was unsuitable, the fuel used by the railways, especially during the early stages, was wood. Extensive use was made of the roots of a shrub called *saksaul*, which grows profusely in the desert and in appearance and height resembles the juniper. Its roots spread over a wide surface and are often as thick as the limbs of an oak, while in calorific value they produce as much heat as good quality coal. In no time at all the desert along the line was stripped of every bush, and further supplies had to be brought on camel back. This of course, was uneconomical, as a camel can carry only about six or seven hundredweights. Wood fuel was superseded by crude oil, easily brought to the Turkestan harbour of Krasnovodsk on the Caspian from the oil fields of Baku. Subsequently, large quantities of oil were found in Fergana, but the output of the wells, promptly acquired by the Oil Trust, was purposely restricted to prevent a fall in world prices.

The rate of railway construction in Turkestan increased as, one by one, the difficulties facing the engineers were overcome. The two main lines, built and completed by the state, were in full operation when I first visited the region. One, begun by General Annenkov in 1879, led from Krasnovodsk on the eastern side of the Caspian, via Ashkhabad, Merv, Chardzhou, Bukhara, and Samarkand to Tashkent and Andizhan. The other, several thousand kilometres long, started from Samara and ran via Orenburg and Perovsk to Tashkent, bridging the Volga, the Ural, the Syr-Dar'ya and several other rivers. On either of them four days could be spent in travelling within the borders of the Turkestan region. Merchandise in large quantities was brought to the railheads, and the amount of freight offered rapidly surpassed the most sanguine estimates. Cotton was, of course, the main item of export to Europe, but there was no lack in other kinds of local produce, including minerals such as uranium and ozokerite. A great trade in fruit soon developed, whole trainloads of it being taken to European Russia where it commenced to displace foreign imports. Shortly before the war the construction of another trunk line was taken in hand. Many thousands of kilometres long, it was to run from Arys via Vernyy and Semipalatinsk till it joined the great Siberian trans-continental railway, thereby on the one hand providing an outlet for the cereals, fruit, furs and minerals which abounded in the northern parts of Turkestan, and on the other supplying the cotton-growing regions with cheap grain.

These railways were really only the first meshes of a vast network which, it was intended, would convey the produce of torrid Central Asia to the markets of the world.

One of the results of the rapid expansion of the cotton market in the last few decades preceding the 1914 war was an increase in wealth of the local population and a concentration of capital, calculated literally in millions, in the hands of the inhabitants. At first, there appeared to be no outlet for all this money, as the mere spending of it on luxuries made little or no appeal to a people accustomed to a patriarchal and modest form of life. There is, after all, not such a great difference between the mode of life of a wealthy Kirgiz or Sart and that of his less fortunate brother. At best he might perhaps own a few more wives. But a larger harem called for no heavy expenditure if one thinks of the long established tradition of a self-sufficing economy. The frequent earthquakes confined both rich and poor to a uniform type of adobe dwelling and precluded the possibility of building luxurious and many-storied buildings. The women's attire did not fall heavily upon the purse of their lord, as their dresses were of home-spun material and cost him next to nothing; while their diet, if I am to believe the stories I was told, was vegetarian. Only on special occasions when there was feasting in the men's quarters were the women favoured with a few morsels of roasted lamb or goat graciously sent to the harem by their lord and master. A stage was eventually reached in the early days of this bonanza when the wealthy Sarts, Turkmen, or Kirgiz literally did not know what to do with the piles of roubles which kept flowing in from the sales of their cotton. One must remember that they were reared in a tradition by which every petty despot was always on the lookout for plunder at the slightest sign of affluence. Accordingly, the safest thing to do with money was to tuck it away where it could not be detected. A Turkmen once told me the story of how he had appealed for help to the District Officer against the mice which were devouring the paper money he had secreted in his garden. When he went to the bank, as advised, and there emptied his sacks and salvaged the valid notes, he found himself the possessor of well over half a million roubles.

However, it was not long before the wealthy natives, particularly the Sarts, ventured into commerce and in no time built up a flourishing trade in local produce. Sarts and Bukharans became a common sight at the great trade fair of Nizhniy-Novgorod on the Volga, where they exchanged their wares against Russian manufactured goods for resale in the markets of West China, Persia, and Afghanistan. Russian china, in particular, cleverly designed to suit the local taste, was highly prized in these countries.

The growing commercial activity among the natives soon attracted the attention of some of the larger banking houses in Russia. Credit on generous terms was offered, local branches opened all over the region and a local bank was founded in Bukhara shortly before the war. Savings accumulated at the banks, and the natives, progressively mounting in financial stature, now turned their attention to mining, industrial undertakings, and the building of narrow-gauge railways. Cotton-cleaning and pressing mills sprang up like mushrooms all over the country, and at the time of my visit to Fergana the majority were owned by native capitalists. It was, however, the narrow-gauge railways which presented the greatest attraction to native capital because of the huge dividends they yielded. The fantastic crops of cotton harvested in the relatively constricted irrigated area of Fergana, where the population is as dense as in Belgium, were crying out for rapid means of removal. Roads and light railways were the answer. Consequently, any money invested in the construction of a narrow-gauge railway was assured a profitable and rapid return. Native capital seized upon this chance, and in the last decades preceding the war a whole network of approach railways spread over the province, all owned by the natives. One of the most important was that put through the district of Namangan. At the time of my visit, and before the line was built, the only link between the district and its market town at Old Margelan on the Tashkent–Andizhan railway was the caravan route over the Amu-Dar'ya, where camels, horses, and carts were laboriously ferried across the river. Another route, 100 kilometres away and over a ford usable only in favourable weather, was unpopular because of the mountainous country through which it led.

Cotton is harvested in October. It takes a month to clean, bale, and pack it. Transportation to the market centres, therefore, never begins before November or December, when the rivers are usually swollen and much time is lost in ferrying the cotton across. The ferries are really flat rafts made of tree trunks lashed together, and the accepted *modus operandi* is as follows: first, the loaded ferry is pushed for about half a kilometre upstream by a collection of men armed with long staves who shove it laboriously against the strong current. It is then allowed to drift down and is steered diagonally across the river by means of a long tiller to a point on the opposite bank, approximately facing the original point of departure. Here it is grounded, and the tricky business of unloading begins. As soon as the ferry approaches the bank all hell seems to break loose: swearing men, anxious to be the first ashore, bucking, stubborn beasts refusing to step into the shallow water, snarling camels snapping at each other—the whole scene is one of unmitigated confusion and noise. I had at one time a snapshot of a caravan of camels waiting to be ferried across the river. Thousands of them were stretched out along the bank, flank to flank, for as far as the eye could see. Beside them, squatting on the ground, were their drovers, resignedly waiting their turn to be ferried over the river, which could not be before a few weeks if the traffic was heavy. Stacked alongside were the bales of precious cotton. The time wasted was incalculable, and nowhere but in the Orient would such conditions be tolerated.

Narrow-gauge railway construction, then, on a large scale, especially in Fergana within the last five pre-war years, was the factor which contributed most to the expansion of cotton-growing in the district as against a noticeable decrease of production between 1905 and 1910. Originally, following General Kaufman's farsighted policy, cotton-growing had been given a powerful fillip by the settlers from European Russia. Banks had been granted special facilities for financing the production of cotton and for erecting cleaning and pressing plants, and under these conditions the necessary funds, liberally voted by the directors, were always available. To increase their turnover the mills themselves offered all sorts of credit facilities to the local producers for the purchase of cotton and corn, the whole bringing about a steady expansion of the area under cotton during the last decades of the nineteenth century. Every available parcel of irrigated land was put under cotton, with a resultant shrinkage in the acreage under cereals. There arose a shortage of corn, and consequently of bread, which in this region had previously been ridiculously cheap. Bread prices rose, and cereals once again came into their own. At about this time, too, the banks ceased to be as interested in cotton as before, having found a lucrative investment for their funds in the mining industry and in the overall technical development of the region. Added to this, at the turn of the century, the soil in the irrigated areas best suited to cotton-growing had become virtually exhausted by haphazard and unsystematic methods of cultivation. Irrigation, although encouraging the productivity of the soil, could not restore the precious elements of which it had been robbed. The crops dwindled, and fell to half their previous yield per hectare. Salvation lay in the supply of fresh loam, but this had to be brought by cart and spread on the fields, a costly operation impeded by the rise in the price of labour, in its turn dependent on increasingly expensive bread.

It must be remembered that cotton production had never developed into a properly regulated industry. Instead, it depended entirely on the cumulative efforts of a multitude of small producers, usually poor and devoid of any capital resources. Any calamity or any failure of their crops, whether due to natural causes or a plague of locusts, at once brought about their ruin or placed them at the mercy of the unscrupulous usurers, both large and small. Henceforward the unfortunate debtor, slaving the year round to keep these sharks at bay, could no longer call his soul his own.

I was anxious to inform myself of the true nature of the debtor-creditor relationship existing between an owner of a typical holding and these money-lenders, and called for a report on the extent of indebtedness of the inhabitants of a specific district. Anyone living in an ordered society would be amazed at the terms of credit established over years, as revealed by the report submitted to me; 60 and even 100 per cent was admitted as a fair rate of interest and one for which the debtor was supposed to be grateful to his creditor. I well remember, for instance, the case of a village in the Namangan district where the debts of the inhabitants registered by the Kadi amounted within one month to 800,000 roubles. To remedy the situation I proposed to establish a chain of banks to be devoted entirely to the granting of petty credit facilities. The scheme was sanctioned and in every way encouraged by the Ministry of Finance in the capital, but never bore fruit because of the outbreak of war in 1914. Notwithstanding the chaotic conditions I have described, the banks were able to take an active and lucrative part in the financial life of the region; I was once told by the manager of the local branch of the Russo-Asian Bank that he had never had occasion to protest a bill of exchange issued by a native, and that as far as the inhabitants were concerned the 12.5 per cent interest charged by his bank was considered by them as a veritable boon. It is, however, to be regretted that much of the credit granted in this way went to large scale usurers who had no scruples about extorting exorbitant rates of interest from the small fry lower down the scale of money-lenders with whom they dealt.

That the Russian Government's rooted policy of excluding foreign capital from participation in capital investments had a crippling effect on Turkestan's economic development cannot be denied. An effort was made to induce the natives to place their accumulated, and by now considerable, savings in the local Savings and sundry smaller banks. Two years before the war, a magnificently laid out bank had been founded in Bukhara for the purpose of financing large irrigation projects connected with cotton-growing and with the development of vast landed estates.

As we have seen, the possibilities open to the cotton-grower owing to the peculiar properties of the soil in this region are practically unlimited. Throughout a vast area of Turkestan, hilly ground apart, every single hectare produces a bumper crop provided there is sufficient water. As with the Nile in Egypt, the two main rivers, the Amu-Dar'ya and Syr-Dar'ya, might have been utilized to enrich the soil had there been a proper system of irrigation. The whole thing was a question of money, and shortly before 1914 a great deal of capital was being invested in irrigation works. This occurred a few years after my tour of inspection. Whilst I was in Turkestan private capital still shrank from this form of investment, mostly from a feeling of insecurity since there was no established government policy for regulating the supply of water, a factor which might otherwise have encouraged and even guaranteed private investment in an enterprise of this kind. What capital was being invested went into the mining industry, which was both more lucrative and easier to develop. That the valley of Fergana and its surrounding mountains did indeed offer an attractive field to the enterprising investor I was able to see for myself when I visited the main mining centres of the province.

This was in June 1909, just after the three weeks I had spent in Tashkent presiding over the gathering of mullas with whom I had been examining the Shariat and the Holy Sunna of Mohammed with the object of translating the Arabic text into legally precise Russian. The recollection of those ascetic, long-bearded leaders of Mohammedan thought is still very vivid in my mind, though I must admit that for a European it was no easy task to sit day in day out in a temperature ranging round 100° and keep one's mind fixed on a spate of legal intricacies. What a relief it was, after the work had been completed and the resultant material checked and rechecked, to be seated once again in my saloon car and to watch, as we rolled to the hills, the flourishing gardens and cotton fields gliding by, an eloquent testimony to the unquellable forces of nature and to the toil of an industrious population.

On this occasion our destination was Andizhan, the terminus of the railway which ran via Kokand and Margelan. As we drew nearer to the hills the air became lighter and it was easier to breathe. And at night, with our windows down, it was as cool as in Europe. Pleasant as this was, there were certain drawbacks to our enjoyment. The malarial mosquito, for one thing, is particularly vicious at night in Fergana, as I was shortly to find out.

We were halted for the night at the main station in Margelan. It was blissfully cool and I was fast asleep when I was aroused by a terrific commotion in one of the neighbouring compartments. A few minutes later my secretary rushed in saying that his room-mate, a State Counsellor of the St. Petersburg Supreme Court attached to my suite by the Ministry of Justice, had suddenly gone mad, was raving and had tried to strangle him. I turned out, and after a lengthy search was able to find a local doctor who at once diagnosed the case as one of cerebral malaria. He practically had to fight the patient before he succeeded in giving him an injection of quinine the size of which would have made a European doctor's hair stand on end. In the morning the Counsellor was quite well and we made haste to continue our journey. I later found out that he had served as a young barrister in Margelan about fourteen years before, and had suffered at the time from this form of malaria. The doctors could do nothing for him and he had sought refuge in European Russia. Though in the intervening years he had suffered only occasional bouts of fever, the

three days he spent in Margelan before my arrival had been enough
to bring about a recurrence of the disease.

We reached Andizhan in the evening, and after a brief tour of
sightseeing on the following morning proceeded on our journey to
Osh, our party comfortably distributed in ten troikas. The Governor,
with whom I rode, was a real 'Turkestanian', a man risen from the
ranks to his present position on merit alone and who had spent his
life in the region. A fluent linguist, he read and spoke Sart, Kirgiz,
Tadzhik, and Turkmen and could even write in these languages.

The road, as it gradually ascends from Andizhan to Osh, leads
through some of the most fertile parts of Fergana. Seventy kilometres long, and bordered on each side by four rows of plane trees
providing a most welcome shade, the highway is a modern engineering feat originally started by General Skobelev at the time of the
conquest. In those days human life and toil were not worth much in
Asia, and Skobelev adopted the accepted method of impressed labour
regardless of the human toll exacted. As we bowled along in our
troika mounted on rubber-tyred wheels I was told by the Governor
that this wonderful highway, eighty yards across with a metalled
strip of black porphyry in the centre sixty feet wide and laid three
feet deep, had not been repaired for the past seventeen years. The
surface was splendid despite the fact that the road was the main
artery for the exchange of goods between Western China and Europe
and an endless stream of caravans and Chinese arabas flowed along
it on their way from Kashgar.

We were escorted by a convoy of superbly mounted local notables
and white-bearded chieftains, decked out in the most gorgeous satin
kaftans embroidered in gold, with snow-white turbans and the most
handsome ceremonial swords and daggers, sheathed in gold and
silver scabbards. Their saddles, bridles, and stirrups were also
heavily inlaid with gold and silver. The horses, thoroughbred Arabs
with beautiful heads and intelligent-looking eyes, were decked out in
saddle cloths made of brightly coloured material and, although
slightly overladen by all this finery, presented a gallant and striking
sight. When we halted and our escort dismounted, green, blue or red
blankets were thrown over the horses to protect them from the
noonday heat.

A horseman bearing a green silken banner preceded our cortège.
All along the road from Andizhan I had the impression of driving
through one long settlement, so near were the villages one to another.

The individual houses, Asian flat-roofed structures of plaster, were surrounded each by its own orchard of fruit-laden trees, apricots, peaches, pears and apples. The tinkling sound of water running down the irrigation canals accompanied us on our way, while to the right and left of us, fields of maize, corn and sorghum, standing proudly erect, alternated with the bright green of rice and the deeper hues of the cup-shaped and purple-rimmed blossoms of cotton in bloom. On the emerald green mountain meadows great herds were grazing; high above them and through the clouds sparkled the glaciers of the Tyan'-Shan' range, while the majestic Pamir stretched its immense roof right overhead. I would willingly change places with my readers if they might thus enjoy the full beauty of the scene, the golden rays of the sun and the deep blue of the cloudless sky, for no words are adequate to describe the radiance of the landscape that lay before my eyes.

The highway follows a gentle gradient rising imperceptibly along a valley which gets narrower and narrower the higher one mounts. A few miles from Osh it meets an icy-cold mountain stream which comes tumbling down over enormous rocks of green tinted porphyry.

Osh is a small district centre lying on both sides of a valley running through the mountains. It is renowned throughout Turkestan for its genial climate and complete freedom from the malarial mosquito, and is a local spa to which hundreds of Europeans come every year to recoup from their own trying climate and to enjoy the wonderful mountain scenery. It is also famed for its kumys and is visited by many sufferers with lung and chest troubles.

The officers' mess of the battalion garrisoned in Osh is located in a grove of oak trees and is built like a Swiss chalet with large verandas from which there is a splendid view of the whole valley and the surrounding mountains. But for the flat-roofed houses one might easily think one was in some picturesque mountainous region of central Germany or Switzerland, and not in distant Fergana. The impression was heightened as we sat by moonlight on the veranda with dark green woods of oak and plane trees on either side and at our feet the silvery streak of the river, making its precipitous journey down to the valley.

On the road again next day we no longer kept to the highway but drove straight across country, following the slopes of the mountains at first through clearings in the oak woods and later, as we ascended higher and higher, over mountain pastures, our ponies keeping up a steady trot over the springy ground. Osh was soon far behind us, deep down in the valley, and no sooner had we clambered over one ridge than we were confronted by another just ahead, as if waiting to be vaulted. It was like an endless game of slithering down slopes, seeking a way through some narrow defile and climbing again. When at last we left the tree line behind us the snow-capped mountains seemed much nearer, their summits having gained in height and now towering above us.

After more climbing we reached a long, narrow valley with walnut trees growing thickly on both sides. The trees were small, bushy, and resembled hazels. These were the famous state walnut forests, where the Mennonites I have mentioned were employed as foresters. A sponge-like growth on the trunks was, it appeared, a source of considerable revenue to the State, being much prized by wood turners abroad, especially in France. After being carefully removed by contractors it was packed and exported in whole trainloads.

A picturesque spot on the side of a mountain overlooking a vast expanse of country was chosen as the site for our camp at nightfall. We had a hearty meal splendidly prepared by our cook over a cheery fire at the foot of a nearby mound and then relaxed in the luxurious yurts put up for us on the flat expanse of ground, enjoying the cool of evening and the wonderful scenery. Far beneath us we could see the fertile valley dotted with villages and minarets, the fields framed by mulberries and poplars. Farther up, the long valley stretched into the mountains, narrowing in the distance into a deep gorge. Above us the glaciers glowed in the sunset. Far away on the horizon a small black cloud rested on the summit of one of the peaks.

We had unexpected visitors at our meal, among them a Ukrainian, one of the earliest pioneers in Turkestan, who had come to the country in search of gold. Though unsuccessful in this quest he had found many other deposits of valuable minerals which, however, he had not taken the trouble to exploit, but had sold off as soon as he could in order to resume his search for the elusive precious metal. Another of our visitors was an Armenian businessman, keen and conceited, who had just begun to work a coal mine for which he predicted a glowing future. The third, tall and handsome, was a gentleman by the name of Kennedy, who introduced himself as the owner of a coal mine about half a day's journey from the camp. The Governor told us that this Englishman had turned up in the region about three years before, claiming to represent a powerful and influential financial group in Moscow. He was a plausible fellow, though in his puttees and well-cut sports clothes he looked much more like an officer than a rough mining engineer. According to the Governor he knew everybody in the administration in Margelan and was a welcome guest at every party. Later in the evening, when we were discussing future plans, he surprised me by his intimate knowledge of every pass and byway in the vicinity.

After sitting up for some time we retired to our yurts, and the camp was soon deep in peaceful slumber.

I was jolted out of my sleep by a terrific thunder clap and a roaring wind; looking around hastily I saw the walls of my yurt were swaying and bulging in a most dangerous manner. I rushed out clad only in my night attire and found twenty men desperately hanging on to the guy ropes of my tent, which looked like being blown away at any moment by a wind of hurricane force. Not a moment was lost in emptying my tent of its belongings; camp bed, saddle, and the rest were hurriedly carried out, while I made my way in my slippers to another yurt farther down where room was made for me for the rest of the night. All hope of saving my former shelter was given up, and it was allowed to blow away into the night. It was the small black cloud I had noticed earlier on which had wrought all this havoc and unleashed over our camp a storm more severe than anything I had ever experienced in Europe. Mercifully, the remaining yurts were better sheltered than mine, and protected by a shoulder of the mountain we were able to snatch a few hours' sleep. These sudden storms are apparently quite usual in the region.

Early next morning we set out to visit several mines I wanted to see, in particular the one owned by Kennedy, which lay close to the Armenian's pits and not too far out of our way. Three hours' driving over rough country brought us to the mines. Evidence of civilization appeared as we drove through the approaches: miners' houses, canteens, and even a hospital. The mine manager treated us to a sumptuous meal, after which we went down one of the shafts. The field we visited was fairly shallow, as far as I remember, lying some 400 feet underground. The coal extracted was pitch black and looked much like the lighter kinds of Polish coal. It was unsuited to the making of coke but enjoyed a good demand as house fuel and for use in samovars, where it burnt as well as charcoal. A narrow-gauge railway led to the valley, the company intending to link up with the main line later on. The coal was brought down on flat trolleys, each accompanied downhill by two horses which pulled the empty trolleys back to the coal pits. There was also another field, 100 feet deeper, where the coal was of better quality, but work here had only just commenced.

Later in the day I was taken to another mine. The installation was primitive, though it was evident that exploitation had originally been planned on a fairly vast scale. An overhead cable railway stopped two kilometres short of the station where the coal was to be unloaded, the construction having been halted through shortage of funds. It was an incongruous sight—the solitary pylons sticking up to no purpose in the desert-like country, and the trolleys, forlornly suspended from the cables, seeming sleepily to watch the flocks of sheep and goats that grazed in the valley below, tended by their shaggy Kirgiz herdsmen.

We were delayed in a mountain village by a deputation of local inhabitants mustered to extend their greetings, and night was approaching when we sighted the buildings of Kennedy's mine, which I was resolved to visit. Earlier on I had been subjected to a concerted attack by Kennedy and the local District Officer, who at all cost wanted me to abandon my original plan. All sorts of excuses were advanced, such as the great distance (a paltry ten kilometres), the lateness of the hour, the hazards and dangers of the road in the dark, the desirability of inspecting something more interesting, etc., etc. However, I was adamant in my decision and told them to move on. Now Kennedy came at me again, making excuses for his mine and saying that in fact he really had no mine in the accepted sense of the word, that he had only sunk a few bore holes and that there was really nothing to show; he was sorry, but there had been some hitch about the transfer of money by his company; he would have it by the autumn, straight from London. The Governor wryly remarked that Mr. Kennedy had been expecting a transfer from London for the past three years, yet apparently the only thing he did was travel round the country and prospect. Here I gave up, for by now the true nature of his activities was perfectly clear. Not in the least abashed he accompanied me for another few days, was a most charming travelling companion, an expert at roasting spitted mutton over a coal fire, and had a better knowledge of the mountain trails than any of the local guides. He made no secret about his wanderings through most of the Altay passes, the Pamir, and Afghanistan. He spoke Russian and Kirgiz fluently. As the agent of an allegedly Russian company he had apparently obtained permission from St. Petersburg to prospect for minerals in this region, though in my opinion there was very little doubt as to his identity: quite obviously, he was a British Intelligence Officer.

On the morrow we had a most interesting day. We started off by driving deep into the mountains till we came to a high-lying meadow, traversed by a rapidly flowing stream. We pitched camp on one of its banks, close to a house built like a Swiss châlet and belonging to the Ukrainian gold-prospector who had visited us two days before. A couple of years earlier, when he had come on a new kind of ore in the neighbourhood, he had rented the meadow from the Kirgiz owner and started building a house for his family. He had named the place 'Olgin Lug' (Olga's Meadow) after his wife, and proudly explained that it was the highest Russian settlement in the world. By sunrise on the following morning he had us mounted on brisk mountain ponies and riding up precipitous paths through wild and fascinating country. It required a strong head to keep to what looked like mere goat tracks winding along the ledges of rugged precipices. Every now and again a halt was called to allow our ponies to get their breath, the stops becoming more frequent as our long string of riders mounted higher and higher, the horses having a hard time in the rarefied atmosphere.

After several hours we reached our goal, a small plateau containing the entrance to a cave. The entrance had been enlarged, and the way led down a long tunnel, fairly even at first and terminating at a row of steps hewn out of the rock and going steeply down. By the dim light of wax candles held by our guides we negotiated the steps with some difficulty, as each was well over a metre in depth. We descended for some time and came to another passage, narrower than the first, which brought us into a second cave, with a dome-like ceiling. The ground at our feet was perfectly dry, without a trace of moisture. In the light of the candles the walls all around the cave glittered with a bright, multi-coloured metallic sheen which reminded me of the fairy stories of my childhood.

Here I heard the most extraordinary story from the prospector, in answer to my questions about the origin of his find. This is what he said: 'In the course of my travels on horseback all over the country I was once told by a wandering group of Kirgiz of certain caves in which the spirits were supposed to have hidden quantities of gold, and was eventually brought by them to this place. At the time

I had befriended a French mining engineer, then down on his luck mainly through drink, who sometimes helped me in my work. He and I crawled through the mouth of the cave, which was then much narrower than it is now, clambered down the steps and came to this chamber. We at once realized that the place had been worked at an earlier stage, but had no inkling as to the kind of ore it contained. You see those red and blue veins running down the walls, and also the yellow streaks? Well, we took samples of the yellow rock and hoped it contained the gold we were searching for. Further exploration led us to the beginnings of a shaft, blocked by a subsequent fall of rock. After we had cleared this away we found a curious-looking pick, apparently made of iron, and perfectly preserved in this airtight chamber though the handle had long since crumbled into dust. We fitted a haft from one of our own picks to our find, and used it to break up the ore we wanted to take away. To our amazement the metal was like the best quality steel. We removed the pick and the samples and the Frenchman analysed them in his diminutive laboratory in town. It turned out that the ore was uranium, and that the pick was made of an alloy of uranium and iron. We concluded that some earlier inhabitants, most probably the Chinese, had used uranium from this mine to reinforce their steel and had then abandoned the works because of some political upheaval.'

Outside, he showed me another shaft, about two metres deep, from which the metal had been mined and also abandoned, probably at the time when the Chinese were driven out by the nomads, approximately 2,000 years B.C.

The wretched prospector had sold the proprietary rights in the mine for 20,000 roubles to a limited liability company which in the first year of its existence had made a clear (net) profit of 200,000 roubles from it, although at that height the mine could only be worked for three months in the year.

The ore was brought in tin containers to Andizhan and from there was shipped to St. Petersburg, where the uranium was separated from the other components.

As we were taking our leave the next day the prospector turned to me and said: 'It doesn't look to me as if I'll ever find any gold. I've been after it for more than thirty years now. But never mind, I have sons, both born in this land. I've sent them to the mining academy and they'll find it, all right. I just haven't the technical knowledge. After all, I ran away from home when I'd only done four grades at school. The Lord knows, I've found rich deposits of iron, copper, sulphur, rock salt, quicksilver, and heaps of other metals all over the place. But gold, no! Only a little, in the rivers. D'you know, the earth here is so full of treasures that any enterprising man could easily make his fortune. For my part, I'll stick to gold; and meanwhile, my family and I will manage somehow.'

Here I should like to explain the provisions of Russian legislation as it affected the prospector. Following a law laid down by Peter the Great and still in force, the finder of any mineral deposits, wherever they might be, was entitled to claim ownership providing the claim was clearly staked out, at once reported to the nearest office of a Crown Lands administrator, and that no previous claim had been lodged by someone else. The location was then entered on a special map and the claim to a clear title checked. This procedure established the finder's title to ownership and left him free, if he so wished, to sell or cede his rights to a third party under the obligatory condition that exploitation of the deposits would commence within two years, failing which the proprietary rights reverted to the Crown. This stipulation could, of course, only be complied with if the finder obtained the consent of the owner of the land on which the deposits were located to proceed with the work. Because of these antiquated provisions, and the difficulties and misunderstandings they entailed, our friend never retained his finds but sold his rights to eager capital investors for amounts far below their real market value.

Though I wasted a whole day in visiting the uranium mine the impression left by the excursion there was quite unforgettable. Never have I seen such wonderful mountain scenery, not even in Switzerland.

The descent from these heights was not negotiated without some risk. (We were right up against the glaciers, in a region covered in thick snow by August, when all work is brought to a standstill.) We followed a trail which in places ran along the very brink of a deep precipice, where one false step would have meant certain death and where we had to lie practically flat on the backs of our ponies for what seemed hours on end pressing for all we were worth against the stirrup irons. Our party of forty, which included a few ladies and looked from a distance like some huge snake, laboriously wound its way over ridge after ridge and reached camp late in the evening, dog tired and very ready to enjoy a wonderful meal of mountain partridge we had bagged on the way. This, together with the local wine,

9

fiery and heavy, and some enormous peaches, soon dispelled all traces of fatigue and helped to waft us into other, less prosaic worlds.

When all was quiet I slipped out of my tent unnoticed. It was a heavenly night. The mild mountain breeze was spiced with the smell of the honey-laden meadows which stretched out before me as I followed the silvery line of the stream on its tempestuous course from boulder to boulder to the valley below. When I reached a spot where the stream thundered into the valley between two huge rocks I stopped, arrested by the beauty of the scene. The gap between the black porphyry rocks, tall as a cathedral spire, looked quite narrow and one felt that by stretching out one's arms it would be possible to touch both sides at once. Next day I found that this was only a trick of my imagination, for the rocks were well over one hundred feet apart. But at night the slit between them looked like the narrow entrance into another world. To add enchantment to the scene the moon suddenly appeared from behind some clouds, turning the rocks into two sentinels guarding the portals of a distant fairyland. The silvery rays of the moon gliding over the gushing waters, the long reach of the Alpine meadows, clad now in sombre green, our camp fires in the distance above me and the lofty peaks clad in their eternal vestments of white, banished the cares and worries of everyday life into a soothing remoteness as I stood in this dreamland of beauty, this realm of the Spirit of the Mountain and his buried treasure.

When I returned I found the camp in a state of uproar. My absence had been duly discovered by the guardians of the law, who just could not understand how and whither I had so mysteriously vanished.

At daybreak on the following morning we were once again seated in our troikas rolling over meadows along the course of the stream and heading, somewhat to my surprise, straight for the gap between the two guardian cliffs. How we were supposed to get through was something I did not even pretend to solve. But, nothing daunted, we plunged into the river, bouncing and careering over boulders and stones, the water reaching up to our horses' bellies and splashing over the floors of our coaches. After driving like this through the narrow and dark defile with only a strip of sky visible far above us for over a kilometre we emerged into another valley, where we faced another climb. Our escort dismounted, harnessed their horses to our victorias with horsehair traces, remounted, and charged the mountain at a gallop, each carriage drawn by sixteen panting and sweating animals. This unusual operation was followed by a gruelling and jolting descent negotiated without any brakes, the middle horse of the troika alone bearing the full weight of the carriage.

Five or six hours later we reached the plain, or rather a plateau. The landscape had changed and was more like a desert, with only an occasional tamarisk shrub here and there, and the colour of the soil was gradually changing from a yellowish grey to a dirty blue. Once, when I got out of my carriage I noticed fragments of sea shells, shaped like snails, in the marl under my feet and all along the route there were large oily patches on the surface. The whole region was dotted over with marked and numbered poles.

We had reached the region of the Chimion oil wells. In the far distance we could see the outline of the drilling rigs, and smoke pouring out of tall stacks.

The first man to find oil in Fergana was a railroad engineer called Kovalevskiy, who was employed in the construction of the Tashkent–Andizhan line. In partnership with a colleague, Maksimov, he tried to exploit his discovery but failed through shortage of funds. The two men hoped to raise the money by inviting the co-operation of the cotton kings in nearby Kokand but discovered that the latter were in no way interested in mining and that they thought the whole scheme was nothing but a colossal swindle. Eventually, however, Kovalevskiy and Maksimov somehow contrived to form a limited liability company with a paid-up capital of 300,000 roubles and started working the Chimion wells in earnest. For themselves they reserved 8,000,000 roubles' worth of shares without paying a penny for them, and distributed gratis another 200,000 roubles' worth among the authorities and stock exchange brokers, so ensuring a friendly and sympathetic attitude toward their undertaking.

They were lucky. At the second drilling they struck oil. The entire region was at once overrun by a crowd of adventurers and every patch of oil on the surface was immediately pegged out and the claim registered. But Kovalevskiy and Maksimov were still well in the lead. From the large revenues flowing in from their wells they built a pipe-line sixteen kilometres long to the nearest railway station and there erected a refinery to extract petrol and paraffin (kerosene). There followed a contract between the Chimion Co. Ltd., and the administration of the Central Asian Railways for the delivery of fuel oil at twenty-five kopecks per pood (40 lbs.) of oil, guaranteed, like all similar contracts with the State, by a clause imposing heavy forfeits for non-fulfilment. The price of twenty-five kopecks per pood was a boon to the railways, which previously were paying the Nobel Company fifty-four kopecks for fuel hauled all the way from Baku.

It would appear that in signing this contract Kovalevskiy and Maksimov, like true railway men, had the interests of the railways more at heart than those of their own shareholders. Nevertheless the company rose in status, and now figured as a competitor of the large oil companies in Baku. The oil produced in Fergana and Baku differs in quality. There is a greater content of kerosene in the Fergana oil, which in consequence is less fluid, and heavier.

Of the oil-producing regions of the province, I have already mentioned the one at Chimion. A second, in the district of Namangan, was brought into production at the instance of the former Minister of Communications, Khilkov, in opposition to the wishes of the oil companies in Baku—Nobel, Mazut, Rothschild and Lianozov. These companies, which supplied the Russian and, in part, the European markets, claimed that the Fergana oilfields were economically unprofitable. While taking out large concessions in the province they were careful to limit annual production to a paltry few poods per individual well, just sufficient to safeguard their concessionary rights. (It will be remembered that according to Russian law, if a registered claim remained undeveloped within a period of two years, ownership of it reverted to the Crown.)

Another oil-bearing region of considerable extent is located in the Caspian District of the Transcaspian Province, extending from the mainland on to Cheleken Island, where it is particularly rich.

At Chimion we were received by the management with the customary pomp, treated to the usual sumptuous repast, the inevitable caviare, champagne, and official speeches, and then taken to inspect the installations. At the time, things were not going well with the company; the main well was out of production and the yields from the secondary wells were poor. During a recent strike a charge of dynamite had been exploded in the main well, destroying the lining and blocking the flow so that the drop in production had nothing to do with natural causes but was solely the result of sabotage. According to information conveyed to me by means of anonymous letters and other sources, I was meant to think that the action was the

work of competing firms. However, I inclined to the opinion that
dissatisfaction was endemic, its roots lying in the far too rapid
development of most of the undertakings which were springing
up like mushrooms all over the province.

But to revert to the Chimion Company. The labour force it had
recruited under pressure of production was composed of ne'er-do-
wells sacked successively by every major and reputable industry
round the globe. In the circumstances there was no chance of
building a solid, responsible core of steady and trained workers, nor
had it been possible in the short time available to make the necessary
provisions for the men's welfare. They were housed in long, wooden
sheds with two rows of bunks along the walls. I must admit that the
sight of the human bodies I saw stretched out on the rough bedding
was anything but reassuring. Russians, Caucasians of every tribe,
Persians, Afghans, Chinese, Italians, Greeks, and Turks—in fact a
motley collection of every race under the sun. With low pay and a
twelve-hour working day of two shifts, the human material at hand
was quite obviously ideal for any form of propaganda. As soon as the
company began to prosper the workers went on strike, accompanying
their demands for better conditions with acts of violence. I am
confident that the fellow who tossed the stick of dynamite into the
well never for a moment thought that he was killing the goose which
laid the egg, even if it were not the proverbial golden one, nor that
he was sounding the company's death knell.

The strike was, of course, suppressed, the more restless elements
thrown out, the improved labour conditions demanded by the
authorities hastily promised, and a higher scale of wages introduced,
But the soap bubble had burst. The oil obstinately refused to flow,
and protracted new drillings overtaxed the company's slender
financial resources. The contracted monthly deliveries to the railway
could no longer be supplied; the railway administration invoked the
heavy fines stipulated, and debited the company with fifty-four
kopecks per pood for the oil it was forced to purchase from Baku.
The price of the company's shares came tumbling down and it was
forced into bankruptcy.

As soon as this happened, one of the large Baku oil companies
struck like a shark. It bought up a small number of Chimion shares
for a few roubles, got in touch with our friends the engineeers
Kovalevskiy and Maksimov, acquired their holdings (originally
obtained gratis) for 400,000 roubles, voted a new board of directors

at the next general meeting, and turned Chimion into a subsidiary branch of the parent company in Baku. The old, old story was then repeated. Naturally the company saw no reason for flooding the Asian market with cheap Fergana oil at twenty-five kopecks per pood when it could sell its own oil from Baku at fifty-four kopecks. This it did. The output from Chimion was limited to a nominal 100 poods per annum, the Central Asian market was secured for Baku and the wells in Fergana allowed to stagnate.

All this happened after my departure. At the time of my visit to Chimion things had not yet reached this stage. The old management was still at the helm and was resorting to all sorts of expedients to retrieve the situation. Messrs. Kovalevskiy and Maksimov were not in evidence, and it seemed that they took little interest in the company's affairs. The firm's business was being run by an extremely able and efficient technical manager, who conducted us round the installation and drillings. After the strike he had sunk several experimental wells but all his efforts were dogged by bad luck. He explained a new method he had adopted in order to hasten the work, but water which seeped into the stratum of oil-bearing shale greatly reduced the content which he brought to the surface. He had also tried to restore the main well by chiselling out the shattered lining and replacing it by a new one, but in this, too, he was unsuccessful, as I was later informed. Shortly after our departure the majority of the labourers were dismissed.

Our next visit was to the up-to-date refinery, joined to the wells by pipeline at the nearest railway station about ten kilometres away. The manager who took us round had tears in his eyes when he spoke of the shortage of supplies and the threatened closedown of the Chimion plant. He was desperately keen on his job and insisted that the petroleum he was refining was the best in the world. At the time we were standing by two tanks. Pointing to one of them, he said: 'The petrol in this tank is of the highest grade by European standards, yet I issue it to lorries. But this', he continued, indicating the second tank, 'really is something you will find nowhere else in the world.' Whereupon he pulled out my handkerchief, and, opening a cock before I could stop him, swamped it with petrol and shoved it under my nose. 'There,' he exclaimed, 'doesn't it smell like violets? I keep it exclusively for use by chemists.' While I was making the expected laudatory remarks I could not help wondering what on earth I was supposed to do with a handkerchief saturated in petrol. But all was well. The stuff was as clear as water and the smell evaporated very quickly.

We left Chimion in the evening of the same day and once again set out for the mountains, this time in order to visit some caves of rock salt mined for export. The plant was of fairly recent date, but on the way we were able to observe a whole encampment of Kirgiz engaged in winning cooking salt from a stream by a very ancient and primitive method. We were travelling through some pretty desolate country with hardly any grass and only scanty signs of vegetation. On our way up, our straining horses drawing us over rough boulders and stones, we caught sight of a great throng of people encamped by a stream and surrounded by their herds of horses and goats. A tall column of smoke rose from the midst of the site and it was some time before we realized what all these people were doing. About 500 or 1,000 Kirgiz were gathered together on a slope on the banks of a stream that wound a tortuous way downhill. I was given some of the water to taste, and one sip was enough to show how very salty it was. Several hundred small clay cooking stoves had been set up along the course of the stream. On these, flat copper cauldrons about two and a half feet in diameter and four inches deep, filled with water from the stream, were boiling, tended by the women of the tribe, both old and young. Pails filled with water were set beside each woman, who was responsible for three stoves and whose business it was to ladle water into the cauldrons, where it evaporated leaving a deposit of clear white salt at the bottom. Saturation point between the cauldrons was reached in stages, and was so timed that the liquid in one of the containers was usually the consistency of a thick brew. While the women were engaged day and night in raking the fires, their men folk kept them supplied with fuel. This was brought down from great distances in the mountains by strings of pack horses and yaks led by a rider on horseback whose own mount was also laden. Young women and children a little farther away were busy breaking up the salt, which was then packed into sacks and dispatched for sale to the towns and bazaars. The Governor told me that the administration of the State forests had repeatedly complained to him about the wastage of timber involved, yet the livelihood of so many families depended on the trade in salt that he could not bring himself to put an end to the practice. Besides, he thought the archaic procedure followed by the nomads was bound to die out in competition with the modern methods being introduced.

During the next few days I visited several other mining plants, the majority of them small undertakings, usually undercapitalized and primitively equipped technically. I was also shown a number of derelict mines that had been destroyed either by flooding or fire, particularly the coal mines. The cause, generally, was either inefficiency or carelessness, for there was at that time no proper technical inspection of mines in Russian Asia. With some of the engineers overseeing districts as large as Germany, slapdash methods were the rule. In most of the workings good profits were earned in the early stages, as the ore usually lay near to the surface; but as soon as difficulties were encountered the enterprise failed and was simply abandoned and allowed to fall into a state of decay.

The size and potential wealth of the coal fields in this region are quite fantastic, and coal of every kind is to hand from brown and light to anthracite and the heavy varieties suitable for making coke. As I saw it the main obstacles in the way of developing all this wealth were the lack of adequate communications, the ban on foreign capital investments imposed by the Government, and the low cultural level of the native population.

During this tour, undertaken with the purpose of gaining an insight, however superficial, into the mining potential of the region, I visited the beautiful city of Kokand, the former capital of independent Khans. One of its brightly painted minarets, which still stands erect pointing to Heaven, is renowned in history through the cruelty of Kokand's most fabulous tyrant, Khudayar, who had his victims hurled down from its summit. According to legend one of his wives was murdered like this in his presence, and he sat gloating over her agonized cries as she writhed for three days suspended from a cornice that is still exhibited.

The cruel Khan's palace, still well preserved, has lofty halls, and walls adorned with superb carpeted mosaic. The throne room, converted by the Russian conquerors into a Greek Orthodox Church, still retains the original quotations from the Koran, set out in gaudy mosaic Arabic lettering.

Like all other cities in Turkestan, Kokand is divided into native and European quarters. The native part of the town is dirty, full of narrow streets, mosques, and windowless houses. The European sector is most imposing, with wide, straight streets lined with rows of trees planted four deep, and many-storied houses. The life of the town is dominated by the cotton kings thanks to whom the European quarter was built with the rapidity of an American mining city. I was greatly impressed by the District Officer in Kokand, who read and wrote fluently in several local languages while his wife was an authority on Mohammedan customs and well acquainted with many of the native women in the harems.

We stayed in Kokand for one night only and set out on the following afternoon to inspect a copper mine, this entailing an easy journey of five hours in my saloon railway coach to be followed by a drive of fourteen kilometres overland. We alighted from the train towards dusk and after the usual dastarkhan and reception by local deputations drove off seated comfortably in landaus with rubber-rimmed wheels, escorted by jigits and Sart notables decked out in picturesque oriental finery and mounted on superb Karabairs.

For the first seven kilometres the road ran through well-kept cotton fields and painstakingly irrigated gardens, but as soon as we reached the boundary of the irrigated area the country took on a desolate aspect. (In Central Asia one soon becomes accustomed to these rapid transitions of scenery.) Meanwhile, night had fallen, and by casting a reddish glow over the landscape the rising moon strangely transformed the scenery around us. We were following the valley of the Syr-Dar'ya, and from afar its silvery waters looked like a glittering white streak on the horizon, while the yellow sand under our feet took on a red-tinted, golden hue. On both sides of the road jagged rocks of sandstone rose up in tall, irregularly shaped pillars, looking for all the world like antediluvian monsters. Some resembled fantastic bears, formed from two gigantic outcrops coupled by a third joining them together; others, monstrous stags shaped out of heavy boulders uncannily rearing up on spindle-like supports; or yet again, serrated rows of dragons' teeth pointing to heaven. I was reminded of a painting I had once seen, by an abstract painter, depicting the end of the world, where everything was supernatural, parched, and bathed in carmine rays.

After driving like this for about half an hour, with the glittering line of the Syr-Dar'ya now appreciably nearer, we caught sight of a row of lighted windows in a long, rambling, flat-roofed building. As we approached we were confronted by the spectacle of an elegantly clad Westerner in the act of alighting from a shooting drozhki, very like those one meets in Prussia or Poland, parked alongside a European veranda. The vehicle was harnessed to a pair of handsome Ardennes horses in Cracow-style trappings, with a liveried coachman in a top hat seated on the box. It appeared we had arrived at the farmstead of Count K., the Polish director of the mine, who had driven out to meet us and who now proposed to escort us to the works. It would be difficult to think of anything more contrasting than this Western outfit amid the bewitching scenery around us, the Russian troikas and our white-turbaned escort in gold-spangled kaftans. As we drove up to the veranda three more gentlemen clad in European dress hastened to bid us welcome, in perfect French. They were the other directors of the mine, all Poles and belonging to some of the best Polish families, the sons of landowners, who had taken up engineering as a profession and had come to this remote region of the Empire to make their fortunes. In the hall we were received by several women in low-cut Parisian evening gowns, who very kindly invited my companions and me to dinner.

The room to which I was conducted to tidy up before the meal was luxuriously furnished. There were soft chairs, bright French woollen window-curtains and a pale blue Aubusson rug on the floor; on the walls hung beautiful reproductions of pictures of the Madonna. But this was typical of Asia, where one is so often unexpectedly brought back to Europe.

The 'modest' dinner to which we had been graciously invited turned out to be a sumptuous meal and a triumph of French culinary art; it was, of course, preceded by Polish *starka* and the inevitable bowls of fresh caviare. At table only French and Polish were spoken, out of regard for other members of the administration and their wives who understood no Russian. Champagne was served immediately after the soup, and really there was nothing to indicate that we were feasting on the banks of the Syr-Dar'ya in the heart of Asia. But after dinner, over coffee and brandy served on the veranda, the noise of the crickets, the silhouettes of our jigits pacing along the river, and the snow-capped mountains in the distance dispelled the illusion and brought us back to the foot of the Pamir.

At sunrise on the following morning I was taken to inspect the mine. During our walk there of about half a kilometre along the banks of the Syr-Dar'ya, streaks of green were plainly visible in the sand, a sure sign that we were in the presence of copper. Next we were faced with a descent down a shaft some six fathoms deep. There was no hoist, nor even a lift of any kind, and the workmen suggested lowering me down seated in a bucket attached to a long rope. The mining engineer who accompanied us apparently did not relish the idea of entrusting my person to so primitive a method and eventually we all went down the thirty-six feet by means of ladders. We soon reached a long gallery, where the unwonted absence of pitprops was accounted for by the exceptional plasticity of the soil, precluding any danger of cave-ins. We were supplied with lamps, and the light, refracted from the walls, gave the scene a warm, roseate colouring. The ventilation was perfect and after the great heat above it was even unpleasantly cool, nor did I see any signs of water, as in the coal mines.

The excavated gravel was loaded into trolleys, then hoisted up in buckets, reloaded into another set of trolleys and brought to the bank of the river. Here, in a long building roofed in against the burning rays of the sun it was emptied onto a flat, moving, and vibrating conveyor-tray where it was sluiced by powerful jets of water, the lighter gravel being washed away while the heavier particles of copper remained on the conveyor. These particles contained admixtures of other metals not exceeding ten per cent. The copper thus obtained was granulated, and varied in size from grains as big as peas down to fine dust. The ore was then smelted and refined in a coke-fuelled oven erected nearby, the water necessary for the whole installation being pumped straight from the Syr-Dar'ya. Production costs were thus reduced to a minimum. On enquiry I was told that profits were lower than had originally been expected and were somewhat disappointing, but this was explained by the heavy downgrading in the price of copper imposed by the Trust. The directors were, however, optimistic about the future. They told me of their difficulties in getting suitable labour and in housing their workers when they had them. An attempt had even been made to import labour from home, but this was hampered by the enormous distances involved.

The inspection lasted a full day. As I was about to take my after-luncheon siesta a delightful sight met my eyes. Outside, a group of my host's children aged from eight to fourteen were playing robbers, mounted on diminutive ponies. They had nothing on except narrow loin cloths round their waists and rode bare-back, like circus performers. Most of them were fair-haired, but their sturdy little limbs were burnt to a dark brown. Later Countess K. told me that the local climate was absolutely wonderful for children and that her daughter, who in Poland had been anaemic and sickly, had so improved in two years as to be hardly recognizable, thanks to the sunlight.

The visit to the small copper mine terminated my short tour. I photographed much of what I saw in the mountains of Fergana, but now, unfortunately, have nothing to show. However, I cannot but stress that Fergana, with its immense stores of minerals, is a land full of exceptional promise for the enterprising mining engineer.

So long as the country was ruled by despotic Asian tyrants the treasures it contained lay dormant and fallow, and the native population, in spite of all the inborn thrift, initiative, and industry of the Sarts, could do no better than merely exist under the miserable conditions forced upon them by grasping, tithe-collecting Beks. The improvement in the people's standard of living under Russian rule, brought about in a matter of years by the introduction of the basic principles of Western civilization, was truly remarkable. It is sad to think of all those gains now being wasted by a system of government which has so much in common with the despotic methods previously common to Asia. Under normal conditions Fergana could have been turned into a fertile field, richly rewarding both for the application of the Westerner's spirit of enterprise and the development of his technical knowledge.

⚔ V ⚔

TRANSCASPIA

WHEN I think of Transcaspia I have a mental picture of sands, deserts, limitless sun-baked stretches of country, mirages. I see immense flocks of sheep and camels; handsome, tall, dignified-looking men dressed in long, pink, silk kaftans and wearing shaggy Persian fur caps. I see a few scattered shady oases and dusty towns. But, more than all this, I can still feel the blistering sun and sense the all-pervading heat which seems to penetrate the very marrow of one's bones, searing the soul, scorching everything, engendering a state of permanent spleen. In all my life I have never had to face a more difficult or a sadder task than the inspection I was called upon to conduct of that region's administrative machine and its personnel.

Unpleasant rumours of widespread embezzlement, bribery, and unbelievable arbitrariness by the authorities of Transcaspia had reached me while I was still in Vernyy. At the time I was too busy in the other four provinces to pay immediate attention to these matters; moreover, my medical advisers strongly dissuaded me from a journey in the full heat of summer to a region that was notoriously malarial and overwhelmingly hot. Most Europeans are advised that it is better to get acclimatized to local conditions gradually. Thus it was not until August that I set out on my visit to Ashkhabad and Krasnovodsk.

The Transcaspian Province is nearly as big as Germany and is bordered on the west by the Caspian Sea, by deserts and the Sea of Aral in the north, by Bukhara and Afghanistan in the east and by Persia in the south. Broadly speaking the entire region lacks any outstanding features apart from the Hindu Kush range, distantly visible in the south. Otherwise, it is mostly a sandy desert composed of finely granulated loess. A few rivers run down from the glaciers of the Hindu Kush in a northerly direction, but all of them peter out in the sands and none reach the Caspian Sea. The two largest are the

Tedzhen and the Murgab. Their waters and those of a few smaller rivers are used for irrigation and by this means a number of oases have been formed, the most important of which are Ashkhabad, Merv and Geok-Tepe. The region is traversed by that stupendous technical achievement, the Annenkov railway line.

Ashkhabad is the administrative centre of the Province, and at the time of my visit the Governor was both head of the administration and Commander-in-Chief. The machinery of government was wholly subordinate to the military and rested upon an Imperial decree of 1889. As a matter of fact this decree, consisting of four paragraphs, was still the only statute with the force of law in the land, General Kuropatkin, who was Governor at the time of its promulgation, having endowed it with the highest sanctions. It stated that the Head of Administration was authorized to make statutory orders, to issue decrees and lay down instructions that were legally binding on the authorities in the territories under his jurisdiction, including the Courts of Law.

Two months before going to the region I had dispatched several members of my staff there and as a result of much hard work on their part I was in possession of a very thorough report on the situation. The picture was pretty horrifying: extortions, corruption, bribery, and arbitrariness. It was with a heavy heart, therefore, that I set out on my journey.

In those days it took two days to reach Ashkhabad from Tashkent. The line runs south via Samarkand through Bukharan territory, crossing the Amu-Dar'ya at Chardzhou and thence entering the Province of Transcaspia. Most of the way lies through the desert, but at some distance from Merv,[1] at Bairam Ali, one skirts the fringe of the Merv oasis and is once again greeted by the sight of cotton fields, almond orchards, and the usual signs of cultivation. Here, too, can be seen the ruins of the ancient city of Margiana, or Merv, alleged to have been inhabited by a million people in the days of Alexander the Great. Over the entire stretch of the thirty kilometres separating Bairam Ali from Merv the train runs through the crumbled streets of the old city, where the rubble of ancient brick-built buildings juts out from hillocks overgrown with thorns. The formation and composition of these bricks is unusual: they are only one and

---

[1] In Pahlen's day the name Merv was used for both the new city and the old historic site some twenty miles to the east. The latter is still called Merv, but the modern city was renamed Mary in 1937.

a half inches deep though over a foot long and nine inches wide, and are made of a baked clay which when broken up is seen to resemble porcelain. The railway station at Bairam Ali and two others are built of these bricks, though I was told by a local architect that no clay of this sort is to be found in the Merv oasis and that similar bricks can be seen in China. Be this as it may, they were extensively used in Margiana and went to build the big dam higher up the Murgab which controlled the supply of water to the oasis.

After leaving Merv the train runs over another sixty kilometres of ruins, which shows that at one time the city covered an area of some ninety kilometres. There is always something a little saddening about a ruined city, reminding one as it does of a derelict graveyard. In its day Margiana was finally conquered by Tamerlane, and subsequent repeated revolts were put down with ruthless cruelty. A nephew of Tamerlane's ordered the massacre of the entire population, a task his warriors had been unable to accomplish by the end of three months of slaughter. To wipe out the remnants he had the dam over the Murgab river destroyed. Everything died for lack of water, and the inhabitants starved to death. Other peoples and nomads came and made half-hearted attempts to bring the oasis back to life. At the beginning of the nineteenth century it was seized by some tribes of Turkmen origin, the Tokhtamysh and the Akhtamysh, under the leadership of an apparently outstanding man, the Sirdar Khan, who founded a new city and built a fortress on the site of present-day Merv. The walls of the fortress can still be seen, embracing an area of over ten kilometres. Built of packed soil, they stand as tall as a two-storeyed house and were so broad that two lanes of carts could travel along the top. It was here that the Turkmens invariably sought refuge during raids by Khivans, Bukharans, and Afghans.

The capture of the fortress, hitherto considered impregnable, by Skobelev, and his victory at Geok-Tepe, made a terrific impression on the Turkmen. Skobelev followed up his success by dispatching Colonel Alikhanov, an astute Caucasian and a Mohammedan, to Merv on a diplomatic mission aimed at securing the occupation of the oasis. The tribesmen in Merv were divided; some advised surrender, others wanted to continue the fight with the Russians, while all the time refugees from Geok-Tepe and stragglers from the corps dispatched to succour the beleaguered garrison were streaming back with wondrous tales about the White Padishah's general and his soldiers. The old Khan was no longer there to direct affairs, but his

widow, Gul Jemal, had taken over, and her influence over his kins-
folk was paramount. The wily Alikhanov succeeded in gaining her
confidence and talked her into persuading the obdurate Turkmens
to submit, thus enabling the troops to occupy Merv without firing a
shot. According to some of the most competent officers Merv would
have proved a hard nut to crack had it come to real fighting, as the
field guns available were not powerful enough to batter down the
walls of the fortress.

We left Merv at night, and as it would be another eighteen hours
before we reached Ashkhabad I went to my compartment and was
soon fast asleep. Sometime after midnight the train came to a sudden halt in the middle of the desert, and by the excited running to
and fro of the personnel I sensed that something unusual had happened. On enquiring I was told that the hold-up was due to a large
flock of sheep which had lain down for the night all over the embankment. It was fortunate that the engine driver had spotted them in
time for, though we killed some fifty of them, we did avoid the
camels sprawling farther down the line. Had we run into them we
should in all probability have been derailed, for the bones of a camel
are hard enough to overturn a train going at speed, or so the railway
men said. It appeared that the incident was nothing unusual on the
Transcaspian line and was accepted with resignation by the fatalistic
Turkmens. We were not held up for long. No complaints were made;
the shepherds seemed quite indifferent to the loss of their sheep, and I
think I was the one most sorry for the unfortunate animals we had
slaughtered. On the following morning we reached Tedzhen, where
we were greeted by the usual deputations assembled on the platform,
and continued on our way to Ashkhabad later in the day.

Frankly, I did not much look forward to the reception I would be
given there. Even before leaving Tashkent, acting upon the reports
of my officials, I had removed from office several of the administration personnel in Ashkhabad and put them on trial, while others had
been taken into custody by the examining magistrate. I had been
warned to step warily in Ashkhabad, since I ran a serious risk of
assassination. I had received many anonymous letters threatening
my life, and the desk in my car was full of documents containing the
gravest charges against the whole administration of the Transcaspian Province. A mass of damning evidence of wholesale bribery,
corruption, extortion, etc., was in my possession, as well as numerous
complaints against the Assistant Head of the Province, General V.,

the Chief of Police and his underlings, the Inspector of Mines, the Governor of the Prison, the Irrigation engineers, Railway officials, Tax Inspectors, etc., etc. It looked as if two-thirds of the entire administration were quite untrustworthy and profoundly corrupt. This was the charming collection of people I was to meet in full pomp on the following day.

We arrived after noon. From the window of my carriage I saw that the whole length of the platform was covered with priceless carpets and that a large green silk tent had been erected at one end. A guard of honour of Turkmen horsemen with their colours was drawn up outside the station. A group of beribboned generals in full dress, and other officers ranging from colonels down to second lieutenants, was assembled before the tent. Next to them stood the judiciary, in frock coats and stiff silverlaced green collars and three-cornered hats, a bevy of civilian officials, and native deputations in gorgeous kaftans. This display of pomp much excited the curiosity of my retinue, who thronged to the windows of their carriages. It was, in point of fact, a critical moment for all of us, as I had been warned that an attempt would be made on my life when I alighted from the train. But here comedy stepped in to relieve the situation. Instead of halting at the appropriate place my carriage sailed majestically past the bedecked platform, the huge silk tent and the expectant deputations. I was aware of frantic signals being exchanged between the guards on the train and the engine driver, and saw the orderly ranks of generals and officers breaking up in dismay. A few moments later the water tower loomed up beside us and we came to a stop. Any chance of a ceremonial reception was gone for good.

What had occurred was this. The Transcaspian railway was among the many bodies administered by the military authorities, and the latter regarded pneumatic braking as an unnecessary luxury, especially in Asia, where time has little, if any, value. Consequently, no funds were allocated for providing the engines with a pneumatic braking system, a few hand-brakes placed here and there over the train being all that was allowed. My saloon car was exceptionally heavy and the engine driver had miscalculated the time and distance needed to bring the train to a halt; in addition he had, out of regard for my person, refrained from sounding the engine whistle as a signal to the guard on the train to apply the hand-brakes. My companions and I were not in the least put out by this episode and treated the thing as a joke. As we watched the proceedings we caught sight of

10

two beribboned generals detaching themselves from the group and running for all they were worth in pursuit of the train. A little later they were hoisted into the train, puffing and panting, an undignified entry caused by the lack of steps at the water tower. Eventually they were announced as Lieutenant-General E., Governor of the Province, and Major-General V., his Deputy. The former was a cheerful, rotund little excellency, the latter tall and dignified, an unpleasant looking individual who refused to look one straight in the face. I must frankly admit that after I had asked them to be seated the obligation to shake hands with the Major-General was most distasteful. He had been too often mentioned in the reports submitted to me as utterly corrupt, suspected of falsifying official returns, and even of instigation to murder when he thought it expedient to remove an unwanted witness.

While I was exchanging a few words of greeting with the Governor the train was reversed, and my carriage now stood directly opposite the tent; I picked up my hat and stepped onto the gaily decorated platform. The generals and officers of the garrison were presented to me individually, in full compliance with the regulations of Russian etiquette on such occasions. Next came the various officials, and again shaking hands with them was no pleasant task. 'Head of the Administration's Chancellery', boomed General E., introducing me to a colonel designated in my dossier as the leader of an organized group of extorters and the evil genius of the administration; a man who exacted payment for every appointment he made. He was followed by 'District Chief B.', described as a gambler and spendthrift. Then came the Chief of Police, a well-set-up fellow with oriental features; he was a Lesghin from the Caucasus, suspected of murder and brigandage. He, in turn, was followed by 'Councillor of State N.', Headmaster of the local 'gymnasium' (boy's secondary school). In my papers he was described as a pedagogue who made a practice of issuing school leaving certificates for a consideration. And so it went on, my mind reverting constantly to the evidence amassed in my papers. The manner in which these people looked at me was truly painful; it was as if they were mesmerized by some horrible monster about to devour them. After a while I turned my eyes on the general public and the other travellers on the platform, standing behind an orderly row of gendarmes. All these people, at least, wore a benevolent look, which ameliorated the chilly feeling that had gripped my heart.

Ceremonies like this are a tiring business at the best of times. In Russia it was obligatory for senior government officials faced with such an ordeal to exchange a few words with the person presented and to mention and show interest in his work or business. In addition there were the local deputations, each headed by a spokesman who read a welcoming address to which one had to respond in suitable terms. In Ashkhabad, because of the mixed population, these local groups were exceptionally numerous, and colourful. However, we got through the ceremonies at last and, after I had inspected the guard of honour, mounted into our carriages and moved off slowly, preceded by a very smart squadron of Turkmen Cossacks and their colours. Behind us trailed a long procession of carriages filled with local officials escorted by jigits. We made our way through the town and at last reached the lovely garden of the Provincial Governor's palace, where I was to be his guest.

Ashkhabad is a new city, founded and developed after the Russian occupation. There is no native quarter, and at the time of my visit the population numbered about 40,000. The streets are broad and lined by two rows of trees, mostly poplars. The architecture of the houses is European, their windows facing on to the street. The city does not lie near any river and there is a constant shortage of water, which is brought by canals from wells in the mountains forty kilometres away. During his term of office as Governor-General, General Kuropatkin spent close on a million roubles on boring artesian wells but, owing to the geological formation of the soil, with no result. The bore-holes were sunk to incredible depths, but no flow or bed of water was ever located. Because of this dearth of water the streets of Ashkhabad were not sprinkled several times a day, as was obligatory routine in other cities of Turkestan. As a result, the town was unbelievably dusty, the stuff mounting into the air and hanging over it like a fog.

I retired to the rooms that had been put at my disposal in the Governor's palace with a feeling of relief, looking forward to a well-earned rest. But in vain. Almost at once I was visited by the senior officer of the staff working for me in Ashkhabad, who presented me with a detailed report of his investigations and turned my mood into one of grim reality. I signed an order dismissing the Chief of Police, thereby sealing his fate, for he was at once brought before the Examining Magistrate. It transpired that he and other officials of the administration used regularly to remove unfavourable witnesses, either by arresting them and then dispatching them to remote districts of the Province, or even by bribing assassins to have them murdered, the kindhearted General E. dutifully signing any and every paper submitted to him by his Head of Chancery.

Prior to leaving St. Petersburg I had requested the Minister of Justice to assign a special examining magistrate to Ashkhabad. This was most fortunate. The Examining Magistrate quickly charged and indicted the authors of the crimes uncovered by my inspection, and they were all subsequently sentenced by the courts to heavy penalties.

When I was at last alone I found that there was still an hour before I was due at the Governor's banquet and I put the time to good use by getting rid of the desert dust, bathing, and having myself massaged in the handsome Persian marble bathroom. After this came the tedium of hours spent at table, with caviare, champagne, toasts, and idle talk over coffee and liqueurs. Most of the guests were the same people I had met at the station, with whose conduct, thanks to my dossiers, I was only too well acquainted. On this occasion however they were accompanied by their wives, all decked out in the most gorgeous finery with low-cut gowns and smothered in jewellery. The world of officialdom in a colonial setting far from home is a curious sight. One is, willy-nilly, constrained to meet a type of person one would not allow over one's threshold at home, and to converse with women whose proper place is the variety stage and not a seat at the Governor-General's table. One of these creatures, introduced to me as the wife of Major X., was an adventuress whose real husband was certainly not a major, nor did he live in Ashkhabad. Nevertheless she was received everywhere, lived openly with her major, was entertained and herself kept open house, and in general was regarded as an adornment of the social set. However, I am told that one has to put up with this sort of thing in most colonial countries.

The week I spent in Ashkhabad was one of heavy work from early morning till late at night, with fresh evidence of bribery and corruption pouring in from every side and a string of terrified officials constantly before my eyes. Before long I dismissed the Head of the Governor's Chancery and handed him over to the legal authorities. A similar fate befell General V. and a host of minor officials. Every time I signed an order of dismissal I took care to show the supporting evidence to the good-natured General E., or to read it out to him aloud. Every time he expressed the greatest surprise, said he never could have believed so and so capable of such villainy, thanked me profusely for unmasking the scoundrel and then pathetically asked by whom he could possibly be replaced. I did all I could to shorten my stay, but the overall impression was most painful.

On one occasion, when visiting a girls' school one morning I was struck by the brilliant answers of one of the pupils in the senior form but one. She was an exceptionally pretty girl of obvious Caucasian origin, quite grown-up in looks though only fourteen years old. As I was about to leave the classroom at the end of the lesson she unexpectedly stepped forward and handed me a petition, begging me to release her father from prison. It turned out she was the daughter of the Chief of Police, who had been arrested on my orders.

In the next form I visited, I think it was the sixth, a German lesson was in progress and the pupils were reading Goethe's *Hermann und Dorothea*. The teacher questioned the girls one by one and every time the answer came out pat, practically before he had finished speaking. This seemed too good to be quite true, so I stepped in and started to question the girls myself. Two lines farther down the page the text might have been written in double-dutch as far as they were concerned. I came to their rescue as far as I could, and tried to the best of my ability to relieve an awkward situation till the end of the class. Later in the day I was being entertained to a meal by one of the senior officials, whose daughter happened to be my neighbour at table. As one of the senior girls she had been present at the German lesson, and claimed that I had let her down badly when I took over the questioning. 'Long before your arrival,' she confided, 'our teacher warned us that if you should come to one of his lessons he would concentrate on a particular page of *Hermann und Dorothea*. He divided the text between twenty of us, allotting about two lines each, and dictated the questions he would set. We learnt the answers by heart, but of course only those referring to our respective lines. When you did appear everything went off smoothly until you spoilt the show by questioning us yourself. We roared with laughter after you had gone, but the teacher was absolutely furious.' We had a good laugh over the silly incident and the way I had unmasked this childish deception.

After Ashkhabad we went to Krasnovodsk, where I wished to pursue my inspection, the evidence in my possession pointing to the universal state of rottenness of the administrative machine in the whole Province.

The journey took about a day and a half. The landscape, a dismal vista of desert relieved in the south by the outline of the Hindu Kush range of mountains, was uninspiring. At most of the stations there were long trains of wooden water tanks, the only means of supplying this stretch of country in which water is at a premium. We drove through the small oasis of Geok-Tepe, the site of Skobelev's victory a few decades ago which had resulted in the submission to Russia of the whole of the region. Railway repair shops have now been set up in the oasis and it seemed that the labour force was causing a lot of trouble, composed as it was of a collection of craftsmen discharged for various reasons from factories all over Russia, who had somehow drifted down here. On the other hand there were a few intriguing, adventurous, and exceptionally gifted individuals.

One craftsman in particular came to my notice. All his life he had been hounded by the political police for his political views, and was now on the point of being deported. This had been his last refuge after a life of adventure which had led him through most of the countries of the world. Here at last he had found a measure of peace, or so he hoped, and had married. At this time he was busy perfecting an invention of his own for the pulverizing of crude oil in furnaces. An engineer on the railway told me that several locomotives had been fitted with his system and that the resultant economy in fuel consumption was quite considerable. The man was an ordinary craftsman, entirely self-taught, a voracious and indiscriminate reader. In the course of a search, cheap revolutionary literature treating on economics and published in Switzerland had been found in his possession and he was now threatened with deportation. I shuddered at the thought of a man of this type being buried in the heart of Central Asia and of what his life must be like. Cut off from civilization by hundreds of miles of desert, separated from his wife and children, who are housed in the women's quarters, he lives with other workmen in a long shed made of baked mud, and for his bed has to make do with a prisoner's cot. The water he drinks has a briny taste, and he is expected to work day in and day out at the same job in the railway workshops in the blistering heat of badly ventilated premises under an iron roof. And what of the company he has to endure? A revolting collection of tramps and ne'er-do-wells, whose one solace is vodka in the canteen. Outside, nothing but the desert and the scorching sun from March to November, with fog and rain during the remaining months of the year. Under conditions like these it was hardly surprising that tempers were frayed to breaking point, that strike followed upon strike, that drunken brawls over gambling and women, and even murder, were the order of the day, or that the whole place was a seething hotbed of political unrest.

The man came to see me during our halt at the station to plead for my intervention. In the course of a long and pitiful conversation he begged for permission to stay where he was and for the sake of his wife and children whom he adored promised by all that was holy to refrain in the future from politics and agitation. I did all in my power to help him, and as long as I was in Turkestan I watched over him. What became of him when I left I do not know.

We reached the shores of the Caspian by early morning and followed the coast line until mid-afternoon, when we pulled into Krasnovodsk. This stretch along the Caspian is known as the Riviera of Turkestan and is very like the bit between Genoa and Nice, with its many tunnels and glimpses of the sea. We were travelling in a special train accompanied by the Director of the Transcaspian Railway and by railway engineers, who treated us to a regal repast in the restaurant car. For hors d'oeuvres we were given wonderful Caspian crayfish and the freshest of caviare, followed by *beluga* (a fish like sturgeon) and, of course, champagne. The fresh sea breeze with its tang of salt coming in through the windows was a welcome change from the sweltering heat of the desert. In Krasnovodsk, which we reached toward dusk, the train halted at the small station on the pier, where the usual deputations ('the menagerie') were assembled to greet us.

For some time past I had been receiving a number of anonymous letters and sheaves of photographs purporting to be extracts from the books of a large petroleum company on Cheleken Island off the coast and within the administration of Transcaspia. The facts contained in them, dealing with the rigging and allotment of concessions on the island, were hair-raising, and in the circumstances I felt it my duty to investigate the charges personally.

Communications between the mainland and the island were maintained by the Company's ferries, but as in my position I could not very well use them I had asked the Minister of Marine if I might have a torpedo boat of the Caspian Flotilla put at my disposal. His reply, stating that the Admiral's yacht and two escorting torpedo boats had been placed under my orders, reached me when I was still in Ashkhabad. On the way to Krasnovodsk a further wire reached me, this time from the Admiral commanding the flotilla, confirming the order and stating that the steamer *Georgii Astrumi* and two torpedo boats would await my arrival. To this I replied suitably, expressing my appreciation.

When we arrived at the harbour I saw no signs of any warship or torpedo boats, nor were there any naval officers among the group assembled on the pier. Among the representatives of the civilian population and standing last in line I did, however, come across a modest seafaring individual in pilot's garb who in broken Russian informed me that he would take me to Cheleken. I went back to my carriage, where I intended to spend the night, having informed the Chief District Officer that at 5.00 a.m. I would transfer to the steamer sent out for me, which was due to arrive at any moment. On the following morning I learned from a member of my staff that on making enquiries in the harbour the previous night he had been told that a steamer belonging to an Armenian firm (the *Georgii Astrumi*) had docked that day and that her captain had orders to convey me to Cheleken. There seemed nothing else for it so I moved into the ship, and there was my pilot of the previous day, who turned out to be her captain! I soon discovered that he was a Kurlander of Livonian origin. His Russian was not very fluent so I addressed him in Lettish, his native tongue, upon which he at once became more confiding and helped me to clear up the riddle of the boats.

It appeared that the Admiral had in fact received orders from the Minister of Marine to dispatch a warship escorted by two torpedo boats to Krasnovodsk, there to await my orders. 'But,' said the captain, 'the naval officers in Baku are not too fond of putting out to sea. The Admiral's yacht is in dry dock and the two warships are not seaworthy and are having their boilers repaired at the moment.' When I asked about the torpedo boats named in the Admiral's telegram the answer I received, in Russian, was *'oni ne lyubyat plavat'* ' ('they are not fond of sailing'). It transpired that one of the torpedo boats could not raise steam because of a mechanical break-down, while the other had actually sailed from Baku at the same time as the *Georgii Astrumi* but after an hour had signalled that she had damaged her screw and that she was returning to Baku for repairs.

The *Astrumi* was a trawler chartered annually by the Armenian

Company to check and place navigational markers, a task for which the Company was handsomely paid by the Ministry of Marine.

We proceeded cosily on our journey to Cheleken, which took about eight hours. The navigable channels were not always easy to find, but the captain, a real sea-dog and son of a Kurland fisherman, was thoroughly competent and appeared to know these waters like the inside of his pocket. The accommodation on board was fairly cramped: four cabins and a small saloon. As we were a company of twelve the captain, quartermaster, and crew moved out and obligingly put their quarters at our disposal. Jolly-looking photographs of the captain's children adorned the walls of his cabin and on the desk was a letter to their father, written in German, in which the terms 'Daddy' and 'Mummy' kept cropping up. By the companion leading to the upper deck there was a door, securely bolted, which obviously led to another cabin. Our meals, shared by the captain, were prepared by my chef, whom I had taken along on the expedition.

In Cheleken we tied up at the pier, built by the company and situated on their holding. Ashore we were greeted by the local chieftain, a Yomud Turkmen, who was also the representative of the law on the island. He stood at the foot of a runner some 500 metres long which stretched from the pier right down to his *yurt*. It had been made of strips, one and a half metres wide and pieced together, of those famous Yomud carpets, soft as velvet, which even in those days fetched 500 roubles per Russian arshin (0.71 m.). The customary dastarkhan was set inside the yurt.

Cheleken is an island fifteen kilometres long and five kilometres wide, rather like Heligoland in shape, with an unusual geological origin, for it was formed by the crater of an extinct volcano. From a distance the island resembled a huge giant's maw, the teeth composed of rugged crags. Looking down at the cavernous crater from their summits, sometimes quite high, one would think one was looking at the open jaws of a monstrous shark. The rivers of lava which flowed into the sea when the volcano was in eruption are still clearly visible today, though the crater is now half filled with sand blown across from the mainland. Oil seems to well up almost everywhere, and from above it is quite easy to spot the large patches of oil on the surface. Ozokerite abounds in the sand, and at the time of my visit was being extracted by an Austrian firm. In the distant past ozokerite was Cheleken's staple item of export to neighbouring countries. I was told that the whole output for years ahead had been bought up by Hamburg firms and that the ore was dispatched to Germany in large blocks via Baku and Batum.

Turkmen settlements of various sizes were dotted over a broad stretch of sand one or two kilometres in width that had been washed up by the sea. Cattle grazed the thick grass by which it was covered. A few isolated yurts stood at some distance from each of the settlements and I was told that they belonged to banned members of the communities, who were allowed to live no nearer than a voice could carry. In the settlements I was presented with a sturgeon at least six feet in length on which we feasted for several days.

The oil company's agent was most hospitable. He sent a carriage to meet us and allowed us to use his house, which was situated in the centre of the island, as an office during the day. Here were the workmen's shacks, furnished according to the respective nationalities of the inmates; here, too, were the neat-looking quarters of the personnel, the extensive repair shops, and even a hospital on the Nobel concession.

Judging by the company's books the annual output was very meagre, a finding that was confirmed by the small number of workmen engaged. However, I was told that the company could recruit as much labour as it needed at any time. During my tour of the island and the various installations I noticed that most of the rigs were idle and only a few small wells in production.

Five years before, the island had enjoyed an oil boom. Oil companies sprang up like mushrooms and were floated on the Moscow Stock Exchange. Each purported to own valuable wells and to have obtained a concession for their exploitation. Shares rose and fell amid a welter of fantastic stories and the island itself was literally pock-marked by the stakes of hordes of adventurers, all of whom had struck oil. The bogus strikes were promptly registered and the rights sold to promoting companies. During my short stay I saw hundreds of such stakes. Disillusionment set in when it was found that the mooring facilities were poor and the drillings unproductive, often because of deep-lying strata of water, generally mineral. Only nominal traces of oil were found. Even had it been found in profusion it could never have been removed as there were no facilities for loading, no storage tanks, no housing of any sort for labour or personnel. The majority of the companies failed and there was a temporary lull in the oil rush, the Nobel Company alone tackling the problem in a business-like manner. It built a loading wharf reaching far out to sea, provided its employees with adequate quarters and cleared up the mess left by the bankrupt companies. In fact, Nobel were just about to commence production on a large scale when there was a slump on the world market and most of the large oil concerns reduced their output.[1] The story was now being repeated on Cheleken, where on orders from headquarters output was being reduced to a bare minimum.

However, to circumvent Russian mining legislation was no easy matter. According to law, if the output of a concession were to fall below a stipulated minimum the concessionary rights were forfeited and reverted to the Crown. In order to assure a proper yield to capacity of the various mines and wells an annual inspection was made by state district engineers. To circumvent an unsatisfactory report and ensuing reversal of the concession to the State the holder had only two ways open to him: fictitious returns or bribery. On Cheleken, it was my task to ascertain the extent to which these practices were being used.

As was only proper, I was accompanied on my tours of inspection by the District Engineer, Mr. Mayevskiy, which was rather unfortunate as it was his conduct in particular I wished to investigate in view of the evidence that had come into my possession. It appeared that following the orders issued by the oil companies (with the exception of Baku) to reduce the annual output per well to a paltry 400 lbs., he had annually, in his reports, called for the return of the concessions to the State, but had later cancelled them. The reason for this strange behaviour was made apparent by the photographs sent to me anonymously, probably as an act of revenge by a discharged employee of one of the companies. These showed highly compromising letters written by one firm in particular, copies of ledger entries, etc. It transpired that at the time of the oil rush the engineer in question, posing as a private individual, had paid the company large sums of money for its concessionary rights and had had them registered in his own name. As registration was the business of a separate department, this was accomplished without difficulty. Next, he fictitiously acquired yet further concessions and entered them in the names of a collection of brothers, sisters, aunts, uncles, etc. Of course, no attempt at exploiting the wells was ever made, the object of the whole swindle being blackmail—but so cunningly de-

[1] For the methods sometimes employed see my description of the Chimion wells, p. 114–116.

vised as to render prosecution very difficult. Whenever the company showed signs of refusing his demands in went his unfavourable report, to be revoked later when a settlement was reached. This went on for quite some time and resulted in a most piquant exchange of correspondence between the head office and the branch in Cheleken. There was, for instance, an item covering Mr. Mayevskiy's insistence on a new victoria, to be mounted on rubber wheels; another on his demand for a pair of young half-bred horses and 5,000 roubles in cash. After long delays the extortions were complied with and the threatened report cancelled. (Copies of these letters were subsequently found in Mayevskiy's files.) I had him discharged and tried; he received a sentence of three years' imprisonment, as his guilt was proved beyond a shadow of doubt. In this and similar cases there were always a great number of people involved, guilty in the main of accepting hush-money.

I also remember the case of an Armenian prospector who had struck oil close to the shore in a locality previously considered quite unproductive. A former labourer in Baku, he had made a fortune out of salvaging and working derelict wells on the island. Flooded with oil from his new find he nevertheless lacked the means of getting it away and in the end was forced to appeal to Nobel, who owned both a loading wharf and the necessary craft. Needless to say he was made to pay very handsomely for this accommodation.

The oil deposits on Cheleken are apparently very difficult to exploit because of the geological formation of the oil-bearing strata. Owing to volcanic disturbances in pre-historic times these do not run horizontally, as for instance in Baku, but often vertically, the detritus of rock, oil-bearing shale and waterlogged sand being all mixed up together. On the Nobel concession I was shown a well in full production, while five yards away a spring of boiling water gushed up from a foot-wide pipe and cascaded down to the sea.

It took about two days to inspect all the installations on the island. In the evenings we used to return to our steamer, and on the third day we set out for Krasnovodsk. After a jovial midday meal with the captain, who by now had shed all his original reserve, we went up on deck for coffee. After a while he drew me aside and, very red in the face, said: 'There is something I feel I should confess. You see, originally, a naval commander to whom I was to act as subordinate was appointed to take charge of the steamer.' Here I interrupted him and asked the present whereabouts of this officer. 'Down there,' said my Kurlander, pointing to a porthole on the deck. 'I've locked him up down below. There was absolutely no other way out. No sooner had we left Baku than he started drinking, and he rapidly reached a stage when he was no longer responsible for his actions. They probably gave him a lot of money, as he was expected to be your host. The evening you boarded the steamer he came on deck dead drunk and loaded with bottles of wine and brandy, started to fight the crew and kicked up an awful row. I arrested him and locked him up in a cabin, detailing a sentry to watch over him and fed him brandy every time he came to. In that way I managed to keep him quiet. He is sober now, but too ashamed to come on deck.' The captain had tucked him away so efficiently that none of my personnel had heard anything of him, and even his servant had not been allowed to visit him during the three days of our voyage.

Much later, in a private interview with the Minister of Marine I told him about my visit to Cheleken. Though expressing his regrets for the miscarriage of his plans to make my journey comfortable he was not greatly surprised at what had happened. With nothing to do but a bit of police patrolling, the flotilla in the Caspian Sea was used as a dumping ground for the most usless elements of the Navy, and transfer to the flotilla was regarded as a form of punishment. Apparently it was the same in the Army, the commanding generals being fellows it would otherwise have been painful or inconvenient to discard. However, I believe a thorough enquiry into the whole affair was instituted by the Minister and that my would-be host was made to pay for his sins.

In Krasnovodsk my work was no more cheerful. There, I had to investigate the aftermath left by General V., a one-time Chief District Officer and Deputy-Governor of the Province. Though he had by now removed to more exalted spheres, after extorting all he possibly could, his successors continued to persevere, if less efficiently, and through a plethora of minor officials merrily kept the ball rolling. State monies were embezzled, books were falsified, sums belonging to public bodies squandered. Those most guilty were the Governor's staff. Shortly before my arrival in Krasnovodsk one of the potentially dangerous witnesses against General V. was stabbed to death in broad daylight by a Persian who subsequently stated that he had been hired by an unknown individual to commit the murder for the sum of one rouble. At approximately the same time one of my staff received an anonymous letter threatening him with a similar fate if

he persisted in investigating the affairs of 'the honest General V.'
I should like to say here how impressed I was by the exemplary sense
of duty and courage of my examining officials, who continued with
their work quite unruffled, trying to unravel the tangled web of
corruption in this hot-bed of evil.

My return to Ashkhabad was undertaken in a serious mood. From
what I had seen and heard it was quite apparent that the entire
province was being run by a well-organized band directed by the
Head of the Provincial Governor's Chancery, who was, incidentally,
an extremely able man and a tireless worker. After eighteen years
in the province there was little indeed that he did not know about the
foibles, weaknesses, and sins of every man in the administration, and
every appointment had his personal approval.

For the past ten years the post of Provincial Governor and District
Chief had been held in rapid succession by a collection of aged
generals, expert in some particular branch but bad as administrators. They, in turn, had been preceded by General Kuropatkin
(Skobelev's Chief of Staff), who ruled over the Province for many
years. He gave it shape, and organized the administration, to which
he appointed some of his ablest regimental commanders. From the
time he was a junior subaltern his career has been spent in Turkestan,
where by dint of hard work, scrupulous honesty, patience, and devotion to duty he made a name for himself and built up a reputation
which eventually brought him to the post of Minister of War. It was
of him that Skobelev is supposed to have said: 'Kuropatkin is an
ideal Chief of Staff if his Chief happens to be a leader; but woe betide
the Army he is ever called upon to command.' To this I might add:
'Woe betide the province he is ever called upon to govern.' Arbitrary decisions based on a callous disregard for the ethics of government, acquired through years of life in Asia, were the ruling principle
of his administration. At the time of his departure his former com-
rades-in-arms were all nicely ensconced in soft jobs. Protected by his
weighty position in the capital, they were free to do as they pleased.
In those parts of the world the power that is placed in the hands of
any official allows the unscrupulous many opportunities of enrichment, and it must be frankly said that many of Kuropatkin's
nominees were men of bad character. Tropical spleen and the killing
monotony of garrison life were an open invitation to every form of
depravity and to a general lowering of moral standards: to cards,
women, slackness, wine. These excesses all demanded money, and

money could be squeezed out of the population. To the natives this was nothing new, and anyway the abuses in Transcaspia were as nothing compared with the life they had been subjected to by their former masters, the Afghans, Persians, Bukharan beks, and Chinese mandarins.

Back in Ashkhabad I was firmly resolved to clean up these Augean stables, and I began by sacking S., the Head of the Governor's Chancery. Following his dismissal a stack of documents came to light, mostly claims and complaints, which he had held up for years. Some were highly original. There was, for instance, the case of a young Turkmen who had petitioned the Governor (not General E., but his predecessor), to redress a wrong done him by a junior district official. His complaint was just, and supported by irrefutable evidence. In revenge the official reported that the claimant was known to have written an anonymous letter containing threats to the Governor's life. A statement by three witnesses, testifying to the authenticity of the claimant's handwriting, was attached to the report. Piquancy was lent the affair by the document's closing sentence, written in Turkmen, which when literally translated read: 'Signed on behalf of the illiterate (here followed the names of the witnesses) S., Secretary to the District Officer.'

Now, in the first place, it is well-nigh impossible to ascribe authorship of anything written in Arabic, as the characters are drawn, and not written in longhand. Secondly, the final sentence made utter nonsense of the whole report. However, for the Turkmen the sequel was not so funny. For uttering a threat to the Governor he was banished to a waterless region in the steppes, where the chance of survival is, on the average, very slim. The order of deportation was apparently never submitted to the Governor, since it bore only the signature of the Head of Chancery, yet it was sufficient to send a man into the wilderness, to languish there unto death. I had the sentence immediately revoked.

The most lucrative posts, I need hardly add, were all held by close and distant relations of S. Every claim against their conduct was suppressed, their patron raking in the donations in kind and money showered upon him by his grateful protégés. Luck favoured S.; after Kuropatkin, his superiors followed one another in rapid succession and even if they had enquired into his affairs they were removed before they could have done anything effective. Moreover, the majority were soldiers, content to leave the tricky problems of administration to Colonel S. and to confirm anything he ordained. Besides, was he not reputed to be an outstanding authority on local conditions? After his discharge, these abuses all came to light.

All in all, by the time I had finished my inspection I had dismissed about one-third of the civil servants in the province. They were all brought before the courts and none were acquitted; this in spite of the fact that some of the trials were held long after my return to St. Petersburg and the expiration of the extraordinary powers with which I had been endowed.

I could go on with my story of the abuses committed in Trans-caspia, but will recount only one more case, which at the time struck me as a piece of unparalleled effrontery. The protagonist was Lieutenant-Colonel S. of Iolatan, a railway town lying halfway between Merv and Kushka. I think he was the most brazen scoundrel I met in the course of my whole career. As District Officer in the region of Merv, he lorded it over 25,000 Turkmen families. Each family was rated as a separate tax unit known as a *kibitka*, which usually consisted of the head of the family, his wives, and his grown-up and infant children. Also included in this official's district was the town of Iolatan, a mixed European and Asian settlement of about 5,000 inhabitants, a few villages of Russian settlers, and part of the Imperial domain of Murgab, the latter being outside his administration.

The powers vested in a District Officer were very extensive, based on one of Kuropatkin's decrees. He was (a) head of the police, (b) commander of the troops garrisoned in his district, (c) presiding magistrate of the native courts, and (d) principal administrator of the domains belonging to the crown. Further—and this is most important —his duties included the distribution of the available water supplies, and all the water aksakals were subordinate to him.

At the time of my inspection, Lieutenant-Colonel S. had been in office for about four years, but he had already amassed the sum of 300,000 roubles. As his annual salary amounted to 4,000 roubles in cash, with free living quarters, the strongest suspicions were aroused by the fortune he had made so rapidly. Investigations revealed that it was the result of a ruthless and brazenly-applied system of extortion and bribery ranging in size from petty sums to huge amounts. Any and every permit, certificate, etc., issued by him was made the pretext for a bribe. Should a native come to the bazaar to sell his goods, money was squeezed out of him;

should he wish to cross the border, he was made to pay for doing so. Any breaker of the law knew for certain that his freedom of action was assured if he were willing to produce the requisite bribe.

Accustomed as the natives were to being mulcted by dishonest officials, the behaviour of the District Officer was too much even for them to swallow, and after a year of his rule a long list of complaints trickled into Ashkhabad, where a new governor had just taken office. The complaints were, of course, never investigated, for the Governor's Chief Secretary was the District Officer's protector and took good care to see that his protégé came to no harm. There followed a journey to the capital, a presumed monetary transaction of considerable size, the donation of a few valuable rugs, and the District Officer, now promoted to Colonel, was back again at his post. In Iolatan he assembled the native chieftains and informed them that he was tired of his duties and had sent in his resignation. He also told them that a parting gift of one ewe per kibitka would be most acceptable. The hint was taken with alacrity and he thus became the owner of 25,000 sheep, which he asked the chieftains to graze for him temporarily until the time came for his departure. This, too, was readily accepted.

Of course, he never intended to retire. After a year his jigits rode out into the *auls* (villages) to claim the lambs his ewes had borne. Magnanimously, he waived the shearing crop—in payment, as he said, for grazing and fodder. Nor would he insist on the production of the lambs alive: all he wanted was their skins. Now, the sheep in that part of Asia produce a very valuable wool, worth five roubles per skin. In spite of the fact that the District Officer was forced to sell his skins from under the counter the profit he made from this deal was anything but small.

After two years in office at Iolatan the District Officer built himself a cotton carding and baling plant, which failed, however, because of the shortage of water. Undeterred, with the help of a thousand impressed natives he diverted the town's irrigation water to his own plant, neither caring nor worrying about the hardship he was causing, nor about the parched gardens of the unfortunate townspeople. The latter, who included many Russians, set off for Ashkhabad, where they were given short shrift. They were told that they were nothing but a band of subversive elements and revolutionaries, and sent away. Once again the mantle of protection had been spread by the Governor's Chief of Staff over his favourite.

When, on my way from Ashkhabad to Kushka, I was tended the customary greetings at Iolatan railway station, I pointedly refrained from shaking hands with the District Officer. It subsequently transpired that, on his orders, the delegations in their welcoming speeches were to emphasize their gratitude for the fatherly care bestowed on them by their 'beloved' chief. Now, in spite of all his outer semblance of submissiveness, the oriental is as able as any other man to read signs and draw appropriate conclusions. The fact that I had not shaken hands with Lieutenant-Colonel S. was noticed at once, and the result was a serious breakdown in his carefully organized plans. While a few of the delegations came out with the stereotyped speeches in praise of the District Officer, the majority never so much as mentioned his name, and after luncheon in the officers' mess I was besieged by a crowd of petitioners who begged me to redress the wrongs they had suffered at the hands of their 'protector'.

A week later I dismissed him and he was taken into custody by the examining magistrate, which proves that even the best of things cannot last for ever. The magistrate suggested that a full confession might help to mitigate his probable sentence, and after a few days spent in meditation the District Officer was handed pen and paper at his own request. The outcome was a sheaf of closely written pages which read like a novel. He concluded with a series of scathing remarks about my staff, who although they had brought about his arrest had inefficiently overlooked the largest of his swindles, which he then proceeded to describe.

It appeared that as soon as news of an impending senatorial inspection had reached him the District Officer had realized that his days were numbered, and that if he were to make a final catch it must be now or never. I was already in Tashkent when he summoned all his chieftains and explained to them that the 'White Tsar' had lost a great deal of money over the war with Japan. The treasury was bare and must be replenished. It had, therefore, been ordained that a 'voluntary' contribution of five roubles per kibitka would be levied. By this final swindle he had, in the space of three months, collected over 30,000 roubles.

Even in prison this crook made an attempt to coin a dishonest penny after an attachment order on his property had been issued by the magistrate. He dispatched a letter to one of his fellow District

Officers demanding 15,000 roubles under threat of exposure to me of certain of his misdeeds, all carefully detailed in the epistle. The money was to be paid to the bearer of a specifically designated five-rouble bank note. The list was certainly impressive, but paled in comparison with the epic exploits of our friend. The letter was impounded by the Governor of the prison and used by the Prosecuting Attorney to institute proceedings against the luckless friend of the Lieutenant-Colonel. A subsequent search produced the specified five-rouble note.

S. was sentenced to a long term of imprisonment and deprived of his rank. After his arrest a flood of letters came pouring in, in which victims of his from every class expressed their relief at the end of his reign.

The fate of the Hero of Iolatan was shared by another of his colleagues. On this occasion we were dealing with a plain robber, who plundered his district of every penny he could lay hands on. A family man, he lived on a lavish scale, and some of his exploits as revealed by the indictment were positively past belief. On one occasion he had fallen so low as to rob one of the native schools of a built-in iron cooking-range, sell it, and pocket the proceeds. When the range was being removed the protests of the schoolmaster, who incidentally was a Russian and not a native, were met by the short retort that his wife could cook out-of-doors and dispense with the luxury of a range. To his chief, to whom the schoolmaster appealed for redress, he explained that the range was rusty and he had had it removed to prevent a possible fire. His greatest guilt, however, lay in the manner in which he quashed the evidence against criminals who were prepared to pay the exorbitant sums he demanded. There was evidence to show that for a suitable consideration he was even prepared to allow murderers to commit their crimes with impunity. There was the case of a murdered Russian boy (something to do with homosexuality, I believe), where the father of the victim himself succeeded in tracing the authors of the crime and took action against them. The District Officer had them released, and arranged for their flight to Persia. The father's repeated appeals, some of which eventually reached St. Petersburg, had no ill effects at all on the career of the District Officer, protected as he was by the all powerful Chief Secretary, whose niece he had married, and by the fact that she was also the daughter of one of Kuropatkin's brother officers.

Awareness of the nature of my work, namely to try and root out corruption, spread through the district, and the distasteful impressions I was to carry away greatly spoilt my stay in Transcaspia. Nevertheless, the insight I gained into the people and their customs gave me much satisfaction. I was also interested in seeing the early effects on the natives of an alien civilization based on a European cultural tradition which, in spite of all the shortcomings of a corrupt administration, was beginning to exercise a beneficial influence.

I stayed in the province longer than I had originally intended, though not in the capital, Ashkhabad, where the authorities spent their time in official receptions and banquets, but in neighbouring Merv, on the Imperial domain of Murgab. Unfortunately, even here I was called upon to investigate a series of abuses. From Murgab I made several tours of inspection to Kushka, on the Afghan frontier, and Khiva, bordering on Transcaspia.

The Imperial estate of Murgab was a creation of the Emperor Alexander III. A few years after the conquest of Transcaspia by Skobelev a chance audience had brought a Russian engineer, one Poklevskiy-Kozel, to the notice of the monarch. In the course of this audience Poklevskiy-Kozel, who had then returned from a scientific survey of the region undertaken at his own expense, described the great Sultan dam to the Emperor, telling him how in the past it had been used to irrigate the whole of the Merv Oasis, and about its destruction by a nephew of Tamerlane's. He maintained that the dam could be rebuilt relatively cheaply and the district thus restored to its former beauty. The idea appealed to the imagination of the Tsar, who entrusted Poklevskiy-Kozel with the work of restoration and assigned him the necessary funds from his privy purse. Poklevskiy-Kozel promptly accepted and took the work in hand.

The Sultan dam, which dates back to times earlier than Darius, spans the valley of the Murgab and was conceived on a magnificent scale by the Persian kings of old. The Murgab river, with head waters in the glaciers of the Hindu Kush, flows at first down the valleys of Afghanistan. Upon emerging from the hills its route is barred by two gigantic cliffs—a phenomenon I have often noticed in Central Asia—and what was a narrow valley is thus transformed into a large natural reservoir. At this spot the Persian kings, or perhaps even their predecessors, erected a superb dam, built of those astonishing bricks I have described elsewhere. How this was achieved with the technical means then available I have never been able to comprehend. The magnitude of the structure is illustrated by the mention in some old chronicles of 10,000 men who were employed in the work. It rests on a fine loess soil, which when damped looks like liquid mortar.

When Poklevskiy started work the old dam was still standing, with the exception of a portion to one side that had been destroyed by Tamerlane's nephew. The opening had subsequently been enlarged by the action of the rushing waters of the Murgab, which had washed away the exposed foundation. Originally it had been proposed to restore the standing structure but this plan was abandoned as it soon became obvious that to engage in repairs on the existing foundation would be unsafe. A plan for a new dam some 600 feet farther upstream was consequently projected.

Because of the steepness of the banks Poklevskiy did not anchor the sides of the dam to the two cliffs mentioned above, and the result of this omission was catastrophic. By the time it was completed the dam had cost nearer a million roubles than the originally estimated 400,000. It was opened in circumstances of great pomp and ceremonial feasting; the sluices down the river were closed, and the water poured majestically into the reservoir. A few days later it was full and, as planned, the overflow began cascading over the lip of the dam. Following what he had learnt in Europe, Poklevskiy had built a staggered concrete fall for the water between the old and new dams, but it proved too short. The gushing waters churned up the soft soil at the end of the spillway and hit the Persian dam with terrific force. A breach in the latter was made with dynamite but the size of the opening was insufficient to take the volume of water coming down. A terrifying whirlpool tore up the whole of the concrete spillway and threatened the foundation of the new dam. Efforts were made to divert the flow, which was exceptionally heavy because of melting snows, into a side channel, but this too proved unsuccessful. The narrow stream rapidly turned into a raging torrent that bored into the desert and carried away all the water, eventually leaving the dam standing high and dry. The whole enterprise ended in unqualified disaster.

In the meantime, in anticipation of an abundant supply of water, a model settlement had been laid out at Bairam Ali, some sixty kilometres to the north. It was being irrigated provisionally by water diverted from the Merv Oasis, while the inhabitants had been told

that they would have all the water they could wish for as soon as the
Sultan dam came into operation. The settlement was embellished
by an ornate palace newly-built in Moorish style, and handsome
gardens had been generously endowed with cotton fields and an
almond orchard. The system of irrigation canals followed the layout
adopted by the British in India and Egypt: there were concrete dams
on the canals, corrugated-iron sluice gates and inter-communicating
telephones. All this elaborate installation was, as I have mentioned,
fed by water withdrawn from the township of Merv and the surrounding Turkmen settlements.

Poklevskiy-Kozel's reputation as an engineer was of course
seriously damaged by the failure of the Sultan dam project, but
being a man of means he was able simply to withdraw.

Thereafter, the Murgab domain went through a lean period, the
Keepers of the Privy Purse treating it for the next fifteen years as a
sort of ward. New men were sent out, each of whom submitted his
own plans for righting the situation. Photographs and reports were
faked in order to present a rosy picture to the Tsar, whose interest
in the estate was as keen as ever. Numerous projects were launched,
the majority of them makeshift undertakings; subsidiary dams were
built and additional reservoirs excavated as a safeguard against
flooding in spring. All this cost a great deal of money, with little or
nothing to show. Instead of the projected 100,000 hectares, only two
or three thousand hectares of cotton were actually irrigated. In
addition, the owner harvested only a half or two-thirds of the crop,
following the fellah system of share-cropping adopted in Egypt and
India. The position was further aggravated by the fact that many of
the share-croppers, some of them officers of the Department of State
Domains in St. Petersburg, sublet their holdings to smaller men for a
percentage of the harvest due to them and thus earned a supple-
mentary income without incurring the slightest risk.

By the time I visited Murgab the reserve catchment areas were
mostly silted up, quite useless, and the Sultan dam was in the process of being rebuilt as a result of a personal inspection of the estate
by the energetic and able Keeper of the Privy Purse, Prince Koch-
ubey. On this occasion the engineers employed were experts at their
work, with experience gained in India and Egypt, and there were
no mistakes. What I saw of the vast project was most impressive.
The dam now rested on a ferro-concrete foundation sunk deep below
the loamy surface of the soil, right down to rock bottom. I was

amazed by the depth, but equally so by the cost, which ran into millions. The whole project was completed either in 1911 or 1912.

Looking out from the dam one could trace the dried-out bed of a large canal, called Sultan Jab by the natives, which in the days of the Persians had been the main artery of the Margiana irrigation system. I drove down the whole length of this canal and even did some pheasant shooting in the surrounding scrub. The technical ability of the men who, thousands of years ago, laid out the irrigation system was positively astounding. When, on completion of the dam, the water was finally supplied to Bairam Ali, modern instrumentation proved that the best distribution was obtained by restoring and using the network of ancient subsidiary canals and ditches, still distinctly traceable in the desert.

To the north of Sultan dam lies the little township and railway station of Tash-Kepri. It was here that in 1885 General Komarov inflicted a resounding defeat on the Afghans and upheld the lustre of Russian arms in Asia for the last time, all but precipitating a war between England and Russia. In the course of his pursuit of the defeated Afghans, Komarov seized the oasis of Kushka and was on his way to Herat when he was halted by orders from St. Petersburg. England demanded the withdrawal of the Russian troops from Kushka and Herat, and the Ministry of Foreign Affairs went as far as drafting an *aide mémoire* acceding to these demands and submitting it to the Emperor. 'The M. of For. Affs. has turned very cowardly', wrote the Emperor on the margin, laconically. But Russia did not retreat, and the gains won by Komarov were not relinquished.

The battle of Tash-Kepri was a piece of incredible daring. The Afghans enjoyed a superiority in numbers of twenty to one over Komarov, who had about 2,000 men under his command. A considerable number of Turkmen horsemen hung about the fringes of the battle, ready to fall on the vanquished, whoever it might be, but well remembering that only a few years previously they themselves had been the bitter foes of Russia. The Afghans were armed by the British, and it was only the discipline of the Russians that won the day. The battle was first described to me by local eye-witnesses, and later I heard another detailed account from a Tokhtamysh Turkmen chieftain, one of the 'neutral' native horsemen, who recounted with glowing eyes how he had joined in the pursuit and had himself hacked down forty Afghans.

The story goes that there was an English instructor attached to the Afghans, called Captain Yates. He urged them to attack and fall upon Komarov, but the latter was too quick for them. When the enemy encampment was taken and the booty checked, a pair of riding boots belonging to Yates was found by the participant who told me this story. Apparently he had ridden away in his slippers, so hasty was his flight. The boots were handed to Komarov, who duly returned them to their owner, with a somewhat sarcastic note, under a flag of truce.

From Tash-Kepri I drove on to Kushka, a small fortress right on the border of Afghanistan. I found two-thirds of the inhabitants and the garrison down with malaria. Here was assembled an immense quantity of supplies in preparation for a possible advance into India, and material for a narrow-gauge railway to Herat. All this was useless, according to the opinion of highly competent officers, as it was literally impossible to invade India via Herat. They found the fears entertained by England in this respect quite incomprehensible. In view of the roughness of the roads in Afghanistan, and the consequent difficulty of maintaining supplies, no expedition exceeding a couple of battalions in strength had any chance of success. Besides, the passes were so narrow that progress could be checked by the most meagre of well-posted forces. I was inclined to share their opinion, judging from what I saw of Afghanistan, which I thought looked a desolate wilderness of grey-brown mountains and hilly deserts with no vegetation or trees.

Of all my recollections of Murgab I cherish the memory of only one event. This was the settling of an age-long feud between two rival branches of Turkmen, which I was instrumental in bringing about.

In days long gone by, when the district of Merv was free of any foreign elements, the Tokhtamysh and Akhtamysh had joined forces, and, led by their talented leader Sirdar Khan had fallen upon their kinsmen, the Saryks who inhabited Merv, paid tribute to the Khan of Khiva, and driven them out of the oasis. They gained recognition by Khiva and the Yomud Turkmen, her vassals. A semblance of a republic was set up under a Tokhtamysh Khan who built a dam across the Murgab and restored the irrigation canals round Merv. At the time, both branches were about equal in numbers, with perhaps a slight predominance of the Tokhtamysh. The total supply of water was divided according to the number of kibitkas in each of the two branches, the Akhtamysh receiving a little less of the all-precious water than their cousins. But as the years went by the disparity in numbers increased, especially after the advent of the Russians. Disliking the new rulers, many of the tribesmen emigrated to Persia and now the Tokhtamysh numbered about 24,000 and the Akhtamysh 15,000. It followed that the latter owned more water per family, and this was a factor of immense importance.

The legal ball was started on its way by the application of the Tokhtamysh to their District Officer, as representative of the Ak-Padishah, for a redistribution of the water rights. There followed a series of decisions based mainly on the subjective appraisal of the problem by each successive occupant of the post or his chief clerk, and the succession of Chief District Officers in Merv. Simultaneously, a representative of one of the feuding parties, hoping to improve matters, handed the case over to the Russian courts. As these were absolutely independent of the local administration two sets of legal machinery were thus set in motion: one, the slow grinding process of European jurisprudence, that is to say the District Court, the High Court in Ashkhabad, the Court of Appeal in Tashkent and finally the Senate in the capital as Supreme Court of Appeal of the Empire; the other, strictly administrative, via the Chief District Officer in Merv, the Government Offices in Ashkhabad, the Regional District Officer, the Governor-General in Tashkent and, lastly, the Plenum of the Senate, sitting as Supreme Administrative Court. The offices of all these courts were filled with individuals hired by the contesting parties to push their respective claims, who were either resignedly hanging about with true oriental patience, making flowery speeches, or else cunningly distributing valuable rugs and cash when they deemed that a present in kind might further their cause and would not be taken amiss.

This glorious legal imbroglio was at its height when I was sent out on my Senatorial inspection. Then I was warned that the rounded and beautifully worded verdict of the Senate was being temporarily withheld in view of fresh representation from the Governor-General at Tashkent, which caused me no grief because, when all was said and done, what did the gentlemen on the banks of the Neva know about *su*, about Asian customs or the actual value of fresh water in Merv? It later transpired that the Governor-General's latest move had been engineered by his Chief of Staff, who had been presented with ten rugs as a spur to action.

When I arrived I was approached by delegates from both parties, who laid their respective claims before me and retired content, quite certain that I, as the Emperor's special envoy, could and would solve the knotty problem. During the previous few months I had had occasion to be in touch with both tribes and it seemed that somehow we (my staff and myself) had gained their confidence. As the smaller fry of local officialdom steered clear of this tribal wrangle I was left a clear field to take whatever action I thought best. I began by securing the help of a few particularly venerated mullas and plunged into the business, which incidentally was quite outside my terms of reference. After a lot of work I at last succeeded in producing a formula acceptable to both parties. The happiness of this outcome was enhanced by the fact that up to that point I had done nothing but criticize. What a joy it was to be able to reconcile and bring together these naïve and knightly children of the desert! Their gratitude knew no bounds, and in accordance with local custom they wanted to suffocate me with presents of precious rugs and other gifts. I think they were genuinely disappointed when I politely but firmly declined to accept them. However, an enormous feast which lasted for four days and was attended by representatives of all the kibitkas was staged in my honour in the plain of Merv.

Unfortunately, I was only able to attend the feast for one day, as owing to pressure of work I was obliged to continue my journey. The assembly presented a most picturesque sight. I and my retinue together with the chieftains and elders, feasted in a huge silk tent on an assortment of national dishes, mostly variations of pilau. (None of the natives used forks or spoons.) The feast proceeded to the accompaniment of a Turkmen orchestra using an odd collection of instruments, from ancient two-reeded Greek flutes to long silver trumpets, each of which sounded only one particular note. There was also a large assortment of drums. When I first heard it I thought the music positively unbearable, but gradually I began to discern an original melody, definitely affecting the senses, which with its scales chromatically executed by the violins, strangely reminded me of the overture to *Tannhäuser*.

Later, a minstrel stepped forward and treated us to a long rhapsody in blank verse which he sang to the accompaniment of a lute, a form of entertainment customary at every feast in the steppes.

For my benefit, the gist of the song was translated. It consisted of verses specially composed for the occasion, representing in symbolical pictures the settlement recently reached, alluding in the most glowing terms to my own humble role as mediator and, lastly, describing the spirit of friendship which had at one time bound Russia and the three brothers, the forbears of the three tribes of Tokhtamysh, Akhtamysh, and Saryks. There then followed a long recital about the arrival in the land of the three brothers. As the story was entirely based on legend and oral tradition I regret that I did not have it taken down at the time. Other minstrels followed, but their contributions lacked originality and consisted mostly of a repetition of the previous theme.

After the meal, when we were comfortably seated on rugs sipping our Turkish coffee we watched a display of wrestling, one of the favourite sports of the Turkmen. All the wrestlers are stripped to the waist. Definite rules must be observed and no departure from them is tolerated, the onlookers working themselves up into a frenzy and betting heavily on their favourites. The object is to lay one's opponent flat on his back; no holds are barred, tripping is allowed, but the hands must at all times be clasped on the opponent's back. Wrestling between boys is also very popular, the contestants being paired off according to age. At the conclusion of the bouts I was asked to present prizes to the victors.

Races, on a course laid out close to our tent, concluded the day's festivities.

Few people in Europe are aware of two superb strains of horses bred by the Turkmen in the course of centuries of independence. Both are of Arabian blood and probably descend from stock left by the Arabs at the time of conquest.

For centuries the Turkmen lived on the booty gained in raids on their neighbours—the Persians, Afghans, and Bukharans living beyond the protective mantle of the desert. These raids went by the name of 'alamans'. The timing of them was decided by the elders of the aul and the young men and horses selected put to a rigorous course of training, for success depended exclusively on speed and the ability to fall on a peaceful population unexpectedly.

Distances of as much as 100 kilometres across the desert were sometimes covered in a single day and followed immediately by a speedy retreat to the initial starting point. The 'alaman' horses were all specially picked, fed and trained, and never used for any other purpose. An original strain was thus evolved, very swift-footed and of immense powers of endurance over long distances. Today the Turkmen horse looks like an English thoroughbred, is of about the same size and differs only in the finer lines of its head and limbs, more resembling those of an Arab. Later, a second strain bred from the same stock was evolved, providing pack-horses for the 'alamans'.

These facts explain the immense popularity of racing among the Turkmen. I noticed that traditional rules and form were strictly observed, while the riders handled their mounts with the skill of professional jockeys, holding them back for a final effort and then suddenly dashing forward with a surge of speed at the finish.

The scene was very colourful. Everyone present was dressed in his best. There were kaftans of pink and striped silk; tall, shaggy fur caps of the finest Persian lamb, perched on clean-shaven heads; heel-less boots of soft morocco leather which are pulled like stockings over the foot. Sparkle and glitter were added to the scene by saddles embossed all over in silver, bridles studded with precious stones, silver stirrups and gaily-coloured saddle blankets, bejewelled yataghans and pistols, tucked into silver sashes, and curved swords in gold and silver scabbards.

I left in the evening, to the sorrow of the elders, who lamented the fact that not all the members of their tribes had been notified in time. There were so many other things they wanted to show me, they said, particularly hunting with falcons, and a *jiran* (gazelle) hunt with their swift-footed greyhounds (a very graceful native breed), all of which had been planned in my honour.

This sounded tempting, but I could not spare the time. His Majesty expected me back in St. Petersburg with a verbal report on the inspection of his domain and, besides, I was anxious to pursue my task of unravelling the threads of the myriad abuses I had un-covered, many of which led straight to the capital.

I did a thorough job of cutting out the dead and rotten wood in Transcaspia. While I was in St. Petersburg a petition from the native inhabitants reached me begging me to request the Emperor to have an inspection similar to mine held regularly every three years and thus prevent a return to former conditions.

No sooner had I left than there was a general drive by the officials I had disciplined to reassert their influence and prove their inno-cence. Many of them had friends in the capital, but on this occasion no amount of wire-pulling proved of any use. The law proceeded on its majestic way in cold-blooded impartiality and meted out punishment where it was deserved. Much, I believe, was changed for the better in the province.

In the context of this brief narrative the descriptions, based on memory and official data, of conditions in Transcaspia might lead to the assumption that I was dealing with something inherently Russian and generally prevalent. In this respect Russia has been much sinned against in tendentious reports and stories by a multitude of travellers. The abuses I brought to light in Transcaspia were a local phenomenon, produced by local causes and conditions.

Primarily it was a phenomenon inseparable from colonial expansion and accentuated when linked to the opening-up of Mohammedan countries, a fact which should compel the attention of both statesmen and pioneers. The mental state known as tropical madness, spleen, or any other name, engendered by climatic conditions, and especially by the assumption of power from oriental forms of despotism, is pretty universal. I need only point to the French colonies in Africa, with their local *Bureaux Arabes*, to the Italian administration of Eritrea, the shocking happenings in India in the first half-century of British rule as witnessed by the trial of Warren Hastings, etc., and the early, groping steps of German colonialism. In this respect we do not have to go back to the days of Cortez and Pizarro.

Colonies are acquired and founded by purposeful, energetic, and talented men. Ethics are disregarded; the existing forms of government, whatever they may be, are torn down and replaced by others evolved by a European civilization.

At the outset, every European putting his shoulder to the task of developing the new acquisition is worth his weight in gold. The halo surrounding the white man glitters to heaven. The white man both feels and factually is a lord thanks to the colour of his skin. A feeling of solidarity among all the whites is rapidly established and, for the sake of prestige, often leads to the concealment of all sorts of abuses and even crimes. The life of a native, his comfort and well-being, become insignificant and lose what little meaning they ever had, while the white man, who feels that he is enriching his mother country with a new possession, is more than apt to take an exaggerated view of his own importance.

The effects of the climate and the traditions of centuries-old despotism which he is called upon to succeed are not without a marked influence upon the character of the colonizer. Under the Khans in India and Turkestan a man considered himself lucky if he retained 10 per cent of his gross income after he had finished dealing with the Beks, acting as emissaries of his rulers. The same conditions prevailed in India under the Moguls, and, at the time of its introduction, the tax of 75 per cent introduced by the British was regarded as a veritable boon.

The Russian conquest of Turkestan brought about an immense alleviation in the lot of the common man. Slavery was abolished, and capital punishment and the lash done away with, while the staggering relief in the burden of taxation was unique and unparalleled anywhere in the East, British possessions included. In Transcaspia the nomads paid an annual tax of three roubles per family, and the settled population five per cent of net income. Peace reigned over the land, and with the advent of Russian troops the previously daily instances of robbery and plunder ceased as if by magic. After centuries of oppression the inhabitants were at last able to gain their livelihood unmolested. The land was rich, and earnings easy. The population was inclined to view the occasional dishonest levy by some official as a form of *bakhshish*, philosophically applying the dictum of 'why fetter the ox when he is threshing'. The fact that these levies were contrary to western ethics did not worry the Asian. Besides, the individual contribution he was called upon to make did not amount to all that much. Five roubles levied from a family represented the value of half a sheep, whereas the head of the family might well be the owner of a few hundred or even thousands of animals.

As I have said, climate and living conditions tended to influence the behaviour of the European. Some time later, on looking through the reports of the trial of Dr.Peters, the former Governor of German Africa, and the statements of some of the witnesses, I fancied myself once again in Transcaspia. 'Why get all worked up over the fate of a negro woman or a few lashes of the whip administered to a boy?'

I think that the climate, coupled with the heat and the scorching rays of the sun, is primarily responsible for engendering a state of mental unbalance which results in a breakdown of the will and a general slackening of morale. The average European usually feels nothing during the first twelve months or so. I know that I hardly noticed the relaxing effects of a temperature averaging 90° in the shade; it was only during the second year of my stay that I realized the harm it could do. Malaria is another scourge that the European has to face in Central Asia, and the use of quinine is unavoidable. Those who have suffered from malaria (and I, too, succumbed to the infection) know only too well what it means, and the suicidal tendencies it produces in some of the more aggravated cases.

I would now ask my readers to picture the life of a civil servant under the following conditions. When he is in his office he is bathed in perspiration; the pen he is using sticks to his clammy fingers. For hours on end he has to sit going through papers, drawing up minutes, deciding cases, or listening to complaints in a foreign tongue. His job is to bring order out of chaos, and to set a pattern for future behaviour. In addition, he probably administers a district whose size would stagger the imagination of a Western colleague or even of his Russian counterpart in Europe. One hundred kilometres in a spring-less tarantas is reckoned a short tour, two to five hundred a long one. I have often met doctors and district officers working busily in their offices who have only just returned from a drive of 300 kilometres each way to investigate a murder.

And what about his home conditions? As likely as not his wife and children are down with malaria, the mother incapable of domestic work. Large numbers of native servants are a downright necessity.

Most of the government employees in Central Asia were, however, either unmarried men or 'grass widowers' who had left their wives behind in European Russia because of the climate. The local clubs, which incidentally were very comfortable, thus became centres where the European community congregated and where it was possible to relax during the hours of leisure. Here were wine, feminine society, cards. But to enjoy these boons one needed money. By Russian standards, salaries were low. A police lieutentant was paid up to 5,000 roubles per year, although he was given army rank, free living quarters, and a decent pension on retirement. A District Officer's salary was double that amount, plus a representation allowance. Money of that order did not take a man very far when a thousand roubles were likely to change hands overnight at the club, when women demanded costly dresses, and the champagne was imported from France. When funds were short one began by delving modestly into government monies, continued by tampering with official returns, and wound up with bribes and extortion. The older officials, who had got to the stage of taking all this for granted and had lost all sense of what was ethically proper in the service, took a criminally indulgent view of their younger colleagues' behaviour. Those higher up in the administration connived by turning a convenient blind eye on anything which might cause scandal.

In Merv I was told the story of a battery commander who had gambled away 40,000 roubles at one sitting. The money he lost was not his, but belonged to the battery. When discussing the case with the Governor, himself an old 'Turkestanian', the only comment I elicited was: 'The poor devil! Well, I suppose I had better wait for a bit before I audit the accounts of the battery.'

'Of course,' he continued, 'I shall retain some of his salary every month; he might even win it back, you know.' As the battery commander's salary amounted to 4,000 a year I wondered how on earth the Governor hoped to recoup the man's losses by the monthly reduction of a third of his wages, which was the maximum amount permitted by law. The old man confided that in his youth, he too, had helped himself to government funds when luck was against him, but had always managed to pay back the sums he had abstracted. In his opinion my views on what was proper and what was not, as applied to life in Turkestan, were both unrealistic and ridiculous.

In Transcaspia, as I have already mentioned, the aftermath of General Kuropatkin's tenure of office was a contributory cause to this deplorable state of affairs. The imprint of his autocratic personality was profound, and though he was scrupulously honest himself, the men he appointed to administer his province were of a very different stamp. Moreover, matters of secondary importance engaged too much of his time. Going through the archives of the government's offices I came across sheaves of papers with profuse marginal comments written in his own hand, all carefully preserved for posterity in rubber sheaths. None of them dealt with really important administrative problems but treated of such matters as advice to gardeners on the best way of planting apricot trees for the settlers, or the colour of the houses of Ashkhabad. He refused to consider the drafts submitted to him with the aim of providing the province with a proper legislative structure, because he could not bear the idea of a curb on his right of final decision. Thus was brought into being a system whereby the local District Officer was allowed unrestricted authority, one which tended to revive the evils of Transcaspia's neighbours such as Persia and Afghanistan.

For as long as he held office as provincial governor, Kuropatkin's untiring zeal kept the machinery of government running fairly smoothly and helped to establish a form of benevolent, patriarchal administration. When, however, he left to become Minister of War, everything went out of gear, and the province was delivered into the hands of smaller officials who had no scruples about exploiting the native population.

In the other provinces of Turkestan the earlier governors, Kaufman and Kolpakovskiy, two really great men, founded a political structure which enabled the region to develop on a magnificent scale and by its statesmanlike provisions minimized the ill-effects of local conditions. I do not wish to say that the administrative apparatus in these provinces was perfect, by any means, yet the number of civil servants I was obliged either to discharge or to discipline was small indeed in comparison to the host of competent, strikingly able, and talented men. I can site K., L., and M., three District Officers in the provinces of Syr-Dar'ya and Samarkand. Any country would be proud to number them among its servants. Besides being learned men, each in his own field was an expert; in addition, they were competent and very efficient administrators. L. was an authority on comparative philology and had written many fascinating books on the subject. M. was responsible for a revealing work on ethnography, though his notes unfortunately never saw the light of day. K. was an authority on the Shariat and could hold his own with avowed native experts on Mohammedan law. In addition, he was a fluent writer and speaker of Arabic, Sart, Turkmen, Kirgiz, Tadzhik, and Persian.

So far I have dealt only with Turkestan officialdom. There was another type of civil servant I was called upon to meet, even less to my liking than the rough brotherhood of Transcaspia. This type belonged to the local administration branches, founded at the beginning of the century, of sundry ministries in St. Petersburg. Recruited from the four corners of the Empire, they were a shady collection of the type known as 'carpet-baggers' and had come here either to draw attention to themselves by exaggerated reports of success, or they were frankly on the lookout for a fortune to be made by any means available. The majority were employees of the newly organized Colonization Department of the Ministry of State Domains and, to make matters worse, the department was placed under the jurisdiction of St. Petersburg and to all intent freed from control by the Governor-General.

I shall deal with the activities of the Colonization Department,

12

directed from the capital, in the chapter on Semirech'ye. However, the instance I shall quote now will illustrate the kind of thing that happened. It concerns a Mr. Timayev, an assessor of mines employed by the Ministry of State Domains. In 1905 he was known to have been seriously implicated in the revolutionary movement in Tashkent. Somehow, he had managed to regain the goodwill of the authorities and to secure his present appointment during the period of expansion following the troubled times of 1905. The mining industry was booming, and new concessions were being granted every day. It will be remembered that every claimant of a new find was required to mark the site with a stake and to report it to the appropriate department (in this case that of State Domains), where claims were entered in chronological order. In cases of dispute between several alleged claimants of an oil or mineral strike the rights of exploitation were granted to the earliest claimant.

As assessor, Timayev kept the register of claims. He also got in touch with an agent connected with the Department of Mines Inspection. When a prospector came to his office with a promising looking claim he would enter it under a few blank spaces, purposely left unfilled. A telephone call would bring the agent to his office, where an antedated claim to the same site would be entered in the blank spaces. At night a jigit rode out from the agent's house and planted a stake next to that of the original finder. Sidelights on the whole procedure were revealed during the legal investigation of the case. A whole cache of iron stakes was found in the agent's house; they had been cleverly treated with acid in such a way as to convey the impression that they had been in the ground for a long time. The stage being thus set, rumour was allowed to spread that several claims, all antedated, of course, to the genuine one, had been filed by the assessor. The prospector was summoned to his office, where the following conversation ensued: 'It appears that you have filed a claim for such and such a site and have requested the grant of a permit of exploitation. Are you aware that Messrs. so-and-so, for whom I am acting as attorney, have previously filed a similar claim? I am, however, authorized to concede their rights to you for such and such a sum. If you refuse to pay what I ask, the permit to work your claim will be withheld.'

Many an unfortunate prospector was robbed of the fruits of his toil, often undertaken at great cost, by methods like this, and the development of Turkestan's mineral riches retarded. During a search in Timayev's quarters account-books were found which revealed an extremely efficient system of book-keeping spread over many years. The amounts he received from his victims, and the sums he paid out to his straw men, were all carefully tabulated. At his trial Timayev pleaded his innocence and claimed that he was being hounded by 'the forces of reaction'. Nevertheless, the court by which I had him tried sentenced him to three years' imprisonment.

⚜ VI ⚜

KHIVA

HIVA is always associated in my mind with my stay in Transcaspia. I went there on the trail of fraudulent practices in the Amu-Dar'ya Flotilla, which was financed by the Treasury, and to look into the legal proceedings about to begin in this connexion. Apart from this, I wished to obtain some additional statistical data in order to complete my official report. I was particularly anxious to ascertain the economic value of the wealthy oasis of Khiva to the other provinces of Turkestan.

The Heir Apparent of Khiva had called on me in Tashkent and begged me, at his father's earnest request, to visit his domain and furnish the White Tsar with a first-hand report on the genuine loyalty of Khiva to Russia, which, he had no doubt, could not fail to impress me.

In 1873 the present Khan of Khiva had fought the Russians in the course of a campaign led by General Kaufman, who with a handful of soldiers had set out from Tashkent on a daring expedition aimed at putting an end once and for all to the raids by the Khan's men. Kaufman and his small band[1] all but perished from thirst in the desert. They were saved by the chance find by a Cossack scout of a well about fifty kilometres distant from the encampment where the exhausted troops had pitched their tents. According to a member of the expedition, when the Cossack scout rode into the camp shouting: 'I have found water', the soldiers jumped to their feet and covered the fifty kilometres in one frightful march of mingled hope and sheer despair. Two days later they reached the Amu-Dar'ya and settled the fate of the campaign, as the oasis of Khiva lay on the opposite bank. Modern methods and modern equipment soon disposed of the Khan's

[1] Kaufman's 'small band' was actually a well-equipped force of about 5,000 men, which came close to disaster because of a last-minute change of the route of march. See Eugene Schuyler: *Turkistan*, vol. 2, pp. 337, 341. London, 1876.

warriors, armed with antiquated flintlocks, and forced the Khan into submission as a vassal of Russia.

In my time the journey to Khiva was not as strenuous. A steamer of the Amu-Dar'ya Flotilla conveyed one downstream from Chardzhou to Petro-Alexandrovsk, situated on the right bank of the river, and thence, seated in a comfortable carriage, one travelled overland to the capital, 100 kilometres away.

By the terms of the peace treaty of 1873, Khiva ceded to Russia a large strip of territory along the right bank of the Amu-Dar'ya reaching as far as the Aral Sea. This considerable gain was added to the governor-generalship of Turkestan, directed from Tashkent. Petro-Alexandrovsk was garrisoned by a squadron of Cossacks and, I believe, a battalion of riflemen, a force adequate to keep the Khan in check; he was allowed a bodyguard not exceeding a hundred men and barred from acquiring modern weapons.

In the distant past the Khanate of Khiva had been overrun by Kirgiz-Uzbeks, who after the fall of the Parthian kingdom conquered and then assimilated a people of mixed Chinese and Persian origin inhabiting the oasis. Remnants of Chinese influence are still met in Khiva today, as, for instance, the *araba* or low two-wheeled cart. The oasis is surrounded by a girdle of terrifying deserts which have saved it from conquest. By vicious raids on the wandering Turkmen in the steppes and on the scattered villages left over from the Arab conquest, the Khans of Khiva turned them into obedient tributaries.

The oasis was well and efficiently tended by its masters. Over the years irrigation was improved, large canals leading inland from the Amu-Dar'ya were excavated, and the work done by the industrious inhabitants in the fields was truly astonishing. The landscape is very reminiscent of Egypt: water from the canals is brought up by the same diminutive camel-driven mills; the same shrill sound of unoiled cogs proclaims the presence of water from afar.

I left Chardzhou in the morning aboard a handsome Finnish steamer and was immediately confronted by the usual inefficiency and short-comings of the Asian administrative machine. The Amu-Dar'ya is a very shallow river, and consequently can only be navigated by boats with a very shallow draft. For reasons I was never able to fathom, the river flotilla was under the control of the General Staff, the intention being, presumably, to use it for ferrying troops to the Afghan border in the event of war with England. A prerequisite were craft that sat high in the water, for the upper reaches of the Amu-Dar'ya were extremely shallow and it was precisely these reaches which were really important from the military point of view. The orders for the steamers stipulated a maximum draft of two and a half feet. They were built by the firm of Krichten in Åbo, in Finland, the trials and handing-over taking place in the Baltic. In sea water the margin specified by contract was obviously met, but in the sweet waters of the river the steamers drew an extra one and a half feet. The steamers were taken over on behalf of the Imperial General Staff by officers detailed from St. Petersburg, who must have drawn a handsome commission on the deal.

The transportation of the steamers from Åbo to Chardzhou, the seat of the Flotilla Board, was a most complicated business which entailed dismantling them, loading them piecemeal onto freight cars, carrying them overland by railway to Chardzhou and then reassembling them in the Flotilla's workshops, run by the Treasury. In its turn, the whole operation provided the officers of the staff in Tashkent with plenty of opportunities for illegal enrichment. A commander with the authority and rank of colonel was in charge of the Flotilla and was directly subordinate to the Commander-in-Chief of Turkestan. On the other hand the purely commercial activities of the Flotilla, which in peace time ferried passengers and goods from Chardzhou to Petro-Alexandrovsk and back, were controlled by the Corps Quartermaster. A convenient source of graft for the officers of three separate military establishments was thus provided, while the Treasury annually forked out subsidies worth several million. The echelon worked this way: first, the representatives of the General Staff in St. Petersburg; second, the Staff Officers in Tashkent, and third, the Quartermaster's Department, likewise in Tashkent.

Word of all these abuses must have come to the ear of the Chief of the Imperial General Staff, General Palitsin, a very thorough and competent man, for at the time of my departure from the capital he particularly asked me to cast an eye over the affairs of the Flotilla.

It was stiflingly hot on the June day when I set out on my journey from Samarkand to Chardzhou and I recollect with horror the temperature of 104° that I had to put up with in the railway carriage.

We rose early in the morning, inspected the workshops and docks on the banks of the river and cast off at nine o'clock. Above the bridge at Chardzhou the Amu-Dar'ya is about one kilometre wide. I found the furnishings of the steamer very impressive, with a luxurious saloon and comfortable cabins. The steamer had been expressly chartered for my use but I was asked if I had any objection to taking on a few passengers, a permission I was only too willing to grant. They turned out to be wealthy local merchants who respectfully kept their distance during the whole length of the trip. On the bridge I met the captain, a pleasant, well-educated German Balt in naval uniform who maintained his ship in perfect order. A great lover of music, he had even contrived to organize a ship's orchestra from among the members of his crew. The latter were drawn from the local railway battalion but wore sailors' uniforms with large red collars. On the fo'c'sle, two guns we were conveying to the Khan of Khiva as a gift from the Emperor gave our craft the appearance of a naval ship.

At the beginning, our course lay between two pylons of the bridge across the Amu-Dar'ya. The engines were none too powerful and we had to battle our way up against the strong current. An expression of relief spread over the captain's face when we emerged safely on the other side. Later he confided that he was always afraid of bumping his ship against the pylons, as the powerful current running under the bridge demanded very careful navigation. Upstream from the bridge the river is much wider; the water is chocolate-brown and takes on a reddish tint over the deeper stretches. The fairway is not marked out at all, as the navigable channel changes course all the time.

We were barely out from under the arches of the bridge when we ran into a sandbank and stuck fast. Though I thought we were about to be wrecked, the captain was quite unperturbed and calmly said that in less than two hours we would be freed and able to proceed, as the current was already washing away the sand from under our keel. He was right. Strong eddies and whirlpools on both sides of the ship removed the sand in a matter of hours and released her. In all my travels I never witnessed anything like this, though I must admit that we did not present a particularly dignified picture, sitting sand-locked within a stone's throw of Chardzhou. For another hour and a half all went well as we chugged upstream, and then we struck another sandbank. A Turkmen pilot armed with a measuring rod was lowered into a small boat and told to look for the fairway. In places the water was only a foot or two deep, and the man was able to get out of his boat and stand on the river bed. But we needed a depth of at least four feet. At last he succeeded in locating a deeper channel, and after we were washed free we continued on our journey.

By evening the same performance had been repeated several times. On some occasions we even reversed over several kilometres in order to find a more suitable channel and be able to resume our painful progress. At dusk the captain pulled inshore, an anchor was dropped into a dinghy, rowed across and secured to the bank, for the bed of the river was much too soft and there was a danger that we might drag our anchor.

We remained moored to the bank all night and had a most pleasant meal on deck, protected by an awning against clouds of small but vicious mosquitoes which made exposure to the open air a torture. The heat in the cabins was appalling, and like a Turkish bath. However, we managed to get a little sleep in the early hours of the morning, stretched out on camp beds on deck after we had cast off.

The whole journey to Petro-Alexandrovsk, spent in running off one sandbank onto another, took seven days. For four days after leaving Chardzhou we saw nothing but steppe country scorched dry by the sun and only met one ridge of hills. Here, the river runs very rapidly in a broad stream between high, sand-covered rocks. The rapids in this passage are the terror of the native boatmen who ply up and down the Amu-Dar'ya. I noticed their craft were very curiously shaped. Unbelievably narrow and long, with a single sail, the bow and stern rising high above the water, they resembled Viking ships. Loaded with freight, it takes them two months to cover the stretch between Petro-Alexandrovsk and Chardzhou. When there is no wind the crews get out and wade, pulling their boats after them. The shallows present no dangers to these boats as none of them draw more than about a foot of water.

On the fifth day of our journey, high above us on the left bank we caught sight of streaming banners in the distance and an array of large green tents. Gradually a huge encampment came into sight, where a path covered with beautiful carpets led down to the river. We were signalled and told to draw up inshore. This was the heir apparent, sent ahead by his father to greet me on the borders of his realm. It meant a delay, of course, but there was nothing else for it. We halted, a gangplank was laid down, I walked across and then mounted the carpeted steps dug in the sandy loam, escorted by the heir, who had come to the water's edge to bid me welcome. At the top we were ushered into a large tent and treated to a dastarkhan followed by a meal *à l'Européenne* with champagne and more familiar dishes.

The heir, a tall young man, slightly round-shouldered, was dressed like the rest of his entourage in a long, dark-red silk kaftan, and had the usual huge black woollen fur cap on his head. He had an aristocratic look about him, and I particularly noticed his delicate hands and features, signs of a finer and nobler race. He was accompanied by his father's trusted man and prime minister of Khiva, a stout, jovial gentleman, swathed in a silken scarf that had been wound tightly round his somewhat protruding stomach and positively bristled with the arsenal of ancient weapons tucked into its folds. The whole assembly had, as a matter of fact, donned their ceremonial curved swords, sheathed in gold and silver scabbards.

As the road overland to Khiva from our present location was long and tiring I invited the heir to accompany me on board. He readily agreed, and I spent two very pleasant days in his company on the way to Petro-Alexandrovsk, as both he and his suite spoke a little Russian. An honoured hostage, he had spent a few years in Russia after the conquest of Khiva as a pupil in one of the military cadet schools. He was very delicate and extremely shy. Much of the time we spent in playing chess, a game greatly favoured, it appeared, at the Khan's court and one in which the prime minister was supposed to be an expert.

Signs of cultivation met our eyes as soon as we reached the borders of Khiva—large canals branching off the river and running deep inland. As we moved upstream the heir acquainted me with the past history of his native country, closely bound, as I could see, to the extension of the canals and improvements to the general system of irrigation. 'That one over there was excavated by one of my for-bears; and the one we are now passing, by another.'

For the next two and a half days we proceeded on our chequered journey of running onto everlasting sandbanks, an occurrence which no longer caused us any concern.

Petro-Alexandrovsk is a typically Russian town of straight streets and the obligatory *Gostinnyi Dvor* (shopping centre, bazaar). At the mooring stage I received the by now familiar menagerie of deputations and stayed a couple of days in the town inspecting government offices and the administration. At this time Petro-Alexandrovsk was a fairly important trading centre with Khiva and the nomad tribes living around the Aral Sea. Most of the middle-men were former deserters from the Ural Cossacks who had sought refuge in Khiva after an abortive mutiny prompted by the introduction of conscription in 1875, which according to them infringed their age-long right of voluntary service. In Khiva they settled down quite happily, and after the conquest were amnestied by the Russian Government. They still proudly wore their military caps and the distinguishing badge of the Ural Cossacks, a broad strip of mauve piping down their trousers.

Three days later we resumed our journey to Khiva. We first crossed to the opposite bank and then proceeded in comfortable rubber-tyred victorias drawn by troikas. On this occasion I was escorted by a squadron of Orenburg Cossacks, in yellow caps and yellow piping, mounted on magnificent horses. Despite the stifling heat they accompanied us over the whole seventy kilometres to the capital singing merrily all the way. At midday we halted in the shade of a mulberry grove on the banks of the Hasavat, one of the largest irrigation canals.

The heir to the throne was here to meet us, and received us in a sumptuous Bukharan tent where we were offered a meal and allowed to rest until the worst of the heat was over. We were right in the centre of the oasis. Village succeeded village, the roads were lined with trees, the orchards past which we drove were full of apples, peaches, apricots, and pears. Every morsel of ground was cultivated and carefully husbanded. The architecture of the houses was most quaint. High, plastered walls, loopholes, and crenellated battlements round the flat roofs made them look for all the world like diminutive forts. The road we followed had been watered in my honour and we thus avoided being half-choked with dust.

At seven kilometres from the capital I was greeted by the Khan in person, who had driven out in a landau presented to him by the Emperor. I got the impression of a man of great authority, very aristocratic-looking and dignified in bearing. In honour of the occasion he wore a black silk kaftan and all his Russian decorations. We drove to his summer palace a short distance away, where I was provided with a tent and thus could freshen up after the journey and don my gold-embroidered court dress. From there we proceeded in full ceremonial to his residence escorted by my Cossacks and the Khan's murids.

Khiva is one of the prettiest native cities in Turkestan and from a distance looks like a huge garden. The streets, as usual, were just narrow lanes winding between high plastered walls. I marvelled at the skill of our coachman and at the way he manoeuvred the carriage in so confined a space.

From outside the Khan's palace rather resembled the Kremlin in Moscow, but once through the main gate in the outer wall one was confronted by a large courtyard surrounded by carved ebony columns that supported the terraces of the flat-roofed buildings. A fountain of spring water occupied the centre. All the inner rooms of the palace opened on a pavement which led round the cloisters a good two feet above the level of the courtyard floor. The room we had been allotted was high, airy and cool, with a carved ebony ceiling, carpeted walls and western furniture. As soon as he had conducted us to our rooms the Khan withdrew, bidding us join him at a banquet in two hours' time.

We profited by this respite to visit the palace gardens, which we had been told were exceptionally lovely. Enclosed by cloisters similar to those in front of our room, they presented a row of open courts profusely irrigated by small channels and gushing fountains, so that in spite of the great heat all around the air was pleasantly cool. Each court had a number of beautiful fruit trees, bowers covered in grape vine, and beds with gorgeous flowers. The rose garden was quite wonderful and was tended by a German with whom I exchanged a few words and from whom I learnt that the Khan's two favourite hobbies were rose growing and falconry. I was shown the spacious chamber where, sitting as Supreme Justice of his realm, the Khan gave judgment every morning in the legal disputes of his subjects, in the manner of Harun al-Rashid in the days of old. In his stables, which we also visited, his thoroughbred horses, covered by the finest of blankets and with their long manes and tails often dyed red, fed out of marble mangers.

It turned out later that it was the Khan's intention to present me with six of his choicest stallions. To accept a gift of this kind was out of the question, yet I had much difficulty in tactfully explaining to His Highness that a Senator who commits government officials to trial for accepting unsolicited gifts cannot very well himself be the recipient of bounties of this kind. He was, he said, debarred from bestowing decorations, and it pained him to see his guest depart without some mark of his esteem. Eventually we settled for a ceremonial sword and yataghan, which I saw no way of refusing though I did not much approve of the golden scabbards inset with precious stones in which they were sheathed. Some time later I did my best to reciprocate by sending him a collection of the choicest rose bushes I could order for his rose garden.

The banquet, served in the cloisters of the main court, was much like the one I had attended in Bukhara, and lasted for two or three hours. After coffee the Khan retired, and his son, the heir, asked me if I would like to see their national ballet. Tired as I was, I could not refuse. Cushions and rugs were fetched, on which we gratefully reclined, great carpets were spread over the court, the natives puffed at their narghiles, politely offering them to us, and the famous Khivan *bachehs* made their entrance. Backstage, an orchestra mainly composed of twin flutes, kettle drums, and half a dozen man-sized silver trumpets took up its stand. Opposite us a door left slightly ajar led to the harem quarters. We caught a glimpse of flashing eyes as the inmates thronged to the door to have a good look at us and watch the performance.

The orchestra started up with a curious, plaintive melody, the rhythm being taken up and stressed by the kettle drums, and four bachehs took up their positions on the carpet.

The bachehs are young men specially trained to perform a particular set of dances. Barefoot, and dressed like women in long, brightly-coloured silk smocks reaching below their knees and narrow trousers fastened tightly round their ankles, their arms and hands sparkle with rings and bracelets. They wear their hair long, reaching below the shoulders, though the front part of the head is clean shaven. The nails of the hands and feet are painted red, the eyebrows are jet black and meet over the bridge of the nose. The dances consist of sensuous contortions of the body and a rhythmical pacing to and fro, with the hands and arms raised in a trembling movement. As the ballet proceeded the number of dancers increased, the circle grew in size, the music waxed shriller and shriller and the eyes of the native onlookers shone with admiration, while the bachehs intoned a piercing melody in time with the ever-growing tempo of the music. The Heir explained that they were chanting of love and the beauty of women. Swifter and swifter moved the dancers till they finally sank to the floor, seemingly exhausted and enchanted by love. They were followed by others, but the general theme was usually the same.

In between, we were treated to other types of dances, also accompanied by the orchestra, which were really more like circus turns than anything else. I remember a small boy who was tossed like a ball high into the air by his partners and who never failed to come down on his feet, bowing gracefully to the audience. There were also war dances, with drawn swords glittering in the moonlight. Though I thought the performance very long, my hosts were very excited and seemed to enjoy themselves enormously.

However, the whole scene was most poetic: the cloistered court-yard with its beautifully carved columns lit up by torches held high by grim-looking belted warriors in shaggy fur caps, the dancing shadows imparting a wild fierceness to their features; the disturbing effect of the bubbling fountain, and the sweet smell of burning rosin mixed with the scent of roses. In the intervals between the music sounded the gentle murmur of running water, and the shrill chirping of myriads of the crickets so typical of Turkestan, filling the night with their unending song of love. In the distance were the sounds of the city, of caravans wending their way, of songs on the flat roofs of the houses, the unmelodious braying of donkeys, the barking of dogs and the yapping of jackals. Over the entire scene stretched the jet-black heavens, the astonishing brightness of the Milky Way, the mysterious light of the gentle moon. And everything was permeated by the sensuous melodies of Eastern music. Those melodies con-tinued to haunt me for many a day long afterwards.

After spending a day in Khiva we set out on our return journey to Petro-Alexandrovsk, this time via Urgench. At first the way led through the gardens and fields of the oasis, after which we had twenty kilometres of desert, and in spite of an early start it was un-bearably hot. I was afraid that the escorting Cossacks must be having a pretty bad time of it keeping up with the brisk trot of our carriage horses but their commander, to whom I voiced my thoughts, laugh-ingly replied that they thought nothing of it and that at Urgench they had a surprise in store for me, so delighted had they been with the reception given them in Khiva (a magnificent feast and an indi-vidual present from the Khan to every Cossack as well as handsome yataghans for the officers).

Urgench lay at the end of the twenty kilometre drive through the desert. At that time it was one of the principal trading centres of Khiva, a prominence which it owed to the enterprise of a few wealthy Russian merchants, who after settling there had monopolized the commerce of Khiva. The town was unique from the point of view of administration. Though situated within the boundaries of Khiva it was virtually independent, the affairs of the Russian population being administered by an autonomous Justice of the Peace who settled any disputes between his nationals or between them and the natives. The town itself was run by a Council elected from among the most prominent Russian merchants, which was not interfered with either by the Russians on the opposite side of the river or by the Khivans in the distant capital.

The reception I was given here was one of the warmest I ever received, and one in which Russian and Eastern customs were curiously blended. At the dastarkhan the traditional Russian bread and salt somehow got mixed up with the oriental sweetmeats, melons and grapes. Tea was handed round in glasses; there was a samovar and, to my surprise, iced champagne. A foaming glass in his hand, the senior member of the Council greeted me with a welcoming speech and a toast to the Emperor.

We were all pretty tired after our long journey and I remember the joy with which I quaffed glass after glass of the icy-cold stuff as toast followed toast. However, it was time to leave and to pay our round of calls on the members of the Council. After six hours of exhausting travel a glass of champagne goes easily to one's head and I noticed with some alarm the effect it was having on the members of my entourage. How right, I thought, was Mohammed in forbidding wine to his followers! Imagine my horror when at the Council's reception I caught sight of a silver tray laden with champagne glasses. Obviously great caution and discipline must be observed. Mercifully, there was a stand with *zakuska* (hors d'oeuvres), with some very fine caviare and other Russian delicacies. I declined the vodka and kept sipping my champagne, with a watchful eye on my suite. All told, we visited ten separate commercial houses and in every single one of them were treated to zakuska and iced champagne. This round of visits was followed by an official luncheon and more toasts. To this day I do not understand how I survived the ordeal.

After luncheon the Cossack commander invited me to attend a display of horsemanship (*jigitovka*) that his men wanted to stage in my honour as a token of gratitude for the wonderful presents they had received from the Khan. The show lasted for over an hour and could not have been surpassed by the most daring turns in a circus. No one could possibly believe that the Cossacks and their horses had covered seventy kilometres only a day before and another fifty a few hours back.

We left towards evening, and after a drive of three hours reached the banks of the Amu-Dar'ya. A steamer was waiting for us, and five days later we were back in Chardzhou. I travelled once more to Murgab, and paid another visit to Ashkhabad.

As I write these lines I feel I am back in the past, in those stifling days spent in hard and often galling work amid endless stretches of desert. I see gold-tinted visions of oases; flat-roofed houses with inquisitive women inspecting us from afar; tall, noble-looking men with huge fur caps perched on their shaven heads. I see the searing, piercing rays of the sun shimmering through a cloud of desert dust.

My visit coincided with the first attempts by European civilization, coming as a blessed and a freshening wind, to bring to light the hidden treasures of this land, to restore the shattered ruins of its ancient cities and to change its honest and noble people from nomads and robbers into honest and settled farmers in spite of abuses and the remnants of Asian tyranny. Alas, it seems that all this has relapsed into its former state of chaos and a new breed of loud-mouthed, uncultured barbarians has brought ruin to what had been achieved and replaced it by a new form of tyranny!

⚔ VII ⚔

SEMIRECH'YE

THE Russians call this province 'The Land of the Seven Rivers'.
It might equally well be called 'The Land of Milk and Honey',
for it is a region lavishly endowed by nature, where riches are
to be had for the picking, where the labourer is rewarded a thousand-
fold for his work in field or garden, where prosperity and justice
might reign with ease, where very little need be done to ensure full
development, perpetuating a state of universal plenty. And yet,
looking around, one is amazed at the extent of man's ineptitude, at
his inefficiency, at what he can do to hem in, arrest, and even partly
destroy the wonderful work of nature.

Semirech'ye is the most northern of Turkestan's five provinces.
Its western borders lie along the steppes that stretch eastwards from
the Ural. In the North it almost touches the southern confines of
Siberia. In the east it is cut off from China by a dividing wall 24,000
feet high formed by the Tyan'-Shan' mountains, and in the south it
joins the two 'sister provinces', as they are called, of Syr-Dar'ya and
Fergana.

The southern part of Semirech'ye is all steppe, divided in two by
a spur of the Kara-Tau running from south to north. Small rivers
spill down from the heights of the range, flowing from east to west
till they peter out in the sands of the Ural steppes. These are the
'Seven Rivers' that the Russian conquerors had to cross on their way
from the north, but it was not difficult since in the hot season all are
fordable and barely a foot deep. Slightly to the north another and
much bigger river, the Chu, comes down from the glaciers of the
Tyan'-Shan' and flows through the land in a large arc before it, too,
gets lost in the sands as it reaches the lake of Balkhash. Here the
whole region is one vast marsh overgrown with rushes tall enough to
conceal a man on horseback and forming an impenetrable jungle
which houses the tiger and wild boar and the malarial mosquito,
making it untenable to man. But for the hunter this stretch of

country is a veritable Eldorado teeming with pheasants, geese, duck, and countless other game, not to mention wolves, jackals, and snakes.

For ages the Chu has been one of the most important rivers in Turkestan, and must at one time have emptied into the Caspian Sea. The dried-out bed of the river, which the natives call the Jan-Dar'ya, can still be traced in the steppe, and salt-water fish such as sturgeon are caught in the Chu. I was told that seals inhabit the lower reaches of the river, where it turns into marshland, but I think these are more likely to have been otters.

All along the dried-out bed of the Jany-Dar'ya, which in the summer months is bone-dry, are many ruins of ancient cities, and traces of extensive irrigation. This would seem to indicate that the region was at one time inhabited by a highly-cultured people, farmers and fruit-growers who were at some later date compelled to leave because of unfavourable climatic conditions.

In its upper reaches, as it comes down from the glaciers of the Tyan'-Shan', the Chu follows a southerly course at first, but twelve kilometres from Lake Issyk-Kul' it makes a right-angled bend and goes on to flow from east to west. This sudden change of course is caused by a stony ridge stretching over the whole twelve kilometres, which prevents the waters of the Issyk-Kul' from spilling into the Chu where it flows twenty metres below the level of the lake. Only during the rainy season, when the level of the waters in the lake is high, does it overflow into the Chu along a bed running over the ridge.

It is the opinion of an engineer, supported by survey data of the Chu, that attempts were made at some time to deepen this bed and regulate the flow of water. He also thought that in the distant past the Chu must have flowed through the valley of the Issyk-Kul', gathering on its way the waters which now form the lake and which are rapidly evaporating, and was thus able to reach the sea. There were signs, he said, that after the volcanic upheaval which threw up the barrier between the river and the lake the inhabitants had made superhuman efforts to avert the catastrophe which threatened their valley by trying to pierce the twelve kilometre-long ridge. Apparently the task was insuperable with the technical means then available and the inhabitants were driven out of the land and settled elsewhere. The engineer claimed to have studied the ancient Hindu Vedas, and said that their description of this part of the country unmistakably pointed to the Jany-Dar'ya and the Chu. The theory that the plain covered by Lake Issyk-Kul' was once inhabited is further strengthened by the many domestic articles washed ashore in stormy weather, such as fragments of quaint-looking barrels, copper vessels of all sorts, etc., now exhibited in the museum at Przheval'sk or to be seen in the posting inns strung along the shore of the lake.

After the withdrawal of the Aryans the land became a desert and for centuries was overrun by nomadic Mongolian and Finnish tribes. Some of the old chronicles in the Kaufman Library in Tashkent mention a Chinese domination of Semirech'ye of several hundred years' duration. This was succeeded by a large Hunnish state which sprawled over the whole of Turkestan, causing the Germanic tribes to migrate and starting them on their trek to the West. The Kalmyks then appeared on the scene from Mongolia and Eastern Siberia, pressing the Huns and sending Attila to ravage Europe. Genghis Khan's Tatars followed, and having broken the Kalmyks, they took over the land. After the death of the great conqueror his realm fell asunder and splintered into puny sultanates. Genghis Khan was the last to incorporate Semirech'ye into a unified empire; after him, all semblance of order vanished for centuries. Nomad peoples, stateless and recognizing only the ties of tribe and kinship, roamed the land, never settling anywhere but just driving their herds before them, following the seasons in their quest for pastures. Such, then, were conditions at the beginning of the nineteenth century.

The nomad population was of Kirgiz origin, divided into three distinct stems: the Kara-Kirgiz in the east, the Kaisak-Kirgiz (or Kazakhs) in the west, and between them a third stem of no definite name. The tribal elders were known as sultans or manaps, and were blindly obeyed by their kinsmen. The frequent raids north made by the Kirgiz, and their infringement of the grazing rights of the Kalmyks, who were Russian subjects, prompted the southward push of the Russians from Siberia. To counter the Kirgiz raids the Russians successfully applied colonizing tactics developed over a couple of centuries in struggles with border nomads. Small forts were built in the steppe, far ahead of the frontier, to which Cossack villages (*stanitsas*) were after a time transferred by order of the sovereign.

Most of my readers probably know that the Cossacks were an armed militia, obliged to put cavalry regiments into the field in time of war. Every Cossack owned his mount, the distinctive uniform of his unit and all his accoutrement, only his rifle being supplied by the state. Against this duty the Cossacks paid no taxes and enjoyed a large measure of autonomy in the management of their communal affairs; and every mounted man was granted 200 hectares of land. The whole of the Cossack structure in Russia was divided into separate 'cossack hosts', named after the regions they inhabited. Each host was militarily under the command of an 'Ataman', appointed by the Emperor, while each village was represented by an elected ataman but administered by an elected village council. Following an age-long tradition, long upright poles indicated the approach to a Cossack village. When set alight, the bundle of straw fixed to the top of these poles used to serve as a signal that the enemy was approaching and as a call to arms.

As time went on, whenever there arose a need for a standing force on some distant frontier the Cossacks were allotted new areas, and thus new Cossack 'hosts' were brought into being such as the Siberian Cossacks, the Amur Cossacks and, in the course of the nineteenth century, the Semirech'ye Cossacks, the latter originating in the manner I shall now describe.

By order of the Ataman of a given Cossack host 'voluntary' emigrants would be called for. Wives and children would be left behind for the first few years, while the men went off to the designated region where they would found a new settlement, bring the soil under cultivation, defend themselves against unruly tribes and even wage war against them.

An old Cossack of Semirech'ye told me the story of his experiences.

'I was twenty years old at the time.' he said, 'and had to leave my young wife behind me in the stanitsa in Siberia. The authorities ordered every stanitsa, according to its size, to produce so many young men for emigrating to Semirech'ye. We were promised good land, and I and twenty other youngsters came to this stanitsa, on the river Ili. The younger generation have no idea of what we had to put up with. We were told that we were expected within three years to build a sufficient number of houses, and to lay in supplies of corn and oats sufficient to provide bread and fodder until the next harvest, for three times our number together with their and our own families. Those were hard times. We toiled in the fields by day, spent the night chasing off the Kirgiz who grazed our lands and raided us, built houses and dug wells. It took ten long years to make life more bearable.'

When I visited it, his stanitsa was a flourishing village. Every

Cossack owned cattle and horses; the sons and daughters of several were studying in the gymnasium or at a university. The houses were spotlessly clean and well-built; some even had pianos, and every home was surrounded by its own orchard.

All through the nineteenth century the Cossack cordon round Semipalatinsk went on extending farther south. The towns of Kopal and Vernyy were founded, and gradually populated by Russian townspeople. I need hardly say that these pioneers were a mixed and motley lot, deriving from the most varied strata of European Russia, many of them with records best left uninvestigated. There were also quite a few keen tradesmen, who bartered their goods with the natives and piled up huge profits, as well as some craftsmen and intellectuals. In metropolitan Russia police surveillance at the time was pretty thorough; out here the authorities were less inquisitive, prepared to accept anyone as a citizen and to register him under any name he chose to adopt. What he was called at home was not their business, neither was his marital status. Under these conditions many a shattered life was forgotten for good and a new life built up under the benign protection of a rapidly growing province.

After a few years of life in Vernyy, Pishpek, or any of the local townships many of the settlers wandered off into the open country-side, prompted either by homesickness, a spirit of adventure, or just plain lust for gain. Some of them had made contact with the Kirgiz, who pretended to ownership of the vast stretches of country over which they grazed their herds and were taken seriously. Deals were struck and land rented for next to nothing. Houses went up in the valleys, farming was started, high-lying land was ploughed up, sum-mer crops were sown during the spring. By the following July the settler knew whether his crop was worth harvesting, whether there had been enough rain to justify his labour. Simultaneously, new methods of cultivation were adopted, such as the 'dry method', where the seeds were sown so sparsely that the blades stood more than a metre apart. This, it was found, enabled the corn to withstand the drought better.

The settlers also took up cattle-breeding on a large scale. Land was available in hundreds and thousands of acres; all around the valleys there was an ample supply of grass for grazing which the manaps were quite willing to rent to the Russians. In the process the Kirgiz learnt something new: haymaking, and the laying in of sup-plies for the winter. At first they treated the idea as a huge joke (hadn't God provided animals with hooves for raking away the snow over the frozen grass in winter?). But when, in frosty weather following a thaw, the steppes were covered with a thin coating of ice which the cattle could not break, their beasts died by the hundred, while the Russian herds came through unscathed on the hay made in summer. It took several decades to convince them, but when I was there most of the Kirgiz had provided themselves with scythes bought from the Russians, and some of the manaps even owned horse rakes and mowing machines.

There was also another branch of farming in which the Russians excelled and which the natives were not long in copying: this was beekeeping. Some of the settlers went in for this industry, at which they were experts at home, from the very beginning, turning it into a profitable business. An added inducement was the fact that some of the grasses and shrubs growing on the mountain slopes in northern Semirech'ye were particularly rich in honey. This explained the large apiaries set up in many of the valleys. One beekeeper I met, an ordinary Russian peasant now registered as a citizen of Vernyy, alone owned 1,200 beehives. In 1909, when I was in the province, the maximum price of a pound of honey was six kopeks, yet even at that price a good apiary brought in quite a considerable income. The winters were short; the bees went about their work for nine months of the year, or even longer, while the revenue from each hive was anything but negligible. The Kirgiz lost no time in following suit. Out hunting near Przheval'sk I met one of them, who pointed with pride to his 600 hives and the field of buckwheat, covering several hectares, which he grew to feed his bees.

In those years of the nineteenth century most of the pioneers who slowly colonized the northern regions of Semirech'ye belonged to the settled urban population. In the plains they felt insecure, mainly because of the Sarts, who were steadily pushing their way north-ward, led by those outstanding warriors of Central Asia, Yakub Khan and Khudayar of Kokand. A clash between the two waves, of Russians driving south and Sarts pressed in the opposite direction, was inevitable and matters came to a head when a forceful person-ality, General Kolpakovskiy, took control of the steppe regions. The traces left of his activity all point to a man exceptionally thorough, outstandingly gifted and statesmanlike in his outlook. The natives spoke of him with awe and respect, calling him 'the General of the iron thighs' (the literal translation is slightly more realistic), because of his fame as a long-distance rider. He is reported to have made a practice of rising early and, accompanied by only one Cossack, riding some hundred kilometres to inspect a subordinate, or a project being carried out on his orders, and then, after a light meal of bread and milk, riding back and presiding over an important meeting or council.

A self-made man in the truest sense of the word, Kolpakovskiy came from a poor family of peasants in far-off Voronezh. His father was illiterate, and his mother a simple peasant woman. He began his military career as a private in the ranks and slowly made his way up to commissioned rank, an extremely rare occurrence in the Russian army of those days. Under his energetic leadership Russia's penetration southward gained in momentum. With a handful of troops he came up against a numerically vastly superior force of Kokand warriors between Pishpek and Auliye-Ata; having beaten them and put them to flight he then went to the support of yet another Russian force, pushing eastward from Perovsk.

Appointment as Governor of the province of Semirech'ye gave Kolpakovskiy the chance to apply his innate talent for statesmanship to the development of the regions he had conquered. In this his success was outstanding, for at the time of his death Semirech'ye was far ahead, in westernization, of any of the other provinces of Turkestan. It is sad to record that his successors were mostly men of no vision and often grossly incompetent. However, Kolpakovskiy built soundly, and the work he so skilfully began endured in spite of many reverses. Colonization was one of his strong points but he was careful to uphold the advantages of a wise policy of emigration, so obvious to him, by limiting admission to the province under his care to genuinely willing pioneers. His keenness to maintain the standard of potential settlers is demonstrated by the journey he made to his native Ukraine in order to select applicants personally from the many who came before him. On his return he surveyed the best land he could find, and himself conducted negotiations with the local inhabitants in order to ensure from the start a friendly understanding between the natives and the newcomers.

He also founded agricultural colleges in every district, with the aim of building up a body of technical experts who would help the immigrants adapt themselves to their new surroundings, and instruct them in the best methods of cultivation. Under his guidance particular attention was devoted in the colleges to fruit growing;

beekeeping, and the raising of silkworms, while the best varieties of fruit trees were imported from Tyrol, Germany, and France. His surmise that the loamy soil of Semirech'ye, with its greater content of lime as compared with the other provinces of Turkestan, was particularly suited to fruit-growing proved correct; the biggest and best apples and pears I have ever eaten were grown there.

As was only natural, in due course the settlements founded by Kolpakoviskiy began to attract other emigrants from European Russia. Village after village sprang up throughout the province. There was a constant influx of pioneers, and emigration took on a definite pattern. And this in spite of the central government's firm policy, adopted in the eighteen-sixties, to discourage emigration to the Central Asian provinces. This policy, prompted by the fear of still further reducing the sparsely populated parts of Russia lying to the west of the Urals, overlooked the fact that a spirit of enterprise cannot be killed by compelling people to live at home if conditions there are less satisfactory than elsewhere.

An opposite trend, pursued with equal zeal by the ministries concerned, set in at a time when the first rumblings of political unrest were heard at home, a trend dealt with in a bureaucratic and indeed a markedly Byzantine manner.

Travelling through Siberia when he was still heir to the throne, Emperor Nicholas II was profoundly shocked by the empty stretches of land which met his eye and expressed a wish to see them settled as soon as possible. There was also the precedent of the south of Russia, which the Empress Catherine II had by a series of decrees colonized with thrifty settlers who included a great number of Germans.

The wish of the heir apparent initiated a spate of great activity in every ministry. The Ministry of the Interior created a brand new 'Department of Colonization', later enlarged and transferred to the reorganized Ministry of Agriculture and State Domains; the Ministry of Finance readily allocated vast sums to the enterprise; an army of employees was brought into being; schemes, circulars and regulations were drafted and, on paper, there blossomed forth a wonderful, but purely artificial, creation supported by rows of gratifying statistical tables.

Regional emigration centres were set up to the east of the Urals and generously staffed with personnel paid five times the salaries received by less fortunate local officials in other government branches and in the Department of Justice. Moreover, the staffs of these centres took their orders direct from St. Petersburg and were not subordinate to the local authorities. Attracted by high salaries, experts of many varieties were only too keen to offer their services to the Emigration Department: doctors, medical orderlies, veterinary surgeons, architects, road and waterworks engineers, foresters, bacteriologists, chemists, authorities on natural science, botanists, statisticians, etc. etc. This legion of bureaucrats naturally had its trail of wives, children, entire families and, of course, the pleiad of servants customary in Russia.

The new emigration officers arrived at their respective posts already prejudiced against resident local authorities and rapidly made themselves unpopular by boasting about their influential connexions in the capital. By recklessly and often stupidly spending state money they aroused the jealousy of the resident officials, who had been vainly trying, often for years, to obtain the necessary credits for schemes and projects of real importance. The arrival in any town of a group of these newly-baked civil servants was immediately followed by a rise in rents and a mounting spiral in the price of all commodities, as well as by a general falling off in morals, and by feasting and debauchery in music halls, restaurants, and hotels. This deplorable state of affairs was entirely and directly attributable to overstaffing in the capital.

Wretched attempts to settle a few emigrants of dubious character on some strip of land gave rise to bombastic reports which were dispatched to St. Petersburg accompanied by columns of padded figures. The old truth that colonization by order cannot succeed was proved to the hilt, enhanced on this occasion by a plethora of ignorant and incompetent officials who turned the whole operation into a farce.

After 1905 the problem of emigration became increasingly acute. In European Russia, the agrarian population, hemmed in economically by the system of the *Mir*, or village commune, found no outlet for expansion and was insisting on reform. The demand, as represented by the best and most forceful elements in the countryside, was for the private ownership of land. The need to divert this urge to possibilities other than those held out by the revolutionaries prompted the very able Russian Prime Minister Stolypin to direct his attention to emigration. At that time, Turkestan's reputation as a land of wealth was high and had been rendered doubly attractive since the completion of the Orenburg-Tashkent line by the increased transportation facilities this offered. So the call went out from St. Petersburg: 'Produce land for the settler.'

A Regional Colonization Department embracing the whole of Turkestan was set up and placed under a revolutionary turncoat named Veletskiy. Scarcely a year later both he and his subordinates were being fought tooth and nail by all the authorities in the province. Until then, theirs was the power and theirs the right to unquestioned authority. The attitude of the old-established civil servant to the Russian settler was one of resentment towards an interloper who had appeared from nowhere to interfere with his plans. What was needed was to settle the fellow as quickly as possible to get him accustomed to local conditions, but, above all, to discipline him. As compared with the slavelike, submissive natives, the independently minded Russian settlers with all their ideas of privileges due them as of right were a thorn in the flesh and a source of nuisance with their constant demands, complaints, and reproaches. I have heard minor officials talk with rage of the settlers and have known them do everything in their power to oust them from their districts, for a single Russian village was a source of more trouble than a few hundred native settlements. On the other hand, the type of emigrant they brought over was of little or no concern to the emigration authorities; for aught they cared, they might be thieves, robbers, tramps or just idlers. It was numbers that counted, and provided that satisfactory reports could be sent off to St. Petersburg all was well.

Before long a state of open warfare between the Governor-General and the Department of Colonization was well under way. The Governor-General demanded the recall of Mr. Veletskiy, while the latter penned yard-long letters to his own chief. This first exchange resulted in the flight of the Governor-General. The next move was made by the Minister of State Domains, who summoned the Head Administrator of State Domains in Turkestan to St. Petersburg. From this competent and able civil servant the Minister got the brutal truth, underlined by a speech made by the Administrator in the Imperial Duma in which he called Veletskiy's reports a compilation of lies. The Head of the Colonization Department, likewise under the Minister of State Domains, chose to regard the statements of the Administrator as a personal insult to himself and started to campaign against him. The campaign was successful and ended with the removal of the Administrator, who had in the meantime returned to his post and was thus unable to defend himself.

When, before leaving on my tour of inspection, I was asked by the Minister to investigate all these matters *in situ*, the picture of intrigue and counter-intrigue by dyed-in-the-wool bureaucrats with which I was confronted was most depressing. The Minister, the very able Mr. Krivoshein, had only one aim in view: to get emigration to the rich regions of Turkestan put on a workable and efficient footing; personalities and intrigues were to be of no consideration. He told me that he had sent an Under Secretary to Turkestan two years previously, but that after a lifetime of office in the Ministry in the capital, this worthy official failed to obtain a proper appreciation of the situation and could only report that: 'Everything appeared to be in order'. This statement caused me and my staff no little amusement when the contents of a letter, written at the time of the Under Secretary's visit by a colonization officer subsequently put on trial, were disclosed. Part of the letter read as follows: 'We have had the Under Secretary with us today. He visited our offices and was shown over the settlements. Everything was, of course, done to pull the wool over his eyes.' (The literal translation from the Russian is 'To grind his spectacles into his eyes'. Later, in describing my travels through Semirech'ye, I shall describe the efforts made to subject me to the same kind of operation.)

From the earliest days of my stay in Tashkent the main topic of conversation at every interview with the Governor-General or his assistants was the problem of colonization and the feud raging between his departments and the new authorities. Thus I had many opportunities to hear the administration's side of the question. However, I was determined to apply the principal of *audiatur et altera pars* and intended personally to investigate the activities of Mr. Veletskiy and his subordinates. I therefore pressed on with all possible speed with arrangements for a tour of Semirech'ye, where Veletskiy had his main office, and from where he reported such gratifying results.

The journey I was about to undertake had been described to me as very strenuous. Construction of a railway line which would join Vernyy to Arys was begun only a year or two before the 1914 war. In my time one travelled north by rail from Tashkent to Kabul-sai and then covered the remaining 850 kilometres to Vernyy by *tarantass*. My way led even farther, across the Kopal Region to Dzharkent on the Chinese border, then to Karkara in the mountains, Przhevalsk, the Buam Pass, and back to Tashkent over the Kara-Tau. All in all I was setting out on a journey of some 3500 kilometres overland, and it was on this undertaking that my staff and I were now busily engaged. On this tour I was accompanied by a few members of my staff as well as by the Administrators of State Domains, our caravan consisting of five troikas.

Has the reader any idea what the vehicle called a *tarantass* in Russian is really like? Capable of being driven over rocks, boulders or, as a matter of fact, over any imaginable surface, it must have been invented in the days when no roads existed at all. It consists of two long, springy poles, about four inches thick, placed parallel and bridging the two wheel axles to which they are attached. A large wicker-work body, broad enough to hold two people, is placed between the two poles in the centre between the axles. A light seat is sometimes fixed inside the body, and the more luxurious tarantasses are provided with a hood. The coachman perches on a small seat over the fore-axle and the whole contraption is harnessed to three horses, the one in the centre running between two shafts. When passengers are about to leave a posting inn, a mattress covered with a feather blanket is spread over the bottom of the body. With a little luck one is able to snatch some sleep stretched out at full length provided the going is not too rough. In theory, the springy poles are supposed to take up the bumping, but in actual practice they are usually so stiff and strong for the sake of solidity that one is mercilessly jolted about or bounced to and fro if the pace is hot. Because of this, and the fact that as an inspecting Senator and consequently an important personage I was always driven at top speed, we called the tarantass 'a horse-powered liver-massaging device'.

After the comfort of the saloon railway-carriage which had conveyed our party to Kabul-sai the transition to the mode of locomotion I have just depicted was something of a shock. We spent a considerable time in stowing away our travelling impedimenta and securing everything properly with ropes of plaited horsehair under the watchful eyes of my valet and cook, whom I had brought with me. The cook in particular took great pains to see that all his paraphernalia, such as saucepans, pots and pans, were nicely bedded in hay and placed in strong wooden crates. Before we had gone a few kilometres every crate was smashed to splinters and with great amusement we watched the cook distributing the contents among the native horsemen. Anything more ridiculous than the sight of these wild-looking sons of the desert each gingerly trying to balance a coffee-can or some other cooking utensil is hard to imagine. At the next inn everything was repacked into felt blankets and stowed away inside the tarantasses.

Our departure from the inn was quite dramatic. First I was asked to take my seat in one of the unhitched vehicles, and then a Kirgiz coachman appeared and mounted the so-called box. He was dressed in a long kaftan, which looked for all the world like a dressing-gown, round which was wound a broad sash. On his head he had a small cap made of white felt and shaped like the little paper-boats we used to make as children. Round the top of the cap was a broad black band, much favoured by the local coach-drivers. Next, he made ready with a length of measly-looking horsehair rope, presumably the reins. Suddenly a door, of what looked like a keep or fort, was thrown open and out rushed three shaggy horses, wild-eyed and neighing, with about eight men hanging on to each—screaming, yelling, and trying to hold them in. This first glimpse of a scene later to become so familiar was really very diverting: the kicking and rearing horses, the little brown men in long kaftans doing their best to get at the horses' heads, the hubbub in a foreign tongue and the utter phlegm of the onlookers. After a lot of hard work the middle horse was at last backed into the shafts which were then quickly strapped to the collar and secured by the *duga* (a curved wooden bow over the horse's head). The coachman threw the reins to his assistants, who tied them to the bit; the off-horses were rushed up, their traces fastened, and, with a loud '*Aida!*' (forward!) from the driver we set off. The entire harness was made up of knotted bits and pieces, like the reins, and how it held is a mystery; but anyway it stood the strain of the first wild jerk into a gallop and continued to hold as we drove off as fast as the horses could carry us.

There was no question of skilful driving. The tarantass went bumping up and down like a boat on a rough sea and the only thing we, the unfortunate passengers, could do was to sit tight and try to avoid being hurled out. After about three kilometres the horses calmed down and took up a steady trot. Mercifully, the driver had somehow managed to keep to the road, a mere track consisting of two ruts. The worst roads in western Europe are better than anything one meets in Turkestan. 'Road' is really not the correct word; one just drove anywhere, following well-worn ruts leading in the right direction. When things got too uncomfortable and jolty one turned aside and drove over the sun-scorched grass of the fields, the meadows, or the steppe. The amount of dust raised by the fine, loamy soil would horrify a westerner. A following wind smothered one in a thick layer which clung to hair, beard, and clothes, turning one into the parody of a powdered actor and colouring one's face a sickly yellow-brown. If the road was stony, as was often the case, the tarantasses bounced all over the place; the number of screws, bolts, clamps, and spokes we lost is past reckoning. The one thing I am certain of is that at the end of the journey I was presented with a handsome bill for repairs and that at every posting inn there was a lot of hammering, joining, and repairing.

We kept to a steady pace of from fifteen to twenty kilometres per hour and usually stopped at a posting inn every twenty or twenty-five kilometres to change horses. At all these inns there was a clean waiting-room where one was handed a long fresh towel to rub the dust off one's face. Washing, I was told, was not recommended, for fear of blisters. There was also a boiling samovar, and tea on request was dispensed by a friendly, motherly creature. At the beginning of our journey we used to get out of our carriages at these roadside inns to avail ourselves of the comforts they offered, but after a while we became indifferent to the dirt and dust and sat patiently in our respective carriages, thereby speeding up the change of horses.

Following the established Russian custom, the local Chief of Police preceded us when we drove out of Kabul-sai. He was also the head of the native community, mounted and accompanied by a whole troop of horsemen. The appearance of this worthy was rather comical. As the son of a very wealthy Kirgiz manap he considered that it befitted his dignity to ride carrying an immense open umbrella of raw silk which contrasted oddly with his velvet, gold-embroidered kaftan and the assortment of weapons with which he was festooned.

From Kabul-sai the road runs east for seventy kilometres through one of the most arid deserts of Turkestan till it reaches the district town of Chimkent, lying in an oasis of the same name. It took us three hours to cover this distance, including the time spent in changing horses.

This particular stretch of desert is noteworthy as the home of artemisia, a plant of the wormwood family, the juice of which is used for making santonin, the cure for worm diseases. It is reputed to be so bitter that even the camels, who eat everything else growing in the desert, will not touch it. From time immemorial the right to harvest the seeds of artemisia was a monopoly held by the lord owning the land. Now the Russian government had taken over, and had leased the monopoly to a number of holders. The revenue accruing to the state as a result was quite considerable, for this is the only place in the world where artemisia grows thickly enough to warrant a harvest. Even before the Russian conquest the seeds had been bought by German pharmaceutical firms to produce a medicine in crystallized form. In more recent times some Hamburg firms had acquired an option on the entire crop for several years ahead. At the beginning of this century a wealthy Moscow businessman, who was destined to become the last tenant, built a factory in Chimkent for manufacturing santonin on a large scale, thereby depriving the exporters of their handsome income. Threatened in their interests, they bribed an influential official in the chancellery of the Governor-General in Tashkent and arranged for certain rumours to reach his ear about the time when the lease should expire. According to these rumours the grazing rights over the land where the artemisia flourished belonged to the Kirgiz; consequently, the monopoly was an infringement of their rights. There must be revision in order to establish the proper form the future lease should take. (The fact that not even the camels would look at the plant was not disclosed to the Governor-General.) The result was that the exclusive rights were brought to an end and the free harvesting of the seeds was authorized. The factory in Chimkent was forced to close down, it being no longer able to compete with an uncontrolled trade in artemisia seeds.

The Administration of State Domains took up the cudgels and protested vigorously to the Governor-General, with the result that an acrimonious exchange of correspondence took place, spreading over several years. By the time I left on my tour of inspection the wrangle between the interested ministries was so acute that the matter was actually being investigated by the Council of Ministers, and I was instructed to submit a report on all its aspects—historical, legal, topical and economic. This required a visit to Chimkent, where I should be able to obtain first-hand information from the local inhabitants regarding the possibilities of developing production of this most valuable medicinal plant.

Chimkent lies on the banks of a relatively shallow stream coming down from the Kara-Tau, and is divided into two distinctive and loosely bound sectors, native and Russian. The native quarter is full of mosques, minarets and windowless streets, and has a bazaar. The latter is, in reality, just another narrow street, roofed over with thatch and lined on both sides with raised steps on which the vendors vociferously display their wares. Down its length camels, donkeys, and cattle move in an endless stream; men ride past mounted on splendid Karabair horses, and figures in billowing grey garments slink timidly along the walls, leading their children and bargaining in low voices with the merchants. Every so often the line of stalls is broken by a cheery *chaikhane*, or tea-house. The floor is spread with carpets on which turbaned men sit cross-legged, majestically puffing at their narghiles and discussing the latest coffee-house gossip of the town.

In the European quarter (the Russian town, as it is called) the streets are like broad alleys of poplars, with irrigation runnels all along their length, and one sees drozhkis stationed at the street corners. In the centre of the town an imposing two-storeyed building houses the District Officer and the various Government offices. Native petitioners loll on the steps waiting to be admitted by the High and Mighty One, while Kirgiz jigits sit about in the shade, their mounts hitched to the trees. There are some quite good shops, with attractive window displays, in the main street, and from the nearby public gardens one sees the distant steppe and the sparsely-wooded slopes of the Kara-Tau on the eastern horizon. Most of the European houses are owned by retired army officers. The local club is the social centre and here people meet of an evening to sing, drink, and play cards and generally enjoy themselves till the early hours of the morning. Of late a new European set has made its appearance and in the streets one sees men wearing the cap-badge of the Colonization Department. Most of them have adopted what was known in Russia as a Gorki shirt—a long black blouse tied round the waist by a silken cord, the two ends dangling down on either side.

At the time of my stay the employees of the Department were new arrivals in Chimkent, and they were engaged in collecting statistical information on regional economics and in surveying the land destined for the emigrants. This was to allow the Department to assess the number of hectares it could take away from the Kirgiz, the ancient fructuaries of the land, to hand over to the settlers.

Before I go further with the description of my journey through

Semirech'ye I should like to pause and consider the agrarian conditions particular to Turkestan.

Prior to the Russian occupation all the land was owned by the Mohammedan rulers, the Khans and Emirs. This ownership was based on the tenets of the Shariat, which distinguished sharply between the right to possession and of actual use. According to the Shariat only he who brought the land to life ('made it live'), that is irrigated it, was entitled to be regarded as a hereditary user, who was obliged to pay the owner a tithe of his income. The definition was fairly easy to interpret when applied to agriculture; it was when agriculture and cattle-raising were involved simultaneously that matters became slightly more complicated. Since time immemorial the nomads had parcelled out and divided into grazing strips the whole of the enormous steppe stretching from the shores of the Aral Sea to the borders of Siberia, just as had been done in Palestine in Biblical times. It was, however, an established tradition that no cattle were ever permitted to graze on land which had been 'brought to life', i.e. on land snatched from the steppe and made arable by irrigation.

The concept of water as a title to ownership was not grasped by the Russian authorities in the early days. At home, agriculture rested on ownership of the land and not on water. It thus came about that no distinction was made between farmer and cattle-breeder, and that on the maps and plans of the region both were entered, without discrimination, as 'owners' of the land they used. Further confusion was caused by the fact that the terms 'my land', or 'my pasturage', were often employed by the users in their dealings with the authorities. As most of such dealings were conducted by the tribal manaps and khans the impression gained at the outset by the Russians was that the whole of the steppe was an agglomeration of gigantic latifundia, owned by the various lordlings. Succeeding official acts and documents perpetuated the error, which as time went by was gradually accepted by the users, who now regarded themselves as the actual owners of the land.

The next stage was opened by the arrival of Russian settlers in quest of land. For as long as the emigration movement was sporadic and undirected from St. Petersburg all went well, the settlers being anxious to adapt their own ideas of farming to local customs. The majority of them disposed of some capital and, in order to avoid a lot of tiresome formalities with the authorities, dealt directly with the presumed owners, the Kirgiz tribal manaps, renting from them the land they required at prices that were unbelievably low. They built their villages, learned the local art of irrigation and lived on the friendliest of terms with the natives, to whom they duly paid their annual rents. The first wave of uncontrolled emigration served to strengthen the sense of ownership dawning on the manaps and confirmed them in the view that the *nudum jus* of the conqueror as translated to the Ak-Padishah, the Emperor of Russia, need no longer be taken into account.

The Colonization Department now entered upon the scene as a new element of authority, absolutely independent of the Governor-General, the Provincial and District Officers, and staffed by a personnel holding principles diametrically opposed to those on which the historical development of the rights of ownership were based. The majority were political fanatics who wanted at all cost to blend the doctrines of Karl Marx, which had been instilled into them by their parents from their earliest youth, with the orthodox principles and learning they had taken away from school. Here, at last, they were in a land which seemed to offer them unlimited scope for applying their ideals; a land freshly conquered and undisputed. They would divide it, split it up, give to each man toiling on the soil a parcel of land, in accordance with abstract formulae. On paper and in theory nothing could be simpler.

These magic formulae were to be derived from statistical research which would show the exact number of acres needed by a 'toiler' in any given district (smaller administrative units were considered unreliable as regards data) in order to be able to follow the latest scientific methods of husbandry with the means at his disposal. So far as I remember the figures produced by a learned statistician with a long record of work in the Government of Orenburg were thirty hectares or thereabouts per nomad, old and young inclusive, and six hectares per farmer. The following reasoning was then applied. Here is a district belonging to the Tsar: it contains X number of hectares and is inhabited by Y number of nomads. As each nomad is entitled to thirty hectares, the total amount of land due to them is Y multiplied by thirty. Deduct that figure from the total acreage of the area and you have a balance N which should be handed over to the settlers. *Q.E.D.*

This arbitrary way of reckoning is best illustrated by an example. Between Lake Issyk-Kul' and a high mountain, all crags and

14   (20 pp.)

porphyry rock, lay a small strip fifty kilometres wide, split up into little valleys. The grazing in the valleys was good, and there was a flourishing bee-farming industry. The land in the immediate vicinity of the lake consisted of rock detritus, rather primitively irrigated by the Kirgiz and used by them for growing a few cereals; in the summer months the cattle was grazed in the valleys. This strip of land was inhabited by a Kirgiz community numbering about 500. They owned a good deal of cattle; the amount of arable land, as I have said, was restricted, and when divided came to about half a hectare per head. On the maps the area occupied by the community was shown as covering fifteen kilometres of shore-line running from fifty to sixty kilometres inland and figuring features such as hills 14,000 feet above sea level, rising as high as Mont Blanc. At the headquarters of the Department of Colonization the estimates I was shown concerning this particular group of nomads provided for 15,000 hectares to be allocated to them and 100,000 hectares to be retained and distributed among the settlers. In practice, it was intended to deprive the Kirgiz of all the arable land they had irrigated and were now farming and compel them to search for other land in the mountains to which they withdrew with their herds every summer. This order, if executed, would have amounted to condemning the Kirgiz to death, as to grow cereals in the mountains was impossible and the grazing period lasted for about three months in the summer. When I took the matter up with the Director of Colonization the latter, after consulting his files, turned to me and said arrogantly: 'I would point out, Your Excellency, that we are doing the Kirgiz no wrong. Although we are depriving them of 250 hectares which we want for the settlers because they lie in proximity to a town, we are offering them the use of 15,000 hectares in an area covering 100,000 hectares.' The fact that these 250 hectares were the only bit of land suitable for farming, or that the Kirgiz had made it productive by irrigation and so, by oriental reckoning, had 'given it life', meant nothing to the Director, and his subordinates, who were only interested in manipulating impressive-looking statistical tables, or in following figures arrived at by means of abstract formulae.

All in all, the activities of the Colonization Authorities in Turkestan lasted for fifteen years. Their effect upon the local population was so disturbing that the friendly relations that had hitherto existed between the Russians and natives were brought to an end. When I was in the region rebellion was not far off, and it was only fear of the bayonets which prevented the situation from exploding into open revolt. In 1916 there were horrible blood-baths and the wholesale slaughter of entire settler villages by the natives. In Chimkent I found the situation, as yet, comparatively quiet: the representatives of the Colonization Authorities, though strongly permeated by revolutionary elements, had only recently arrived and still kept themselves aloof from the local world of officialdom. Subsequently the Okhrana uncovered in their midst a nest of revolutionary propaganda and a well-organized plot to raid the local revenue offices for several million roubles, with the aim of obtaining funds to further their seditious plans.

I stayed in Chimkent for the day, and in the evening set out on my travels farther north. The surface of the road, which ran across a plain at the foot of Kara-Tau, was perfectly abominable—bumpy and full of potholes. The clouds of dust we raised were unbelievable, so that at sunrise, when we pulled up at a posting-inn, called *Karabatai*, we were utterly exhausted.

I well remember that particular morning. We were in a lovely meadow, quite close to the mountains, from behind which the sun was just coming up, blood-red in a cloudless sky. Numerous herds were grazing on the slopes; above, witness to a Russian settlement, were orderly rectangles of wheat, now bathed in pale crimson light. In the far distance and high up in the sky gleamed the snow-decked chain of the Tyan'-Shan', and to the left, stretching as far as the eye could see, lay the golden-yellow sands of the desert. On the horizon shimmered the distorted outline of a mirage of palms and water.

When I turned to look at my companions as we drove up to the inn I realized that we presented a sorry picture. The carriages, our clothing and our faces were smothered in a thick layer of dust, quite dark where it lay bedded in facial wrinkles. Our eyes looked dull, and mine, accustomed as I was to the comforts of city life, were bloodshot and quite without expression. I fell in with my companions' plea that the time allotted for our rest should be extended, and together we went inside, where after using a mound of towels we soon shed the fatigue of the trying night over a cheerful glass of tea.

A little later I left the inn and set out on foot along the road we were to follow. After a couple of kilometres I came upon a newly-built village of Russian settlers and visited some of them in their *izbas*, glad of the opportunity to meet them in their own surroundings. The majority had nothing but complaints to offer: the loans they had been given were too small, they were short of water for irrigation, there was nothing they could buy in the neighbourhood, etc., etc. The cabins were poor, and it was obvious that the settlers were townsfolk unaccustomed to life in the country. They claimed that they had been promised mountains of gold by the Colonization people, yet they were forced to wait for over a year in Tashkent before receiving their allotments. The cabins of sun-baked clay in which they lived had been built by themselves with the assistance of the Kirgiz. Every man had been allocated a few hectares of irrigated land previously worked and cultivated by the natives who, having been removed by the Colonization authorities, had found and irrigated another bit of land a little distance away. The settlers also complained of the seed they had been given: it was rye, and would not grow on irrigated soil. The Kirgiz advised them to try their hand at oats, but they could not find any seed-oats. Some of the settlers had wandered off to the neighbouring town of Auliye-Ata and were earning good money there as day labourers. Some of the cattle they owned had been donated by the Kirgiz. It appeared that shortly before their arrival the District Officer had summoned the natives and sternly told them to be friendly to the newcomers, who were 'the beloved children of the Tsar'.

At one end of the village, and set quite apart, I found a group of twenty houses, neat-looking and clean. The women were friendly and spoke a language I could not understand. It turned out that they were Slovaks. Instead of emigrating to America they had decided to come to Russia, the protectress of the Slavs. All the inhabitants of this settlement were vine-growers: they had already planted a fair number of vines and were looking forward to harvesting bumper crops in the near future. I was impressed by the well-cared-for appearance of a vineyard I visited.

Farther down the road we came to a large, handsome village founded in the days of Kolpakovskiy. It was a typical Little-Russian (Ukrainian) village of white *khatas* (cottages) with thatched roofs and lovely gardens around the houses. There was also a church, in front of which I was offered the traditional Russian bread and salt as well as platters of splendid apples, pears, and honey-combs and, thank God, no dastarkhan.

The response of the local soil to cultivation is astounding. Every apple, be it never so common or of a variety I would not have looked at in Europe, is wonderfully tender, and tastes like the best Tyrolean or Californian fruit. The size to which things grow is also overwhelming, and extraordinary to a Westerner. How we used to welcome the sight of these magnificent, freshly-picked apples and pears that were offered to us along with the bread and salt whenever we halted on our hot and dusty journey!

Along the whole length of the arterial road which leads from Chimkent over Auliye-Ata and Pishpek to Vernyy we came across village after village of Russian settlers dating from the early days of conquest. Most of them were inhabited by Ukrainians and went back to the time of Kolpakovskiy. All were prosperous, and their population had increased notably since the days of their foundation.

At the time of my visit the cry was for 'more land', just as in metropolitan Russia but with a different background. There was plenty of land to be had, but the antiquated irrigation facilities could not furnish the necessary water. Moreover, following the example set by the Russians, an increasing number of Kirgiz were taking up agriculture and diverting to their own use precious water from the common pool. In the parts of the country I visited the system of irrigation differed from the one employed around Tashkent and in Samarkand, Fergana, and Transcaspia. There, most of the water diverted into the plains flowed down from the glaciers of the Tyan'-Shan', the Altay or the Hindu-Kush. Here, at the foot of the Kara-Tau, there was no glacier water to be had. The only source of supply was the streams running down from the narrow ravines higher up in the mountains. These ravines, mostly overgrown with scrub and conifers, contained small reservoirs of water formed during springtime by the melting snows. Most of the water escaped down the slopes in streams of varying size, but some was retained in the shadier parts. A prolonged drought, or lack of rain in the spring, often caused the streams to run dry in summer.

To prevent the water from escaping, the natives had in ancient times painstakingly built small dams across the ravines as best they could. Some of these, of course, have been destroyed over the ages, but many are still effective today. Social divisions among the natives had led to the allocation of one ravine to a particular branch, or tribe, of the Kirgiz, whose responsibility it had become and who in consequence regarded themselves as the owners of the water.

In his day Kolpakovskiy had provided for his settlers by making private arrangements with the various chiefs, fixing the amount of water to be reserved by the tribe or branch for its own use and drawing up a written contract. However, a serious difficulty arose when the demand for more and more water, both for the settlers and the natives, became really acute, the latter striving to cancel the free supply of water and retaining it all for themselves.

The problem was brought to my attention in every village I visited. Only the application of a far-sighted and wise policy could produce a satisfactory solution. But here again one was up against the Colonization Authorities, intent on flooding the country with hordes of emigrants, and that foolish assumption that theory could be translated directly into practice. A General Staff map showing the boundaries of the native communities was hauled out, the number of hectares calculated (including mountains and deserts), thirty hectares per head of population were abstracted and the balance declared state property available for settlement. This was followed by the arrival *in loco* of land surveyors who allotted the nomads thirty hectares of grazing land in the desert and credited the fields and irrigation installations to an emigration pool. The indignation and excitement caused by these measures among the natives can readily be appreciated. They were not alone in protesting, as the rights of the Russian settlers of Kolpakovskiy's time were also being threatened. Over the years they had extended their original holdings by acquiring partly irrigated land as well as meadows in the mountains from the Kirgiz, thus exceeding the norm of fifteen hectares per head allotted to the settled population by the Colonization Authorities. The conflict caused by this chaotic policy was at its height when I was visiting the country, and it is hardly surprising that in every village and in every aul I was beset by anxious questioners voicing their demands and complaining bitterly about the insane conditions in force.

The road from Chimkent to Auliye-Ata runs over the Kara-Tau mountains and the famous Kurdat Pass. Much was told me about this pass. Only a few years previously it had been the scene of a terrible disaster, when a whole battalion was engulfed by an avalanche and perished in the snow. I had been prepared for romantic gorges, crags, and precipices, and was more than surprised by the hillocks and gentle slopes up which we slowly wended our way. Over the steeper gradients we were helped by our escort of sturdy Kirgiz, who wound horsehair ropes round the shafts of our tarantasses, tucked the ends under their knees and dragged us up. Sometimes I counted as many as twenty men harnessed to my carriage, and as soon as we reached the top we usually broke into a headlong gallop. At this time of the year the pass was perfectly safe, the road running over a layer of grass burnt down by the sun.

With the Kara-Tau behind us we proceeded over a flat expanse of arid steppe, wading the rivers we met on the way and driving on through the night (my third on the road in the tarantass). At sunrise we caught sight of the oasis of Auliye-Ata and by early morning we had arrived there, putting up in the rooms reserved for us in the officers' mess. The town was like a large Russian village: there were small, neat-looking wooden houses with carved woodwork round the window-frames, a few western-type roofs painted green, plenty of gardens and open squares. Had it not been for the hot Asian sun, a constant reminder that this was Turkestan, one might have thought that Auliye-Ata lay in some central province of Russia. It was a lovely morning, and we were greeted by the ringing of church bells summoning the people to early service.

As I was in a hurry to get to Vernyy I stayed in Auliye-Ata just long enough to receive the local officials and citizens. The last to be introduced was a deputation of Mennonites. They arrived accompanied by an interpreter and were overjoyed when I addressed them in German. It was strange to meet these tall, fair-haired and blue-eyed men in Central Asia, wearing long frock-coats, embroidered waistcoats and broad-brimmed black felt hats. They spoke a Swabian dialect of German interspersed with Low-German words, though on occasion I was reminded of the High-German of the Baltic Provinces. They wanted me at all cost to visit their village, lying not far from Auliye-Ata, but this I was unable to do. Instead, I sent a member of my staff with instructions to ascertain their needs and investigate their living conditions. He rejoined us delighted with all he had seen and bringing a whole round of cheese which had been given to him by the villagers. These Mennonites had settled there many years ago and originally came from the Mennonite colonies in the south of Russia. Mennonites, as my readers may know, observe a custom similar to the *ver sacrum* of the Romans. As soon as a village becomes over-populated the younger men are sent out to found a sister colony, sometimes far removed from the parent settlement. This was how the colony in Auliye-Ata had originated. A law passed shortly after the conquest of Turkestan had freed every emigrant and his children from military service and was an added inducement to the Mennonites, who are conscientious objectors.

By hard bargaining, conducted with the inborn astuteness of the peasant, the Mennonites of Auliye-Ata had rented a large amount of land from Kirgiz, though I think the latter did very well out of the deal. They built good, solid European houses, and took up farming and dairying on a large scale. The herd of black and white Frisians they owned would have been admired even in East Prussia, and the cheese they made was famed all over the district, the grasses in the valleys where they grazed their cattle being reputed to have the same aroma as those in Switzerland. The colonists had a school of their own, devoutly observed the Sabbath, and paid great attention to the upbringing of their children. My deputy was astonished to hear that none of them had ever been summonsed during all the time they had lived in the district.

Though after Auliye-Ata the way lies for some distance over irrigated fields and the steppe, one feels one is approaching mountainous country. I still think with horror of a stage of sixty kilometres through a gorge between two mountains, with a following wind that smothered us in clouds of driven dust so thick that we were all but stifled and could not even see the jigits riding a few yards ahead of us. The sides of the mountain prevented the dust-cloud from spreading, and the fine particles of friable loam were literally funnelled down the gorge by the wind. With three days and nights of solid driving behind us and the temperature at 104°, travel under such conditions was no pleasure, a fact that was underlined by the flagging and pitiful appearance of my suite, until recently so elegant and still bearing the imprint of the capital from which I had brought them. They pleaded with me to put up at Pishpek, the original target for this part of our journey, and begged me to give them a chance of at least one night's proper rest. But it was getting late and we had another sixty kilometres before us. Nor did I want to stop in a District Town where I would be compelled to spend more than a minimum of my precious time. But just as we were approaching a posting-inn and could discern the village lights we met a column of Cossacks, and behind them the troika of the Military Governor, C. in C. and Ataman of the Cossack Army of Semirech'ye. He had driven out to greet and welcome me as a guest to his province.

General P. was a thorough, earnest, and energetic administrator as well as a good soldier. He came over to my tarantass and we drove together for some time while he persuaded me to change my mind and agree to spend the night in the yurts he had prepared for me some five kilometres from Pishpek. He told me that I was not expected in Vernyy before two days and that my premature arrival would upset the arrangements made for my reception, including those of the Bishop, who wished to greet me at the entrance to the cathedral. Great was the joy of my party when we unexpectedly stopped at the encampment and they were told that they could have a good night's rest on their camp-beds.

On the following morning we drove on to Pishpek, where I was given the customary reception and where I spent half a day in conference with the officials whom I had sent here a month before and who now submitted their reports.

The difference between conditions in Semirech'ye and those I had seen in the southern parts of Turkestan was striking, the administrative machine being by comparison quite European. The town were administered by an elected corporate body of twenty members, the City Dumas (councils), with an executive body of five members headed by the mayor (the City Uprava). The Dumas had done excellent work. The streets were well paved, the workers were properly lodged, there was a hospital, an alms-house, and there were good schools. Here, as in other places, my problem child and main worry were the Colonization Authorities, with whom very much was wrong. At first glance all appeared ultra modern, very liberal, and apparently perfect, but a look behind the scenes revealed that what met the eye was nothing but a façade and sheer bluff. The Senior Colonization Officer, Mr. A., who was responsible for settling the emigrants in this particular locality, complained bitterly to me about the impossible obstacles placed in his way by the administration and insisted that the regional authorities were stubbornly opposed to the admission of Russian emigrants. Where misunderstandings had arisen, investigation showed that in every single case he named they were caused by the demands of the Colonization Authorities, acting via Mr. A., to deport the Kirgiz from their settlements and replace them by Russian emigrants.

However, a closer examination of Mr. A.'s activities disclosed a number of unsavoury facts. Every emigrant was entitled to a loan of one hundred roubles, repayable in ten years, so that a married couple, for instance, with several children and relatives, sometimes drew as much as a thousand roubles. It so happened that around Pishpek emigration was heavy, and hundreds of allotments were divided among the settlers. Many of the first arrivals had by now left and resold their plots to newcomers, without, however, having paid off their loans. The newcomers were in turn granted loans, and so it went on—as many as five and six settler families being entered as occupying one allotment. Thus, inflated numbers of emigrants were reported to the capital, the figures shown bearing no relation to actual fact. In addition, the loss to the Treasury was very heavy and there was no hope of recovery as the loans were granted to each separate individual and were unrelated to the titles of holding. Numbers of rogues made quite a living out of registering in one community after another, each time claiming and drawing a loan. I need hardly add that Mr. A. drew a handsome commission from this racket, while by entering in his books a horde of straw-men who had never even been to Semirech'ye, and pocketing for himself the loans they were alleged to have received, he did even better. Mr. A. was Veletskiy's right-hand man. The latter lived in Vernyy and did everything he could to whitewash his subordinate when I handed him over to justice.

We left Pishpek with the Governor, spent another night in yurts, and on the following evening, five days from Kabul-sai and having covered 880 kilometres, we at last caught sight of the domes of Vernyy cathedral.

The landscape at the approaches to Vernyy is a complete change from what has gone before. The hills are thickly wooded and one is cheered by the sight of well cultivated fields and pretty Cossack villages (stanitsas). The houses are whitewashed and, in contrast to those in the rest of Turkestan, their windows face the street. Friendly-looking people waved to us from them as we drove past. In the main square a large crowd was assembled in front of the cathedral, where the traditional bread and salt are offered to distinguished visitors. There were neither kaftans nor turbans, nor a total absence of women as in the native cities. Instead, there was a mixed and cheerful gathering of people of both sexes. As a matter of fact the feminine element seemed to predominate and was very colourful, the women and girls wearing Ukrainian finery, with white blouses, short orange-yellow skirts and high boots. On the heads of the girls were wreaths of cornflowers and hollyhocks. The sight of such a gathering in Asia is a real tonic to the Western traveller.

Seven kilometres beyond Vernyy the road runs through a damp valley spanned by a narrow dam. The stretch of road over the dam was built by an enterprising engineer on a thick foundation of ballast and in accordance with the latest methods employed in the West. Unfortunately, he did not reckon with the properties of the local soil. After the rains of the very first winter the whole dam sank, ballast and all, the ruins illustrating the difference between theory and practice. We bumped quite happily over the remnants of the dam as we drove down the valley at a gallop.

Vernyy lies in a hollow valley in the foothills of the Tyan'-Shan'. Viewed from the summit of one of the hills that encircle the town it looks like an immense garden, for it is very beautiful. All the houses are built of wood, and are one-storeyed. Only the cathedral and the schools differ. In view of the frequency of earthquakes no buildings of brick or stone are allowed. In the early days ambitious structures of stone had all been rapidly reduced to a heap of rubble by a series of earthquakes. Even the massive cathedral was not spared, and today special precautions in construction are taken. The foundations of larger buildings such as the cathedral, which is very high but also built of wood, are oval-shaped, so that they can absorb and distribute the shocks produced by the tremors. Because of these recurrent catastrophes it was proposed at one time to transfer the government offices to another locality, and a year after my departure a frightful earthquake shook the whole province from end to end. I was told, however, that the cathedral and the wooden houses of Vernyy withstood the shock and remained intact.

A form of reception totally unlike the usual dastarkhan and menagerie of deputations and officials awaited us as we made our entry into Vernyy accompanied by the Governor. I was welcomed by the huge crowd as an envoy of the Emperor. Flowers and petitions rained into my carriage, and at the entrance to the cathedral I was met by the Bishop in full regalia. After a welcoming address to me and a patriotic speech to the multitude, greeted with thunderous cheers, we all trooped inside to attend a *Te Deum* for the Emperor.

My duties in Vernyy took more of my time than I expected, in spite of the very thorough preparatory work done by my envoys prior to my arrival. At the time, Vernyy was the centre of an administrative system that differed radically from that of other parts of Turkestan. The self-government of the city was based on the liberal provisions of the City Ordnances of 1870, later to be much restricted in metropolitan Russia by the reactionary tendencies of the eighteen-eighties. Many of the District Officers were nominees of Kolpakovskiy, and the influence of his personality still made itself felt in the workings of the whole administrative machine. Agrarian conditions, however, were rapidly heading towards catastrophe, thanks to the policy of the Colonization authorities with headquarters in Vernyy. The crux of the problem was the Kirgiz, whose mode of life was being wrecked all over the province by the haphazard transfer of their lands to Russian emigrants. I felt that the magnitude of the impending crisis necessitated a thorough investigation of Veletskiy and his affairs without delay.

As I have mentioned, the officers of the many branches of the Colonization administration were completely independent of the Governor-General's authority and came directly under St. Petersburg, by whom they were invariably upheld and also magnificently paid in comparison to the local government servants. They could have done so much good if only they had done their duty, instead of padding their reports and sending off magnificent dispatches to distant St. Petersburg in the hope of advancement. In Vernyy I was met by a particularly adroit gentleman whose arrival had been arranged by the Department Head in the capital to coincide with mine. He watched my every step and sought to mislead me over every question I asked. It would take too long to describe the ways by which he tried to circumvent me at every turn, and in any case such situations must abound in every state beset by a bureaucracy. I shall, however, quote one instance.

On the second day of my stay I was told by one of my officials that Mr. Veletskiy was particularly proud of a laboratory he had had set up and was very keen to show it to me. The work being done in the laboratory was soil research to ascertain by botanical and bacteriological analyses the potential qualities of the land earmarked for the emigrants. I arranged to visit the place in the afternoon, after my midday meal with the Governor. Arriving at the appointed time, I was met at the entrance by Veletskiy and a number of agriculturalists, chemists, and other employees. The house, requisitioned by the Colonization Department, was spacious, the rooms large, the installation superb. There were beakers, retorts, mortars and test tubes on every bench, flames flickered merrily under vessels in which various substances were boiling, chemists were busy at their tasks, stands round the walls were filled with labelled samples of soil: everything pointed to thorough and competent research.

The laboratory consisted of five rooms, and all had the same efficient appearance. I asked to see the records, which were filed in cupboards, and altogether spent over an hour and a half inspecting everything until I was satisfied that I had made a really thorough survey of the installation. We then repaired to the director's office, magnificently equipped with American office furniture, and here, venturing a shot in the dark, I turned to him abruptly and asked: 'Would you mind telling me how long you have had this laboratory? Is it a week, or two weeks?' Long faces among all present, the patent discomfiture of Mr. Veletskiy, and an evasive reply by the Director followed the direct question. However, after I had repeated it he plucked up courage and admitted that the installation had been completed only a few days before my arrival and that, so far, no work at all had been done in the laboratory. The records were nothing but a compilation of miscellaneous data, and full of errors. The charts on the walls had come from St. Petersburg, and the samples of soil were not authentic.

The thing that had prompted me to ask the question was the impression I had received in going over the laboratory. In my time I have visited many a good laboratory in agricultural colleges and, as a landowner, I know something of the subject. I had never yet visited one so blatantly new. Quite obviously, even the glasses and retorts over the flaming burners had never been used before. There wasn't a stain on the benches, and the floors were spotless. Only the first couple of pages of the records hauled out of the filing cabinets had been filled in, though they purported to contain the collected experimental chemical and physical data. Moreover, all had been written in the same hand.

The tragedy of the incident lay in the fact that these scientists, who had lived here for over a year, had done nothing during that time but draw their pay and dispatch to the capital grandiloquent reports on the possibilities of emigration to districts where in fact no corn could ever grow. After an experience of this sort, how was it possible to believe a word of what these gentlemen said?

Another instance I would like to quote occurred not in Vernyy but farther on my way to Dzharkent, on the Chinese border. In going through Veletskiy's files and sundry papers I had been struck by a lengthy report he had submitted on the desirability of colonizing a large area in the districts of Kopal and Dzharkent to the north of Vernyy. In high-flown phrases he spoke of 100,000 settlers, and millions of hectares of fertile soil only waiting to be turned into luscious cornfields. Attached to the report were laboratory analyses of the soil, the statement of the few Russian settlers of earlier days and the promising figures from yields of experimental sowings. Having just had a taste of Veletskiy's laboratory returns I felt it my duty to investigate the matter personally by questioning the old-timers on the spot and taking a look at the Colonization Department's experimental fields. A slight detour from my proposed route from Vernyy to Dzharkent would take me there and, according to the maps I was shown, I could conveniently visit six of these areas without going too far out of my way.

The first of them lay about a hundred kilometres from Vernyy in the Kopal District, close to a posting-inn where we were to change horses. We arrived about midday and were met by a white-bearded old peasant who was the father of the innkeeper. In the waiting room he had set up a handsome sheaf of long-eared winter wheat, which, he was instructed by the Regional Officer to say, was intended for me as a sample of the yield from the experimental fields. Closer inspection suggested that the ears were too evenly matched and too long and that all the blades had been specially picked. This was a common practice at agricultural exhibitions and I quite understood the wish of the personnel to do a bit of advertising where I was concerned. Accordingly, I went off to the field, which was about half a kilometre away and a hectare in area, to inspect the stubble. It looked pretty miserable; quite obviously the growth must have been very thin, the individual stalks standing about a metre apart. On my return to the inn I asked the old man how many sheaves like the one he had shown me had been garnered off the field.

'Roughly six', was the reply.

'Were there any stalks with smaller ears?'

'Plenty, but I selected the biggest for you.'

'How was the field mown with the growth so thin?'

'By cutting the stalks with sheep-shears.'

One of the Colonization Officers present could throw little light on the subject but suggested that the seed might have germinated badly in the preceding year.

To this the old peasant replied: 'Yes, that's quite right. The sowing was finished at the right time, true enough, but the autumns here are very cold, and we often have snow in September. Only a small portion of the seed could have germinated in the cold soil.'

I was not surprised, as the Kopal plateau lies high and is known for its harsh climate. In fact, it was obvious that the area was totally unsuitable for growing wheat. On the other hand, the mountain grasses that I saw were of excellent quality and the area was ideal for breeding cattle.

Fifty kilometres farther down the road we made a détour and visited another field, which was alleged by the Colonization Officer to be bearing exceptionally well. On this occasion it was summer wheat.

What we saw was a green field, about half a hectare in size, of good-looking corn. The ears were just beginning to form, still in bud and not yet in flower. This was the beginning of September. The Colonization agronomist would not say how long it would take the corn to mature but in reply to my query about when winter set in, the owner of the inn, who had lived here for over twenty years, said: 'The end of September or the first days of October.' He then added: 'In this area wheat is only good for fodder. It never ripens. When I first came to the district I tried it and lost heavily. I have succeeded in harvesting oats only twice in all the time I've lived here. To think about wheat, or rye, is just hopeless. The land I was given is good land—pure humus. It produces quantities of good hay, so I breed horses. You'll soon have a chance of seeing for yourself how fast my horses can run.'

About fifteen kilometres away there was yet a third field we were supposed to inspect. After we had travelled some distance and were about to turn off the main road we were met by the Colonization Officer in charge, who asked us to cancel the visit which, he said, would not be worth while, as the seed sown in the spring had not germinated. I could not but feel sorry for the three men sent by the Colonization Department to accompany me on my tour. I suppose no one in the Department had suspected that I was a landowner and fully qualified to judge the value of what I was being shown.

The road from Vernyy to Dzharkent is 380 kilometres long. At midnight after a farewell dinner given me by the Governor, we left Vernyy accompanied by the local District Officer, who rode with us till we reached the limits of his district. He was a very competent administrator, thoroughly acquainted with everything concerning his territory, a fluent speaker of Chinese and Kirgiz and, by origin, a Siberian Cossack. One of Kolpakovskiy's old guard, he told me a lot about the General, whose traditions he venerated and did his best to follow. He rode at the side of my tarantass all the way, and when we parted showed no signs of fatigue. What is more, he said he needed no rest and would ride straight back to Vernyy. He was a most useful and pleasant companion and I learnt much from him concerning the Kirgiz and also about the methods employed by the Russian administration in the early days in dealing with these nomads.

In the course of my narrative I have often touched upon the customs and life of the Kirgiz. In Semirech'ye the age-long traditions of steppe life, and the written tenets of the Mohammedan law that differ so widely from our European concepts, were of particular importance. The way of life of the Kirgiz is wholly based on the *Adat*, brought down from the hoary past, and in many respects it differs little from that obtaining in the times of Abraham. These rules, which regulate the whole economic and social life of this people, are the outcome of geographical and political factors forced upon the native population by the insecure conditions under which they were constrained to live.

The Kirgiz, as I have already mentioned, live in tightly-bound tribal and family groupings. Inside these groupings the authority of the head is supreme, and he commands the blind obedience of his younger brothers, children and wives. In the economic field his decisions are final. The buying and selling of land, its rent and hire, the changing of grazing sites and removals to other areas, all rest upon his word. The individual tribes winter in the same locality year in, year out, in settlements known to the Russians as *zimovki*. Encircled by mud walls used as a shelter during the winter storms, they usually cover an area large enough to house the cattle belonging to the entire tribe. A section of the enclosure is set aside for the yurts or felt tents in which the tribe lives. Each family has its own set of tents, every woman having the right to a tent of her own. In winter the cattle are turned out into the open steppe and feed as best they can by grazing on the grass under the snow; recently, however, the Kirgiz have begun to follow the example set them by the Russians, and they now lay in small supplies of hay. In spring a few oats are sown round the zimovki and are irrigated by water brought down from the hills in narrow, crude canals. The areas sown per family are tiny and just sufficient to meet the yearly need. As long as the steppe is green, grazing goes on round the zimovki, but as soon as the grass is scorched by the sun the yurts are dismantled, the tents, rugs and poles loaded onto camels or horses, and the whole encampment together with all its herds moves northward. The head man and the women ride on ahead and the animals follow at a slower pace until a new grazing site is found, where a halt is made for a few weeks. In this way the whole tribe moves from one pasturage to another all through the summer, looking for greener fields higher up in the mountains.

Usually, several related families or tribes build their zimovki close together, forming a kind of village, called an *aul*. The oldest member automatically becomes the head of the combined settlement, is recognized by the Russian authorities as such and is treated as the aul's representative. Several auls inhabited by Kirgiz belonging to one particular stem might unite into a kind of clan and here again the same rule would be followed. The oldest member of the clan would become chief and commanded the obedience of his clansmen just as did the old Scottish and Irish chieftains. These lordlings were called manaps or sultans. The next step in the ascending ladder was an agglomeration of clans under a Sultan or Khan—the name depending on the stem—who wielded the powers of an overlord or ruler.

The areas used by any one branch were clearly defined by tradition and no infringement of them by herds belonging to other branches was tolerated. In cases of dispute the ruling of the Sultan or Khan was final.

The way of life described was common both to the Kirgiz and Kalmyks and was centuries old. With the advent of the Russians nothing was much changed at first. The manaps or sultans were recognized by the Governor-General as chieftains of their respective clans and their right to settle inter-tribal disputes was upheld, though the Governor could now be appealed to as the supreme authority in the land and the representative of the White Tsar. In fact he ruled as an autocrat, the role of the chieftains being reduced to that of minor officials. However, these patriarchal forms were superseded in the eighteen-sixties by a tide of liberalism which swept across the country, stemming from metropolitan Russia. Elected officials were introduced, tribal councils set up, and elections instituted. The administrative and legislative branches of government were separated, following European practice. Verdicts passed by the chieftains now required confirmation by an independent People's Judge, who was the final arbiter on the rights or the wrongs of a dispute.

All this brought about a radical change in the social, and especially in the economic, life of the steppe, which was based on and upheld by a tradition a thousand years old. Particularly alien was the system of land commune applied on the pattern that existed in Russia. Something of the same kind occurred in Ireland at the time when England dispossessed the native Irish chieftains and replaced them by Englishmen. Tradition is not, however, so easily shed. The elections were held as ordered, with returns which could have been foreseen. The elders of the tribe were elected to fill all the newly-created posts. Everything reverted to normal, or so at least it seemed, in the early stages of the reform. However, to ensure their election to office the manaps had to resort to a certain amount of bribery, and made promises to the voters which later it proved difficult to keep. Demoralization and disillusionment followed. The issue disputed at the elections was land tenure. Though at the time of my visit the manaps still ruled their respective communities, opposition to them was universally strong and was brought to my attention by a flood of complaints concerning all manner of abuses at the elections.

The prevailing feeling of unrest was further aggravated by the entry upon the scene of the Colonization Authorities, with their stereotyped programme of land dispossession. The foundations underlying the fairly simple principles governing Russian administrative authority had been undermined and the need somehow to regulate the titles of ownership of the nomadic population was patent to everyone, yet there was no one who could solve the problem. In my report to the Emperor I suggested that the land which the Kirgiz farmed in the vicinity of their winter settlements, plus additional areas of pasturage, might be handed over to them and their titles of ownership to these lands fixed by law. I was opposed by the Emigration Authorities, who wished to settle emigrants on land already farmed and irrigated and then to compel the Kirgiz to make fresh areas arable by digging new irrigation systems. The legal basis for this point of view rested on the right, recognized in Central Asia, of the overlord to the ownership of the land and the assumption that the inhabitants of the land were there on sufferance. This policy was bitterly resented by the hitherto loyal Kirgiz; many tribes left Semirech'ye for good and wandered off, settling ultimately in China.

A few kilometres from the town of Dzharkent I was given a tremendous greeting by Yoldash, the chief of the Taranchi tribe of Kirgiz, who gave us a marvellous meal inside a gigantic silk tent. On the table, and erect on its four legs, stood a whole sheep fresh from the baking pit, its blistered skin still glowing red. This original way of serving mutton in no way detracted from the taste, as was very soon proved. The *modus operandi*, as far as I could gather, was as follows. The bottom of a deep pit is filled with stones, the larger ones at the bottom, the smaller ones placed on top. A great fire is built over these and allowed to burn until it turns into ashes. A slaughtered sheep is then carefully skinned and the bowels are removed, after which it is stuffed with oats, rice, onions, and sweet-smelling herbs; the belly is stitched up again and the carcass placed standing on its legs in the ashes. It is further covered with laurel leaves and herbs and left for several hours in the ashes inside the pit, which is topped with earth. When removed the meat is perfectly cooked, the hot stones having acted as an oven. The outside parts are beautifully roasted and as tender as a well-cooked turkey and the whole roast is saturated with fat.

When tea and the welcoming speeches were over, Yoldash drew his yataghan from its sheath, carved the choicest pieces of the roast with amazing skill, and handed them to us with a deep bow. His apparel was most picturesque, consisting of a short jacket of brownish-gold Chinese silk reaching down to the hips; richly-embroidered, baggy white silk trousers, and a broad scarf. On his head he wore a yellow Frisian-shaped hat, trimmed with sable.

Yoldash was the recognized chieftain of the Taranchi tribe of the Kirgiz. In Chinese or Tibetan 'Taranchi' means sheep, and is synonymous with 'farmer', an appellation applied to this particular tribe because of its fame in husbandry. At the time of conquest, when the Russian troops took possession of the entire Kuldzha plain up to the rivers of the Tyan'-Shan' range, the Taranchi were a subjugated people. Their origin is still obscure, and supposedly a mixture of Sarts and the very early inhabitants. The language they use is certainly akin to the Sart. Under Russian rule they quickly began to prosper, and by laying down a good irrigation system around Kuldzha and planting vineyards and orchards, they soon became a wealthy people. This happy situation changed radically when the Russians handed back the province of Kuldzha to the Chinese, who returned animated by a spirit of revenge. By treaty they were supposed to honour the obligations to which the Russians were committed, and to respect the liberties that had been granted to the population. Instead, they butchered those inhabitants who remained faithful to Russia. By raising Yoldash to the rank of mandarin and making alluring promises they succeeded in winning him over to their side. He even went so far as to restrain his clansmen from moving to the remaining Russian sector of Kuldzha and persuaded them to stay in the Chinese part. The mandarins then set other tribes against the Taranchi, provoking them into tribal warfare. Yoldash and his clansmen fled to the Russians. They settled near a small Russian military outpost at Dzharkent, twenty-eight kilometres from the Chinese border. Two years later they had gardens and fields irrigated with water diverted from the Ili. Gradually the place was adopted by the Russian authorities, and Dzharkent eventually became the centre of a district. Yoldash, quite rightly, acquired great status and prominence; he was awarded several Russian orders, visited St. Petersburg once or twice and was received in audience by the Emperor, though his official title was still that of elder of his tribe. Needless to say, he loathed the Chinese.

Dzharkent is quite a modern town of wide streets, barracks, and neat houses, the whole most uninspiring. The surrounding country is famed for the wonderful grapes it produces, which unfortunately cannot be transported and have to be consumed locally. Personally, I was kept pretty busy by the many knotty problems I was called upon to solve which related to colonization and its effects upon the local population. Here in particular I had to deal with a new factor previously absent—that of Chinese Mohammedan settlers brought over by the authorities in Kolpakovskiy's time and now a prosperous element living in their own flourishing villages.

Dzharkent lies within the fifty kilometre customs-free zone between Russia and China and is used by all and sundry as the perfect smugglers' haven. Here Chinese goods can be had for the asking: the best kinds of caravan tea, neatly packed in five pound lots into cunning little leather bags; heavy Chinese silks ranging in colour from the brightest to the most delicate hues, and priceless ancient Chinese pottery. But the staple and, of course, the most lucrative item of contraband was Chinese brandy, adulterated with fusel oil and opium and with a horrible taste.

A very thorough job had been done by officers of my staff before my arrival, the only inspection left to me being that of the Police Department. This did not take long, as it was run by a very honest and competent officer. Conditions in the prison were perfect, which was an exception in Turkestan. Its Governor was a very able man married to an Englishwoman, a former nursery governess. He came from a much better class and had apparently fallen out with his family over his marriage and sought refuge in these distant parts. He had irrigated the prison grounds with the help of prison labour and now employed his charges in gardening. The prison's revenue was increased by the sale of the garden produce. The money thus obtained was used to improve the living conditions of the prisoners and to provide them with better clothing.

Three days later I was on my way back to Tashkent. But before returning I had to visit Issyk-Kul', that mysterious lake, and the town of Przheval'sk, famed for its hot mineral springs.

For the first twenty kilometres we drove along an excellent road as far as the 'Golubovskaya' stanitsa, a charming Cossack village. Then we followed a formidable stretch of country, a hundred kilometres in length, lying in the valley of the river Ili. Some parts were covered with tamarisk, but mostly it was overgrown with immense rushes as thick as a forest and tall enough to conceal a mounted horseman. The road's surface was terribly bumpy and at every inn where we changed horses it took a blacksmith hours to repair the damage suffered by our tarantasses. Tigers are reputed to infest the region and we were even provided with rifles in case of an encounter. Needless to say we saw nothing, and I am inclined to think that the ferocious tigers were invented for our benefit by the escorting Kirgiz.

I did however get a shot at another kind of game. We had already covered over a hundred kilometres from Dzharkent and I had decided to extend the halt at the next inn as I could no longer bear the sensation of being thrown about like a sack from one side of the tarantass to the other. Suddenly a magnificent cock pheasant rose a couple of paces in front of our carriage and settled on the road a little distance away. I snatched up a shot-gun, rammed two cartridges into the breach, and jumped out. As soon as he rose I fired and brought him down. He was a magnificent bird, a lovely specimen of Manchurian pheasant, blue-breasted with a white circle round his neck. I handed him over to the cook, who plucked him on the way, and we ate him roasted on a spit at our next halt. What a wonderful respite after the cruel pommelling we had endured all day!

Mercifully, after this the road improved and we were soon rolling over a fairly even stony surface.

Twenty hours after leaving Dzharkent we reached a high-lying

15

pass. We had been climbing steadily for the last six hours, usually drawn by five horses to each tarantass and thus able to keep up a brisk canter most of the time. The pass, called Timurlyk, lies 9000 feet above sea level and is the only means of entry from this side to the beautiful Karkara valley, 200 kilometres long and fifty kilometres wide. I shall never forget our entry into this valley over the pass. By the time we topped the last ridge of our painful drive up the hills on our way from Dzharkent it was quite dark. The whole length of the valley lay before us, bathed in moonlight, with the snow-capped summits of the Tyan'-Shan' rearing up through the clouds. Far below we could see the silvery streak of a river running through the valley, the crimson glow of camp fires in the small town, and the wavering torches of a Kirgiz escort and delegates from the fair on their way to meet us. On this same spot the great conqueror Tamerlane had stood several centuries before, watching his army of 100,000 men filing past on its way to the conquest of China.

One of the wheels of our tarantass was made fast by a rope to the fore-axle and we started on our descent, zig-zagging down what looked like sheer precipices at a brisk trot. Our Kirgiz driver must have had the eyes of a lynx to follow all the twists and turns of the road down which we were being hurtled, while at every bend I was sure we would topple over and fall into the abyss below. The escorting Kirgiz, who had their work cut out to keep up with us at the gallop, rent the night with piercing yells in order to inform those coming up to meet us of our approach. Altogether, it was a mad drive.

In the valley we were awaited by a dastarkhan, deputations, and, finally, rest.

The Karkara valley has the most lovely mountain pasturage I have ever seen, its soil of rich humus covered over its entire length by luscious, emerald-green grass. Thousands upon thousands of sheep, goats, cattle, camels, and horses were driven here by the nomads every year at the height of summer. Traders from all over Asia assembled here at that time also, and a great trade fair was held. A sprawling and picturesque encampment sprang up in the middle of the valley, where a few permanent buildings made of clap-board were used to warehouse a fantastic amount of assorted stores. Flags of many nations fluttered in the wind. Wares included tea from China, valuable furs from Tibet, bright-coloured and gossamer-like scarves from India, bales of tea and rugs from Bukhara and Kashgar, stacks of the finest Chinese porcelain and, beside them, cotton goods from Moscow, copper cauldrons, articles of steel, handicraft wares, arms, and swords.

Right in the centre an American and a German flag flew over a wooden shack, and huge lettering in at least five languages informed the world that this was Singer's Depot. The agent told me that every year he sold a great number of sewing-machines to nomads from all over Asia, mostly on credit and deferred payment terms, yet he had never had a bad debt, as responsibility for payment was assumed by the purchaser's tribe. He showed me his books, and I was amazed at the amount of monies outstanding. Many of the buyers came from as far afield as West China, Tibet and Kashgar, from the whole of Turkestan and from West Siberia. The fair lasted for about six weeks, until rain and snow threatened to close the passes leading to Karkara. Then the whole assembly dispersed, the nomads and their herds continuing on their way and the traders returning to their distant homes.

This spot, only suitable for grazing, was now coveted by the Colonization Authorities, who wished to split it up and hand it out in allotments to the settlers. In his report to the Minister, Mr. Veletskiy waxed lyrical over the possibilities of wheat-growing on these 100,000 hectares lying 8000 feet above the sea. He also boasted of a trial plot which I drove out to see. The Colonization agricultural-ist who came with me explained that, because of the failure of sum-mer wheat lower down, they had sown winter wheat in the valley. This was three weeks ago. What I found was a miserably tilled field with unploughed sods of grass all over the place, the grain apparently having been just strewn over the ground and roughly ploughed in. Naturally enough, nothing had come up and none of the seeds in the ground had germinated. The thin blades of green that I saw were grass. It was only with difficulty that I managed to keep my temper.

These, apparently, were the same methods that had been used a couple of years earlier to dupe the unsuspecting and office-trained Under-Secretary S., sent out by the Minister.

The following morning, after visiting the fair, we were once again on our way and ready to tackle the Santash Pass, notoriously dangerous in winter. At the top of the pass we drove into a thunder-storm and heavy rain, the first I had met in Turkestan since the previous autumn. We, at any rate, were grateful to the wicked

Santash, which claims so many victims in winter, for this kind of greeting, reminding us as it did of home. On the other side of the pass we drove over an extensive plain, largely cultivated, which lies in the valley of the river Ili. There were vineyards on the slopes, and numerous Cossack villages.

After the gruelling work we had all been doing, I was firmly resolved to take a rest of two days and forget all about official papers and dusty files. We therefore halted in one of the colonists' villages and went to bed early. Next morning we rode out into the mountains in the hope of bagging one of the large roebucks known locally as *Ilik*. The two days that followed provided me with the most interesting hunting experience I have ever had in my life.

We began by climbing up the mountains for several hours, mounted on tough and shaggy little ponies. Their sureness of foot was amazing; like mules, they never put a foot wrong, picking their way up the steepest of climbs and neither slipping nor blundering even when taking a swift mountain stream at a brisk trot. We were placed at the foot of a steep slope while a hundred Kirgiz horsemen, stretched out in line, began a drive down the mountain side from about a kilometre away. The mountains here are wooded but there are large stretches sparsely covered by balsam spruce, rearing up to the sky like tapers. From our stand we could observe the whole row of advancing horsemen, and watch the deer bounding gracefully from crag to crag. The antlers of this species are about three times as large as those of the German roebuck. I managed to get three bucks.

Later, we had breakfast in a lovely meadow with a wonderful view of the Tyan'-Shan', while at our feet lay the immense expanse of Lake Issyk-Kul.' We were very high up and could even discern the buildings in Przheval'sk on the far horizon. I was, however, soon to learn how sudden changes of altitude can affect the human body. On the second day of our hunting expedition, when we were still 11,000 feet up and just about to start on our return journey, I was overtaken by a fit of such severe shivering, giddiness, and weakness that it took me several hours to recover. It was all the more aggravating as I had been looking forward to a fine supper prepared by my cook from the assortment of game with which we had so lavishly supplied him.

Next day we were in Przheval'sk, named after the famous explorer. It was from here that he used to start out on his voyages of discovery, and it was here that he returned to rest, and restore his health by bathing in the healing waters of the place he loved so well. Przheval'sk lies on the shores of Lake Issyk-Kul' and outwardly is very European, like many of the other towns in Semirech'ye; in its suburbs are many villas used by visitors to this Asian spa. The memories I took away from it, however, were not very pleasant, coming as they did after those heavenly days spent in the hills. It was difficult to get back into harness and resume the tedium of office work, rendered doubly distasteful by an investigation into the conduct of a dishonest district officer whom I had to hand over to the courts.

Our way was to take us along the shores of Lake Issyk-Kul' for 150 kilometres, when we should reach the Buam Pass. After covering about half the distance we halted at a monastery, several hundreds of years old, standing at the end of a long spit of land running into the lake. According to tradition, St. Matthew the Evangelist lies buried within its walls.

As far as I could ascertain the monastery was founded by the Nestorians who spread in this locality in Parthian times, and was later left undisturbed by the Mongol overlords. The Russians restored and rebuilt it after the occupation of Turkestan and added to the number of brethren by bringing monks from monasteries in metropolitan Russia.

The monastery buildings were spacious and there were two churches, a large and a smaller one. Surrounded by gardens, the settlement runs down to the shores of the lake, and has a magnificent view reminding one of Lake Geneva. We were greeted by the pealing of church bells and the singing of the choir, and after a *Te Deum* for the Emperor we went for a walk in the gardens accompanied by the Abbot. Later, we were served tea at the lakeside.

The evening was delightfully cool and we sat admiring the view on the opposite shore, which was of foothills surmounted by a green belt of forests above which, towering to a height of 24,000 feet, was the crenellated outline of the Tyan'-Shan'. Beneath us stretched the glassy-surfaced lake, with neither ripple nor sail to dispel the mystery in which it is shrouded or to weaken the belief in the legend we had just heard about the four vanished cities that are said to lie beneath its waters. In the monastery we were shown a fine collection of articles that had been washed up on the shore—ancient glass fragments, Etruscan-looking earthenware vessels, bronze spear-heads, and a variety of copper utensils.

In the evening we were invited to an opulent meal of eight courses, preceded by the obligatory Russian zakuska. However, the three hours we spent at table were not particularly diverting, for according to monastic rule the entire menu consisted of fish and vegetables, cooked in vegetable oil instead of butter. Moreover, it turned out that Lake Issyk-Kul' possesses only two variety of fish, one called sazan and the other uneatable and even alleged to be poisonous. So all the eight courses consisted of sazan. We had sazan boiled, roasted, stewed, fried, smoked, pickled, and salted. And then more sazan. The fish belongs to the carp family and has a rank, bitter taste quite impossible to conceal, even with the best of goodwill.

The monotony of our repast was relieved by a profuse variety of wines and champagne, and I was hard put to it to keep within bounds without offending my hosts.

We left by moonlight, in the most romantic of settings. The troikas were drawn up at the entrance of the church where we had attended a short evening service, the darkness around being illuminated by the flood of light that poured through its wide-open doors. The Abbot, surrounded by his monks, came out from the building and, raising aloft his golden cross, gave us his blessing. The brethren began chanting the 121st Psalm, gently at first and then louder, enveloping us in the lovely harmony of the chant. The well-trained voices sounded beautiful in the night, especially the tenor of a young monk, slim and tall, with long hair falling down to his shoulders, and dark brown eyes. I can still see his face as he sang those lovely words: 'I will lift up mine eyes unto the hills, from whence cometh my help.'

The background to this wonderful scene was the broad expanse of the Issyk-Kul', and the snow-capped mountains. We bareheaded travellers bowed reverently to the cross, and behind us, in kaftans and shaggy caps, with lighted torches in their hands, was a row of wild-looking Kirgiz sitting astride their richly-caparisoned ponies. When the singing was over we slowly mounted into our carriages and drove off, following the line of the shore. Sitting upright in my tarantass I was soon fast asleep.

Opening my eyes only at sunrise, I found that we were still near the lake, bumping over a stony terrain with steep, high mountains about fifty kilometres away to our right. Hares in numbers I have never seen before were jumping up every minute to right and left of the road; at one time I counted fifty of them. They belonged to a species known as stone hares. Smaller than the snow hare, they have sharp pointed heads, and their flesh is reputed to have a bad taste.

By evening we had reached the end of the lake, and we then drove for twelve kilometres along the dried-out bed of a river which had at one time flowed into the Chu over the depression we were following. We were now at the foot of the Buam Pass, and we halted at a posting-inn owned by a very worthy Cossack renowned as a horse-breeder. His stallion was a very valuable animal and his stud consisted of more than a hundred horses.

We spent the night at the inn and were supposed to leave at five o'clock on the following morning. I got up at sunrise, ready to start at the appointed time, and was very surprised at the sight of our carriages standing in front of the house unhitched. I had a long journey before me and was impatient to get away, but could do nothing but wait when told by my servant that the horses penned in for our use the previous evening had broken out and had galloped off into the steppe. The owner, his coachman, and hands had all departed and were trying to round them up. There was nothing for it apparently but to go inside and resign myself to a glass of tea.

After about an hour I heard the welcome sound of horses trampling, the cries of the drovers, and a choice collection of Russian and Kirgiz swear-words. I got hold of the only member of my staff I could find, the others having seemingly joined in the round-up, went outside and seated myself in my tarantass. After a lot of bucking and rearing, five splendid horses were harnessed to the carriage and we literally tore out of the place. A young Cossack boy rode postilion on the front pair of horses, and the rate we were going at can be gauged by the fact that we covered twenty-five kilometres in less than an hour and a half without a single stop. What was even more remarkable, the horses looked quite fresh when we pulled up at the next inn. It also transpired that those five horses had never been harnessed together as a team but had just been picked out at random from the drove in the steppe, as the best. The whole team was a joy to look at, half-bred Cossack Kirgiz with a strong admixture of English blood by a thoroughbred stallion that the owner had bought for a moderate sum from a British officer.

After leaving the inn and driving for about four kilometres we entered the Buam Pass. Negotiating it was quite an adventure. Tamerlane is supposed to have christened it with the dirtiest name he could think of in his disgust at the death of all the camels assembled by him in Samarkand on his way through the pass to China. Here the river Chu flows between two walls of rock, high and forbidding and in some places absolutely vertical. It reminded me of the St. Gotthard and the Devil's Bridge. The gorge, which is fifty kilometres long, is only as broad as the river and there is no room for any sort of road along its banks.

The feat performed by the Russian engineers is truly remarkable. The road they built, broad enough for two vehicles to negotiate comfortably, runs half-way up the mountain side, some sectors having been hewn straight out of the rock-face, with of course no railing or parapet anywhere. Where the walls of rock are too steep, the road crosses to the other side over a swing bridge.

To a Western traveller these bridges are perfectly horrifying. It would seem that the engineers who built the road with such skill, using the cheapest form of impressed labour, ran out of funds when it came to building bridges. Two poles were thrown across the gorge, the ends secured by heaps of stone. A thick layer of willow branches, some still in leaf, were then placed over the poles and fastened down with osier twigs. That was all. One drove over these contraptions at the gallop, wondering how they might best be described, for bridges they certainly were not. The District Officer who accompanied us insisted at first that I should cross them on foot as a matter of precaution, but I soon found that this was a none too pleasant mode of crossing the chasm. One's feet got tangled up in the branches as one stumbled forward, and neither the glimpses of the river hundreds of feet below nor the sight of the following carriage swinging and swaying to either side of the bridge were in any way reassuring and merely made one terribly giddy. I had no time to waste and could not afford these senseless delays, so after a time I just remained where I was and trusted to luck. '*Aida! Nichevo!*'— and we were over! As you see, the bridges held.

Our team had far outdistanced the other carriages, and after the second change of horses we whiled away the time by shooting partridges as we drove by, flushing covey after covey to right and left of us. My companion, a young man untrained in the niceties of shooting game, blazed away at the sitting birds as they squatted pressed hard against the ground and ready to take off. In this way he managed to get as many as five birds with one shot and was frightfully pleased with himself. Indeed, he was deeply shocked when I told him that for conduct like this he would have been fined in my part of the world and asked to contribute handsomely to the funds of whatever club he belonged to. By the time the other carriages joined us we had collected quite a respectable bag but I did not give my companions the chance to try out their marksmanship, insisting instead on driving straight on.

The landscape on the other side of the pass was very pleasant, a well-inhabited zone stretching along the Chu, well irrigated and farmed by the Kirgiz. In Tokmak, the next town on our route, we halted for a short while, just long enough for me to receive and interview a few Kirgiz deputations headed by their tribal chieftains, who complained to me about the unjust treatment meted out to them by the Colonization Authorities. I found it heart-breaking to listen to the tales of woe of these wretched people, who were being evicted from their homesteads. In days gone by many of them had stood fast by Russia in the wars with the Khanate of Kokand. Some had even been decorated; others had been presented with ceremonial kaftans as a gift from the Emperor or given officer's rank in the militia. They simply failed to grasp how government officials of that same Tsar could now be bent on depriving them of the land they had 'brought to life' by irrigation of their fields and their *zimovki*.

From Tokmak I drove out to inspect some outlying settlements called 'The Chu Allotments'. I had already heard a great deal about these settlements from the emigration people, who considered them their showpiece in Semirech'ye. According to these reports they had settled more than 100,000 emigrants and founded fourteen villages in the area. Information collected by my staff, however, suggested that nothing of the kind had ever happened, and I was curious to find out what really was the truth. I therefore hastened to leave Tokmak and arrived in the first village by six o'clock in the evening. It looked very neat and clean, had a church, a school-house, and a small hospital. From talks with the priest and the peasants, who greeted me with bread and salt, I learned that the village had been founded by the then Governor at least ten years before anyone had heard of the Colonization Authorities.

It appeared that the Governor, who was keen on increasing the number of Cossack stanitsas in Semirech'ye, had sent out an appeal to the various Cossack armies in Russia and Siberia calling for voluntary emigrants against a promise of full Semirech'ye Cossack status, that is thirty hectares of land per head and service in the Cossack post. Seven villages had been founded in this way and the process was still going on when the Governor was transferred to another post. The Colonization Department then appeared on the scene. There were at this time, it should be noted, about 100,000 people wandering about the Province, adventurers from Russia, trying their luck and putting their hand to whatever job they could pick up. As the Colonization Department had as yet no land at its disposal, an arrangement was made in St. Petersburg between the Minister of War and the Minister of State Domains (the head of the Colonization Department) whereby the former transferred, by the stroke of a pen, the land settled by the Cossacks to the land fund of the Colonization Department. The Ministry of State Domains undertook to compensate the Cossacks for their expropriated 300,000 hectares with land in other districts, after proper survey and evaluation. As the orders from St. Petersburg to the Governor, who was at the same time the Ataman of the Semirech'ye Cossacks, were issued by the Minister of War, he could do nothing but obey and hand over the land in question to the Colonization Authorities for the settling of 100,000 worthless tramps. The question then arose of what to do with the villages, now factually Cossack stanitsas. The *Krug* (the assembly of Cossack elders) decided to protest and it complained to St. Petersburg, but of course to no avail. Litigation ensued. The legal tangle, however, was quite simply solved by the Colonization Department: the villages along the Chu were rechristened. They were no longer called stanitsas, they were just common peasant villages. The inhabitants were freed from service in the Cossack army, were registered as peasants and were allowed fifteen hectares per head (i.e. half) of the land they had originally owned.

By the time of my visit the inhabitants of the villages no longer belonged to any well-defined group: they were neither real peasants nor real Cossacks nor peasants who had originally emigrated with the intention of becoming Cossacks and receiving the Cossack grant of thirty hectares. It will be easy for the reader to imagine the number of complaints, laments, and claims showered upon me when I paid my first visit to the settlements. Certainly no thanks were due to the Colonization Authorities for the fact that the villages still stood or that they looked trim and prosperous.

I pushed on, then, with my journey, anxious to see the other divisions farther down the Chu which, according to the statements of the Colonization Officer who accompanied me, had been freshly settled two or three years before by genuine emigrants. We arrived, and I was duly shown the three divisions. With regard to the first; on checking the actual number of emigrants against that entered in the register I discovered that half of them had gone away, after drawing their housing and inventory grants. When I investigated the remaining two divisions an amazing picture was revealed, the circumstances which had led to it being described to me by the neighbours of the settlers in question and by the local police officer, who was accompanying me. I found a village earmarked for eighty settlers, and eighty allotments had been properly marked out and entered on a map. But instead of eighty there were only seven home-steads, and this is the story I was told.

Three years before, ten families of Ukrainians had arrived claiming that they were scouts for a far greater number of emigrants who were due to follow shortly. The ten heads of family drew the author-ized grants, while some were given their passage money home to enable them to report on their findings. My informant, the police officer, persuaded the good-natured Kirgiz voluntarily to cede to 'the guests of the Tsar' some of their irrigated fields of lucerne. Within the first year three of the ten families had left for good. To placate the Colonization Authorities, whose protégés the settlers were, the Kirgiz further donated to each family a few head of cattle, sheep, and goats as well as some horses for the use of the community as a whole. After this act of generosity the natives departed on their annual wanderings north. At once, the settlers set about building themselves quite comfortable houses, while spending the week-ends merrily carousing at fairs in the capital of the neighbouring district on the grant-money they had been given. Strangers who showed any wish to settle in the locality were frightened off by tales of poor soil fertility and Kirgiz raids, or they were just driven off by threats. This explained the absence of new arrivals during the following two years and the fact that only seven families occupied an area in-tended for eighty. When their funds began to run low the settlers sold the livestock given them by the Kirgiz.

Upon their return in the autumn the natives found that the settlers had harvested their oat-fields and appropriated the seed. Two years later the settlers claimed the land as their own and told the Kirgiz that they might either surrender their zimovki or pay rent for the use of them as well as for that of their lucerne fields. Some of the natives, accustomed in general to treat Europeans as their masters, submitted to the demands, though some wandered off and laid out new fields of clover farther north. The position I found when I had completed my investigation boiled down to the fact that the seven families now owned a considerable landed property which they refused to share with anybody else, although a further seventy-three settler families were entitled to live in that division. I found, moreover, that not only did the squatters not work the land, but they made the Kirgiz do it for them and pay them a rent to boot. Also, they enjoyed in the district capital a fabulous reputation for the lavish way in which they spent their money. This story rounds off the account of conditions as they really obtained in the Chu allotments so much advertised by Mr. Veletskiy.

The inspection I have just described was the last I personally made in Semirech'ye, as I considered that my month's sojourn in the province had supplied me with enough material to make a correct appraisal of the Colonization problem as it then stood. After this, in collaboration with one of the most competent members of my staff, I spent many hours sifting, classifying, and collating the data I had gathered. His assistance was invaluable at the time, and, after my departure, I entrusted him and several other equally reliable officers with the task of concluding the inspection (which was to last for another few months), with the greatest possible thoroughness.

In order to map out their programme of work I took a few days off, and camped in the lower reaches of the Chu, where I used to spend a few hours immediately after sunrise on short shooting expeditions. Our camping site was located where the river gradually peters out into desert sands in a series of vast marshes overgrown with rushes as tall and as thick as those of the jungle in India and inhabited by a fantastic variety of game: boar, tigers, wild cats, wolves, all kinds of duck, pheasants and bustards, with an occasional stag. In fact, a hunter's paradise. We rode out to the shooting grounds and returned to camp at about ten o'clock. I then took a short siesta, after which I worked for the rest of the day. I was aware of the risk I was taking by camping in the marshes, but the hunter's blood in my veins got the better of my judgment. However, I did not escape the consequences, and paid for my rashness by contracting malarial fever and going down with the first of what were to be many bouts. In spite of this it was a wonderful holiday. We lived in yurts, just like the Kirgiz, experiencing at first hand both the romance and hardships of their mode of life.

One morning I rode out accompanied only by an interpreter, and a Kirgiz jigit to take care of our horses when we dismounted. On that day our target was a stretch of marsh about ten kilometres away, teeming with pheasants. In rice fields along our route threshing was in progress, performed in a most primitive way. The rice was first spread out in a layer on the ground, then threshed by roughly hewn stone rollers drawn by horses driven round in a circle. The straw, chaff, and grain were then raked into a heap and winnowed by being thrown into the air off wooden spades. The wind carried away the straw and chaff, while the grain fell to the ground. The quality of the rice obtained by this method was pretty poor, but the natives maintained that this was due to a shortage of water.

The pheasants were plentiful in the rice fields and stubble, and we flushed four coveys. The problem was to bring the birds down so as to prevent them from falling into the thickets of rushes growing close by, where even our excellent retrievers often failed to find them. By nine o'clock I had bagged twelve splendid cocks, greatly to the amusement of the interpreter, who could not understand why I did not shoot the hens.

It was getting very hot, as we had gone much farther than we originally intended and the sun was fairly high in the sky. A little distance away I saw a few scattered yurts of a Kirgiz aul and wandered over, entering one of the tents in the hope of being able to rest for a while. The owner was out, but we were very hospitably received by his wife. I should add that, in contrast to their Turkmen and Sart sisters, the Kirgiz women are not forbidden to talk to strangers, nor do they wear the same kind of horsehair veil. Instead, they wear a large white turban, the ends wound round the neck and fastened under the chin. Their dress, too, is very picturesque. Generally, it consists of a loose, white woollen smock with broad sleeves reaching down to the knees and handsomely embroidered at the edges, worn with baggy ankle-length trousers and high boots of soft leather dyed in different colours and also embroidered.

Our hostess was a comely, large-eyed woman of under forty, sun-tanned and round-faced, with the typical high cheek-bones of the Kirgiz. My request for permission to rest for an hour was met by the production of fine-looking rugs, hauled out of a large trunk standing in the yurts and gaudily ornamented with a floral design. A mound of cushions, all made of carpeting, followed, and we were soon comfortably reclining on the floor enjoying a drink of cool kumys that we had brought with us in our flasks. After a while we were joined by the woman's brother, accompanied by his pretty sixteen year-old wife and his second, older wife, and a few other couples. We conversed at a great rate thanks to my excellent interpreter and soon all of us were on the friendliest of terms. Our hostess pointed with pride to two plump, healthy looking babies playing unconcernedly at our feet, and told us they were her twin boys, two years old. She was still nursing them though they were running around and were babbling away quite happily. The interpreter told me that it was the custom of the Kirgiz women to nurse their children until they were fully three years old. The two children, one of who was slightly duskier than his twin, reminded me of the story of Jacob and Esau. I amused them by showing them my watch, gold cigarette-case, and a few trinkets I had in my pockets. Everyone wanted to know all about them and how they worked and they were all much intrigued by a cigarette-lighter.

When I was told that the villagers intended to slaughter and roast a sheep in our honour I quickly dispatched a Kirgiz and my jigit to our camp with instructions to the interpreter there to send us some lunch, for I realized that I would not get away before nightfall otherwise. The messengers, accompanied by two other horsemen, were soon back and we sat down in the shade to a copious and pleasant meal watched by a smiling crowd with whom we shared its surplus. The thermos flasks packed in the luncheon baskets were a source of endless surprise. That hot tea and coffee could come out of a stone-cold container was too wonderful for anything. When friendship had been well established questions came raining fast. 'Where did you get those *shaitan* (devil) flasks from?' 'What are those funny-looking knee-high laced boots you have on?' 'How much did you pay for them?' 'How much does your watch cost? And how much did you pay for your gold cigarette case?'

When in reply to this last question I said 'Four hundred roubles', one of the men pointed out that this was a lot of money and that for the same sum I could have bought myself two wives. Every object was, apparently, valued in relation to the price of a wife. When I asked the brother of our hostess how much *kalym* (bridal money) he had paid for his pretty wife, he told me sadly that she came from a very poor family and that because of the meanness of her dowry in carpets, suzanes, and dresses her father had let her go for only fourteen sheep. The others maintained that this was still a stiff price to ask, but then, she was a very pretty girl. I enquired of our hostess if she had any other children.

'I have those two boys', she said.

'Any daughters?'

'Yes, two,' she replied disdainfully. One of them, fifteen years old, was an accomplished needle-woman, who demonstrated her art by skilfully embroidering a strip of linen with coloured silks. We then drew a few flowers for her; she reproduced them at once in the most lovely colours without even tracing the design on the bit of cloth in her hands. Her sister, aged ten, was a delightful child, with large, laughing brown eyes set in a red-cheeked and deeply-tanned little face. She was called Kalipa and was a trusting little soul. Her eyes filled with tears when I asked her if she owned one of those fine fur caps worn by the unmarried Kirgiz women of better families, a cap of sable adorned with heron feathers. Her mother quickly said: 'We are too poor. My husband owns only a hundred horses and two camels. But the elder girl has one.'

She showed me the cap in question, bringing it out of the trunk. At a suitable moment I expressed my admiration for the plaits of Kalipa's sister, which fell below her knees. A heavy key and a pair of scissors were suspended to the ends, while the braids looked like a needle-woman's work-basket, for they were full of needles of different sizes, and silks, all tucked into the meshes. Weights were attached to Kalipa's long plaits as well. This, the mother explained, was always done to girls to make their plaits grow thicker and longer.

The price of one of those fur caps, I was told, was sixteen roubles, and the sable could be bought from the Chinese. I gave the mother the money and told the ecstatic Kalipa that she would now have a cap of her own. Some time later, via the interpreter, I sent our hostess a box of scented soap—a present, it appears, enormously valued by Kirgiz women—and in return received a long letter of thanks, suitably translated. As proof that my commission had been faithfully carried out a photograph of the whole family was enclosed: the father, the two boys, the two sisters, each wearing a fur cap, and the mother with the box of soap on her lap. We took the most touching leave of our hosts and were accompanied the whole way to the camp by the entire family including the girls, on horseback.

Though we had been given a charming picture of nomad life, I could not but feel sad at the thought of poor little Kalipa. For some years past she had been promised in marriage by her father to an old

Kirgiz who had agreed to pay him a substantial kalym and who had already enriched him with a goodly number of sheep in payment on account.

To a Westerner the concept of kalym is quite revolting. A bevy of girls is a source of guaranteed income to the head of the family, while the idea of a dowry instead of the kalym is never even considered in the steppe. A man must buy his wife; that is the rule and he must stick to it. Should the suitor be unable to pay the full sum outright he is allowed to pay by instalments spread over a number of years, but he gets his wife only when he has completed payment of the contracted sum, just as with Laban and Rachel. In the event of death his right to the girl passes to his heir—uncle, brother, or whoever he may be—who assumes the obligations of the deceased, and according to the Adat the father of the bride is obliged to hand her to him as soon as the stipulated kalym has been paid in full. The girl's consent is never sought.

It often happens that the father promises the girl to a second bridegroom and takes a down-payment from him on account, a procedure generally leading to hard-fought litigation and often developing into vendetta and bloodshed. I was told by an expert on Kirgiz affairs that disputes over kalym lead to more murders, robberies, and raids than any other cause. On the other hand, it sometimes happens that the girl follows the promptings of her heart and allows herself to be stolen or abducted by the man of her choice with no payment of any kalym. In that case, though the young couple may flee a great distance into the steppe, it is surprising how unerringly the natives are able to discover their whereabouts, always lending their sympathy and support to the outwitted father who has been deprived of his just kalym.

Going through some files I came across the following case. A girl from Upper Semirech'ye was betrothed to a young man in a neighbouring aul who subsequently died, but who had already paid several instalments of the arranged kalym. His heir was an old uncle, also a Kirgiz but a Chinese subject, who inherited all the possessions of the deceased bridegroom—carpets, yurts, etc.—and his bride, whom he claimed. He lived in the steppe by Kuldzha and had several wives. Negotiations over the transfer of the estate were handled, I believe, by one of his sons, who promptly fell in love with the girl, forsook everything and fled with her to the Przheval'sk district in the far south of the province, where the pair settled and lived quite happily.

The young man had, apparently, some education and eventually got a job in the police. He got himself properly married before a Kadi according to Mohammedan law and nobody would have dreamt that they would be discovered.

However, relations, both of the duped father and of the heir, somehow unearthed their whereabouts, whereupon the old man went to the Russian Consul in Kuldzha and claimed his right under civil law. (Disputes between native Russian and Chinese subjects came under Russian jurisdiction according to the terms of the treaty between Russia and China.) The young man, in the meantime, had become a Russian subject. The roster of nomads living in the Kuldzha Province furnished no reliable information as to the nationality of any individual, as a matter of fact, for the natives yearly wandered in and out of the two countries over hundreds of kilometres with no regard for boundaries. There was nothing easier for any native of Semirech'ye or Kuldzha than to claim or disown his nationality with the police authorities according to his convenience.

The Consul did not take the case very seriously and gave a verdict worthy of Solomon: the girl was to be handed over to the Chinese authorities and restored to the man who had paid the kalym. A letter directing the District Officer in Przheval'sk to detain the girl and dispatch her by stages to Kuldzha was handed by him to the plaintiff. By some means the husband got wind of this letter and of the peril threatening his wife and fled with her to the neighbourhood of the town of Turkestan, where they lived like nomads in the steppe.

In the long run they were tracked down, and the father brought the man before a Kirgiz People's Judge on a charge of horse-stealing. The judge was suitably bribed, evidence was given by a horde of false witnesses and the accused was sentenced to two and a half years in prison. He was taken into custody by the police, acting on the orders of the Russian District Officer, and dispatched to Przheval'sk to serve his sentence. The wife was also sentenced to a term of imprisonment by the Kadi for breaking her marriage vows. In this instance, too, the sentence was passed by a legally elected People's Judge (the Kadi).

The case first came to light in the course of an inspection into the affairs of the prison at Przheval'sk. From a Western ethical viewpoint here were two unfortunate people languishing in jail for no good reason at all. Yet what could I do? The couple had appealed against the sentences to a higher court, the Council of District Kadis, but with no result because to any right-minded Kirgiz, and all the judges were such, it was patently evident that a flagrant breach of the Adat had in fact taken place. According to the law the decisions of the Council of Kadis required the approval of the Russian District Officer who could, if he considered there was ground for an appeal, hand the case to the State Attorney after a given period of time had elapsed. In this instance, however, the verdict of the Kadis' Council had automatically been confirmed by the District Officer, who, like most of the officials in Asia with a long record of service, treated such cases as the present one as a matter of routine. The only thing I could do was to invoke the Imperial prerogative of pardon via the Minister of Justice. I am glad to say that very soon the Emperor was graciously pleased to accede to my request.

Cases like the one described above, of conflicting Western and Asian ethical principles, were inevitably bound to be numerous. To the honour of Russian rule in Asia I must state that the general tendency in matters dealing with native customs and legal procedure was one of introducing and applying Western concepts and, whenever possible, allowing them to exercise a dominating influence. In all matters concerning local administration and the application of norms regulating the native way of life Russian legislation provided for a large measure of autonomy, in striking contrast to the principles applied by the British in India.

In Turkestan all the Europeans were subject to the jurisdiction of the Russian courts and of Western legal procedure introduced by the Russians into the region. However, penal offences, by whomsoever committed, such as murder, theft, forgery, etc., were automatically subject to Russian jurisdiction, as were offences committed by Europeans against natives or, inversely, by natives against Europeans. Offences committed by natives where the damages claimed did not exceed 300 roubles were subject to the jurisdiction of local Kadis elected by the natives themselves, and so were all cases of theft in the steppe which were classed within this category.

Sentences imposed by the Kadis required confirmation by the District Officer. This proviso was introduced in order to prevent the Kadis, whose dishonesty was proverbial, from arrogating unto themselves the right to try cases which otherwise would have come within the competence of a Russian court. Unfortunately, there were always ways and means of circumventing the law. The right of the Kadis to impose sentences of up to two or three years' imprisonment, for instance, was one which they grossly misused. I came across cases of natives condemned to terms of imprisonment for visiting Christian churches, or for drinking spirits and wine. Women were jailed for complaining to the Russian authorities against their husbands for maltreating them, etc. This type of case was especially numerous, and served to underline the difference of approach to the Oriental native of the British, Indian-Mohammedan, and Russian systems of legislation. The Russian régime strove unfailingly to Europeanize the native and never knowingly tolerated the perpetuation of barbaric norms. Within the framework of the autonomy they enjoyed the natives were free to apply their own concepts of justice, but were never permitted to regard as just—or to enforce—measures repugnant to the laws of Russia. These laws forbade slavery, capital punishment, and whipping. In India there were no elected native judges and the local British Magistrate was constrained to pass sentences based on the tenets of the Moham-medan Shariat, whatever their nature. The Shariat permits the chastisement of a wife by her husband. A British magistrate could do nothing but pronounce a man innocent even if the facts proved beyond any doubt that he had grossly maltreated his wife. In Turkestan he would have been sentenced by a judge. That this was the position was very much brought home to me by the mullas with whom I discussed the Shariat; they complained bitterly about the right of the women to seek redress from a Russian magistrate against their husbands for maltreating them by, for instance, beating them with iron chains, a common form of marital punishment in Central Asia. If cases like the ones described did occur in Turkestan they were entirely due to the laxity of some Russian civil servant.

Poor little Kalipa! I often wonder what became of her. She was such a friendly and confiding little soul, that day I spent in the intimacy of the Kirgiz family circle.

No Westerner, I am sure, can appreciate the feeling of utter exhaustion to which one is reduced after bumping and driving over endless stretches of road in the steppe, smothered in dust or mud, roasted by the heat, and plagued by mosquitoes. However great one's original interest in nature and the scenery, even that is gradually deadened and ultimately lost. My mission in Semirech'ye was ful-filled, and I was anxious to get back to Tashkent and to renew contact with the civilized world. But four long days and nights of unbroken driving over familiar ground were still before us.

All of us were obsessed with the wish to move on with all the speed we could. When, slowly ploughing our way through heavy sand, we first caught sight of a long line of telegraph poles following what was unmistakably a railway embankment, about eight kilometres from Kabul-sai, we felt like the warriors of Xenophon when they shouted *Thalassa!* on seeing the waves of the sea. We felt we should never get to the end of those eight kilometres, and I believe it was the only time during the whole journey that I kept urging the driver to go faster.

Our progress in the sand was slow. However, there at last was our dainty white saloon-coach, and letters from home with news from our near and dear ones in neat little piles on the writing desks of our respective compartments. Then came the unbelievable joy of fresh, clean water, and a bath in the luxuriously appointed bathroom of our coach. In the evening, dinner, seated at table—a wonderful meal which started with a clear pheasant broth prepared by my chef as a final tribute to our adventures, accompanied by tasty little patties and followed by a succession of dishes that were the outcome of a culinary art learned in Paris.

For the first and only time during the whole tour of inspection the junior members of my staff were given permission to concoct a peach cup of real German Moselle wine. We were back in Europe!

INDEX